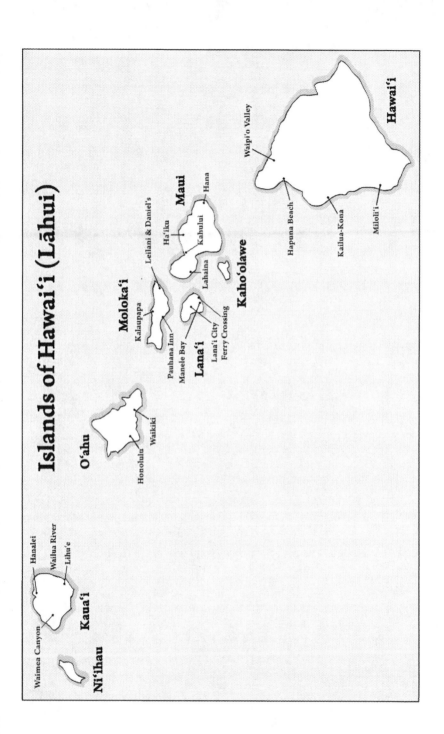

Islands of Hawai'i (Lāhui)

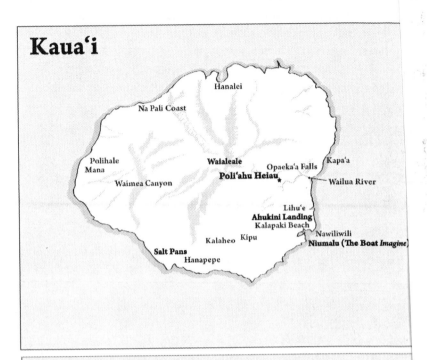

Kaua'i

Hanalei

Na Pali Coast

Polihale
Mana

Waialeale
Poli'ahu Heiau

Opaeka'a Falls

Kapa'a

Wailua River

Waimea Canyon

Lihu'e
Ahukini Landing
Kalapaki Beach

Kalaheo Kipu

Nawiliwili
Niumalu ('The Boat *Imagine***)**

Salt Pans
Hanapepe

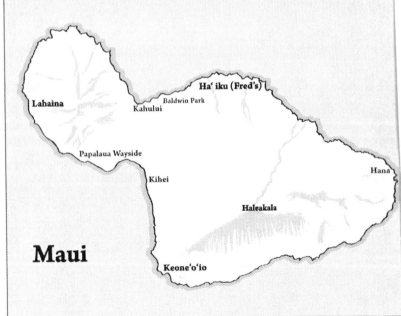

Ha' iku (Fred's)

Lahaina
Kahului Baldwin Park

Papalaua Wayside

Kihei

Hana

Haleakala

Maui

Keone'o'io

GRANDMOTHERS WHISPER

Ancient Voices…

Timeless Wisdom…

A Modern Love Story

INETTE MILLER

Cover Design: Cathi Stevenson:
     www.BookCoverExpress.com
Front Cover Sculpture and Back Cover Photograph:
     Marlene Keller Czajkowski
     www.insacredsilence.com/id79.html
Front Cover Wiliwili Seed Lei:
     Rick Makanaaloha Kia'imeaokekanaka San Nicolas
     www.HawaiianFeathers.com
Maps: Sam Wall:
     www.SamWall.com

Soft Cover ISBN 0-7414-6286-9
Hard Cover ISBN 0-7414-6287-7

Printed in the United States of America

Author's Note: All events described in this book are real. However, some names have been changed.

Published November 2010

INFINITY PUBLISHING
1094 New DeHaven Street, Suite 100
West Conshohocken, PA 19428-2713
Toll-free (877) BUY BOOK
Local Phone (610) 941-9999
Fax (610) 941-9959
Info@buybooksontheweb.com
www.buybooksontheweb.com

To
Mollie Speert Miller
And To
Harry (Hershel) Miller, of blessed memory

CONTENTS

PART TWO
QUESTIONING FAITH: TOGETHER

KA WA MAMUA (WHAT CAME BEFORE)

December, 2010

I was a Jewish woman, living a wonderful, professional life in a progressive northwestern city – Portland. I'd been rearing two bright and loving teenage sons since they'd been toddlers, alone. We lived in a fabulous glass-walled, hilltop home with views of the distant mountains by day, the shimmering city lights at night. I was a writer, a workshop teacher, a good friend, a responsible daughter. My home was filled with laughter, fine food, better books, and antiques I'd collected over thirty years. I wasn't looking to change my life. I knew I was blessed.

I took an impromptu winter vacation to Hawai'i – a reward to myself for three years work on a just completed manuscript – and a rare break from the boys. I was looking for sun, respite, and solitude. I was led instead to 'Iokepa Hanalei 'Īmaikalani, a powerful, silver-haired, brown-skinned *kanaka maoli* (aboriginal Hawaiian) who spoke regularly with his long dead grandmothers – and in the blink of an eye, my life was transformed.

A year later: I had no home, no books, no money, no career, and no friends nearby. I lived like the stranger I was, in Hawai'i. I slept in tents on public beaches, often illegally. I owned and carried no more than would fit into an aging Toyota Camry. I often went hungry.

When I left Portland, I left a trail of friends and family who feared I'd stepped off the deep edge of Middle Earth. They were not far from the mark.

Their fears, I now know, weren't solely for my physical well-being. It was my dependence they grieved – my sacrifice of self for a powerful man's journey.

I spent the next year fulfilling their worst fears. I went on vacation for a week and I stayed for a lifetime.

. . .

"Entreat me not to leave thee and to return from following after thee; for whither thou goest I will go, and where thou lodgest,
I will lodge; thy People shall be my People and thy God my God."

Book of Ruth
The Tanakh, the Hebrew Bible

PART ONE

DISCOVERING FAITH: ALONE

The first time I set eyes on ʻIokepa Hanalei ʻĪmaikalani and heard him speak, it was just after sunrise, Christmas morning, on the Northwestern-most Hawaiian Island of Kauaʻi. An hour earlier I had awakened from a compelling dream. Two weeks earlier any thought of a vacation in Hawaiʻi would have been absurd.

I had never in my entire life harbored the slightest desire to see Hawaiʻi. Twice – separated by twenty-six years – my airplane refueled in the Honolulu airport on its way to somewhere else. In 1970 it was on my way to Vietnam, to marriage, to war, to self acceptance. In 1996, to Bali – and a hesitant first-step into a more spiritual world.

But now, Christmas, 1997, I was on Kauaʻi – an Island I'd never even heard of until a friend of a friend told me her vacation story leaning across a theater seat as we half-listened to John Updike at the lectern. Then, two weeks before Christmas – my new book done, needing a vacation from home and hearth, sending the kids to their Dad's for Christmas – I began thinking *Hawaiʻi* and I couldn't let it go. Away from the resorts, I was sure – something of the real Hawaiʻi (whatever it was and whether it even existed). The Big Island perhaps? Other than that, I couldn't even imagine.

"...a cheap flight and a compact rental car," I told Tina, travel agent and friend these thirteen traveling years since my divorce.

3

"It isn't going to happen," she answered. "Christmas flights are outrageous. But I can get you to Mexico. Or Key West – round trip $129."

"No. I need to go where I've never been. I want the Big Island."

"Look in Sunday's paper," she instructed. "The discounters may have a space left in a package group."

"Yuck."

"It'll get you over there."

But that's not how it happened.

The discounters failed me. Flights to the Big Island evaporated as quickly as the elusive discounter tried to book them. By day's end, the discounter said, "How about Kaua'i?"

"Uh, I don't know a thing about Kaua'i."

"Hiking trails," he tried to pitch to my interests, "Remote beaches, river kayaking...or else, go some other time."

"Oh hell. *Kaua'i* then."

But late the next afternoon, he left this message on my answering machine. "You didn't really want to go to Kaua'i did you?"

Apparently I did. Because after midnight I took on the airline 800 numbers myself, now focused entirely on Kaua'i. United offered me the one seat left, at $200 less than Tina had quoted. I called seven car rental companies. No cars were available at any price at any location on Kaua'i Christmas week. Past one in the morning and exhausted, I dialed the eighth car company. *Thrifty,* it seemed, had opened an office on Kaua'i the week before. "Anything you'd like Ms. Miller..."

I placed a twenty-four hour hold on the last discounted airplane seat, reserved the car, and the next morning looked for a place to stay. I was resolute: neither hotel nor condo. A bed and breakfast – small, cheap, out of the way – I was looking for solitude.

"Everything's full," the woman at the B&B association told me, "except this one – and it's not really a B&B. It's a room in my friend's house on the beach."

"I'll take it."

. . .

The day I touched ground on Kaua'i, I knew that a week wasn't going to be long enough. I had a headache from the stale airplane air, felt a slight case of motion sickness, and was flat-out exhausted from three intense years' work on my last book – twenty-six years in the recollecting. I'd finished it two weeks before I left. Kaua'i was the first vacation without kids in eighteen months. I needed one. I'd been raising Ben and Nathan from age two and five – now fourteen and seventeen – alone.

My first four days on Kaua'i were as restful as I required. I swam, fell asleep on the beach and started on a tan. I hiked a gentle path to a waterfall. I had high-tea at the Princeville Hotel. I'd slept deeply, dreamlessly.

But just before dawn on Christmas Day, I had a dream unlike any I'd ever had. I woke up puzzled, but not frightened.

An hour later, at sunrise, I found myself surrounded by nine or ten strangers – all Western transplants to Hawai'i, except one man. Transparently Hawaiian and powerfully built with a shock of silver hair, he stood out.

We stood on the outside rim of an ancient Hawaiian temple – a *heiau* – on a precipice above the Wailua River. Rachel (with whom I shared the beach-front house) was leading us through a simple daybreak service. At the conclusion, she asked us to touch the remains of the stone walls and close our prayers silently.

I turned, shut my eyes, and reached out both palms to a smooth, foot-wide rock at waist level. I felt a peculiar surge of energy, not unlike the electricity that passed through me once when I touched a plugged-in toaster while standing in a puddle of water. Again, I couldn't let go. Finally, I didn't want to. I was conducting some incredible surge from sky to Earth. I was the lightning rod and it felt powerful.

People have since asked me exactly what I saw. My eyes stayed closed; I saw nothing. It was all feeling.

I have no idea how long I stood connected from Earth to sky by some unseen current. But I heard conversation behind me, and I knew the service had ended.

I ignored the sounds for a minute, then wrenched my hands from the rock with a jolt and turned around. My eyes settled onto the man, now speaking with Rachel eight feet away. He was facing away from me and I heard only a scattering of phrases. "*Wānana*," I heard him say, "means prophecy.

"The prophecy," I heard, "given by the spirits – my ancestors."

I had turned from the magical stones, locked onto his face in profile, and heard only that sprinkling of disconnected words. Then I saw.

I saw it as clearly as I saw the mountain in front of me, the word *TRUTH* spelled out over his head. Literally.

I actually laughed out loud at the improbability. "God," I snickered. "*Whose* truth is this?" Clearly, I was still me – and the person who is *me* laughed and wondered: 'Is it *his* truth? Is it mine?' I was doubly amused by the precision of a God who throws words at a writer.

I didn't doubt it. I didn't challenge it. It was there, and then it was gone. I could not easily ignore the blazing sign.

The man and I had not looked directly at each other, nor had we exchanged a word.

I followed the group back down to our cars. He was standing in front of Rachel's car. I saw her inviting him to dinner that afternoon. He wavered. I had one foot planted in the back of her car; my hands were on the open door.

He turned his head and looked up at me. He says he remembers, first of all, my smile. I remember looking him straight in the eye and saying only, "Come." Maybe then I smiled.

. . .

Our hostess Rachel had assembled a dozen guests for dinner on Christmas afternoon. Most were crowded in conversation into the kitchen she and I were sharing that week. I'd just come downstairs from my bedroom.

Animated by the events at daybreak, I'd walked for miles along the beach that morning. I'd caught sight of a double rainbow; I felt exhilarated.

The man, who I did not yet know as 'Iokepa, entered the dining room: strong, wide, brown, with that lightning bolt of thick white hair brushed back. He wore immaculately pressed jeans, a crisp white T-shirt, and running shoes. He settled at the unset dining room table; I settled across from him. I asked if he'd mind my questions.

He said he did not. He appeared warm, friendly and willing. And like the journalist I'd been for years – less by training, I often think, than by temperament – I barreled questions at the scraps of his story I'd overheard at the sacred *heiau.*

"I heard you say that your dead grandmothers spoke to you. What do you *mean* your dead grandmothers spoke to you? What did they *look* like? How *many* were there? How did you *feel*? Who *else* heard them?"

How did he answer my questions? Directly. Without a shred of defensiveness.

Three grandmothers had spoken to him: a paternal grandmother, great grandmother, and great great grandmother. All had been long-gone when he was born, but they were respected spiritual *kahuna* in their days. (*Kahuna*, he explained, meant practitioners of the sacred aboriginal religion and culture, *Hūnā*. It was my first lesson in the defilement of the Hawaiian language.)

"My grandmothers," he said, "came to me, sat across a table like you are now, and talked to me. I could hear their words like I hear yours. They were shaped by light, clothed in white; their faces were faded. One sat, two stood behind.

"I laughed, and I cried.

"They filled the room with love. For the rest of my life, I'll never forget what that felt like.

"Still," he said, "every morning I hear my grandmothers tell me how much they love me."

When he spoke, the air filled with that love. It lit his brown eyes, his skin, and the space around him. He was the living reflection of his grandmothers' gifts. It was impossible for me not to be moved. It was difficult not to feel the *truth* of him.

Emphatically he spoke of *wānana* – a thousand-year-old, Hawaiian prophecy. He was fulfilling his part at his grandmothers' behest.

A small, serious man sat down next to me – drawn too by 'Iokepa's story. Others came: set down plates, napkins, silver.

"Primal rights," 'Iokepa said. "My grandmothers told me: *The keys to the future lie in the past.* I'm here to reclaim *kanaka maoli* – indigenous Hawaiian – primal rights.

"In Hawaiian, it's called *huliau* – a turning point. When you have moved so far away from where you began, it's important to know how to get back.

"I am a voice of that remembering."

Sometime in that hour or two of rigorous questioning, I told 'Iokepa my dream.

I had awakened Christmas morning at 6:00 a.m. from powerful imagery that felt both momentous and prophetic.

"I'd been sitting in the front passenger seat of a Volkswagen bug," I told him. "Someone else was driving and two others were in the back seat. We were driving a very narrow country road.

"I looked through the windshield and saw a mammoth earthmoving machine coming at us. It was yellow. It filled the entire width of the road, towering like a huge rectangle of glass and metal above and in front of us. I was the only person in the car who saw it bearing down on us."

'Iokepa listened, eyes wide, at full attention.

"There was no chance to avoid the collision or survive it," I said. "But I felt absolutely no fear. I uttered one word: 'God.'

"Then, in the dream, I remember total darkness. I was still in the front seat – curled in a fetal position. When I'd awakened, I knew. I had dreamt about rebirth."

I told 'Iokepa the dream, across the dining room table before dinner, but only after he'd told me he'd been in heavy construction all his American life in Tacoma – maneuvering big dump trucks and other massive machinery. A native Hawaiian, he'd lived most of his life in Washington state.

He laughed his delicious laugh. "So are you saying that I'm an earthmoving machine?"

I blushed. In hindsight, I could have said but did not, "Uh huh. You sure are." I was mesmerized by 'Iokepa – his intensity, his passion – but I was not yet attracted in the conventional way. I felt a magnetism that was utterly unfamiliar – it was in no way recognizable as sexual.

The other guests were setting food on the table. It was time for turkey. 'Iokepa excused himself from dinner. He'd eaten elsewhere, he said. He walked alone to the living room sofa and sat quietly, seemingly contented and relaxed.

From my seat at the table, I looked directly at him fifteen feet away. I filled my plate but I couldn't swallow or speak or follow the dinner conversation. I sat in my silent pool, alone, but connected as if by wire to the brown man who radiated energy.

Rachel's boyfriend asked me from across the table, "Are you all right, Inette?" "Sure," I smiled, "just a bit contemplative."

The morning's strangers were starting to take shape. At the dinner table were: Rachel, originally from England but six years on Kaua'i; her current boyfriend; her most recent past one, and the recent past one's current girlfriend. At dinner, too, were: Veronica (whose house Rachel and I had rented this week) – seven months estranged from her husband – with her nine year old daughter. There were also: a man, who said he'd been waiting ten years to follow his heart to Kaua'i; a woman who'd followed her friend and spiritual healer, Rachel, here; a man who flew helicopters; and a man who painted large canvases of the Kaua'i landscape. There was 'Iokepa and there was me.

Only he and I were strangers to the group. The others were friends. On a whim, the landscape artist had invited 'Iokepa to the *heiau* the night before. Guided always by the grandmothers, 'Iokepa accepted. Rachel invited me.

'Iokepa's ride, the artist, left right after dinner. "I'm leaving," he said. "I'm sure you'll catch a way home."

"I'll take him," I thought. So after dinner when the others shifted toward the living room and towards 'Iokepa, at first I did not. I stayed for several minutes, riveted at the empty dining room table barely saying a word, because I imagined the others might think I was coming on to him. I didn't think I was.

Even more self-conscious alone, and wanting finally to be part of the conversation, I went over. I joined the crowd and sat in the one remaining empty seat, next to 'Iokepa.

Mostly I listened: to their questions and to his answers.

He said. "We've let Western ways distract us. Cell phones, computers, televisions, noise. We are born knowing – all of us. We need to be quiet to listen, to remember.

"The *kanaka maoli* – my people – know how to listen to the Creator and to the spirit inside all creation. It's in our *koko* (our blood), our *na'au* (our gut), our *pu'uwai* (our heart)."

He spread his arms straight and wide apart over his head. "*This* is our genealogy. These are our ancestors' lives. And we're down here." He drew his hands down into a funnel shape, and touched his heart.

"*All* they lived and knew – all their wisdom and experiences – are in us, recorded in our DNA. All the things we know in our gut but don't know how we know them, it's from the ancestors.

"But we've been trained to focus on – to know – only what's out here." He waved his hands into the air. "We forget what's in here." He punched his own chest.

"My grandmothers told me. *When you speak to people's ears, we will speak to their hearts.*"

The tall helicopter pilot asked. "What do you Hawaiians *want*? What's *sovereignty*, anyway?

'Iokepa was silent for a full minute. "Freedom," he said finally. "People will be sovereign – free – when they individually and collectively know who they are. They will be free when they remember fully who they once were – and who they still are. It is first of all about identity."

Sitting directly across from 'Iokepa, Rachel rocked back on two chair legs and abruptly shifted the conversation to herself.

Without a trace of self-consciousness or even the most perfunctory good manners, she told the imposing Hawaiian that she planned to cart sacred *heiau* stones from Kaua'i to Stonehenge – and bring England's stones to Hawai'i. "The vibrations," the Englishwoman said, "are much the same." She was, "balancing the planet."

I looked at 'Iokepa and I felt the others turn to look at him as well. I heard an audible, collective intake of breath – reaction to Rachel's intentions. She was oblivious to the fact that removing stones from the Islands was a violation of more than state law, but a desecration of something essential and Hawaiian.

'Iokepa reached for the beautifully carved, whale-tooth fishhook hanging by twine around his neck. And he said very deliberately, very quietly. "I am touching this," as he ran his thick brown fingers over the gap in the hook, "to remind myself to stay open."

Perhaps he said more. She, too, must have. But the force and energy of his restraint were overwhelming. I was impressed by what he did not say.

An hour later people rose to leave. The party was over. We all walked outside. I offered 'Iokepa a ride home.

"No," he said, "I'll walk up to the road."

"Are you sure?" I asked again.

He hesitated just long enough for me to say, "Where do you live anyway? How long a drive?"

"Fifteen minutes," he said.

"I'm afraid that I'd get lost," I said. "I've driven here at night just once, from the airport."

"That's okay. I'll walk or I'll get a ride on the road." He hoisted his duffel from the porch to his shoulder.

"Goodnight," I said, and I opened the screen door, walked through the living room, and climbed halfway up the stairs to my bedroom. But I was stopped short. Unseen hands turned me around, marched me back through the living room, and pushed me out the screen door onto the porch.

"I've changed my mind," I said.

I asked him to drive. It was warm, and we drove with the windows down to catch the steady trade winds. The night was clear and I could see a black sky thick with stars through the open window. I smelled pungent flowers that I couldn't name.

We talked directions the entire route. He drove the last stretch of the narrow, winding road twice – in and out and in again. He assured me, "You will never get lost on this Island." I focused hard: right, left, right, left, left, left.

So 'Iokepa drove himself home over gravel roads and past boat harbors to the middle of a grassy field where he was living on a fifty-five foot sailboat, eighteen feet off the ground. It looked like the ark in construction before the flood, up on a wooden erector set – a *cradle*, sailors call it – with an eighteen foot ladder leaning against the stern for entry.

He turned my white Dodge Neon around for easy exit, parked on the grass next to the ladder, cut the engine and got out. I walked around to the driver's side. He asked if I'd like him to show me his Island the next day.

"Yes, I'd like that very much." A Hawaiian showing me around the Island, "I'll be down by 9:00."

"Whenever..." he assured me.

Standing there, making small talk and morning plans, abruptly he stopped speaking. After a moment of absolute stillness, he offered me this:

"I don't know who's speaking to me – this has never hap-pened to me before. But he is saying that I am to tell you that he loves you very much, that he's very proud of you, and that your life is about to change." He continued with more words that I couldn't avoid recognizing.

I had told 'Iokepa absolutely nothing about myself other than my morning dream. He didn't know that my father had died less than two years before.

I felt like someone had picked up a hammer, hit me on the side of the head, and screamed: *Pay attention!*

I was emphatically telling myself. "Girl, get yourself home to your own bed." It was that sudden and that strong. I reached up and touched his cheek. Then I climbed into the driver's seat and said goodnight.

When I arrived on the road to 'Iokepa's boat in daylight the next day, fifteen minutes later than I'd agreed to, I was surprised to see him already walking up the road to meet me. He wore no watch, followed no timetables. We met; I drove back to the boat as he asked me to, parked between the ladder and a small grove of coconut palms, and sat in the car. He sat in the passenger seat.

"I need to tell you something before we go," he said. His light brown eyes assessed my darker ones. "I can't not tell you and go through the day with you.

"Last night when you left and then again this morning, I wanted to make love to you. I still want to make love to you."

I turned away and stared straight ahead through the windshield, up at the enormous sailboat hovering in the air. I said nothing; gave nothing away with my face. But I was filled with, "Me too!"

"That doesn't mean anything has to happen," he answered himself. "I don't expect anything. It's fine, if this isn't what you want. I just needed to tell you – I couldn't *not* tell you."

Several days later, he said. "Ten months on the beaches here with almost naked women. Ten months and I've felt nothing! I've asked the grandmothers, "*Why?* Why do you put me here...and nothing? Nothing in me.

"Until you."

Until me.

I remember everything about that night – December 26, 1997, almost thirteen years ago. We'd returned from a magnificent day touring. I remember the eighteen foot ladder leaning against the sailboat called *Imagine*. I have always been afraid of heights. "Can you climb the ladder?" he asked. "I'll hold it for you."

"Yeah, you hold it...I can do it."

I swallowed my fear, climbed the wobbly ladder, and straddled the word *Imagine*. I climbed bravely (without looking down), stepped over the rail on the stern, balanced carefully across the deck, and then went down the steps inside. Past caution. Always before, I'd been vigilant; I had two sons to rear.

"I've been with just one woman for nine years," 'Iokepa told me.

"I've been three years without a date," I answered.

Past resistance; I took seven steps down. As my son Nathan wrote in a short story: "A thought for every step."

Inside, the boat had been scrubbed bare by the hurricane of '92: no leather benches or *koa* wood cabinetry or foldout beds remained – none of it. But it was clean and warm, neat and homey. There was a reading lamp, a neatly made mattress, hanging clothes, pictures on the wall, refrigerator, shelves and stove top. Everything was in its place. This man knew how to make a home. Later, I would learn the degree to which that was true.

It felt just right. He felt right. He was tan and I was pale. He had wide feet, huge hands, thick fingers. He tapered solidly from shoulder to hip. Momentarily, I wished I tapered for him. Then I let it go.

We didn't undress each other. Not those groping, secret handfuls. He undressed; then I did. We presented ourselves to one another standing naked – wide-eyed and open. But we didn't touch or speak until we were lying on the carefully arranged mattress.

The touching was utterly free. "I love how you do that," he said. "How did you know...?"

"I was inspired."

He laughed at that. But I was nothing short of inspired touching this handsome Hawaiian man.

There was the matter of his being Hawaiian – consummately – but also not. Hawaiian to his toes – walking and running the streets, the beaches – yet still, an all-American, working-class boy. The working-class boy was almost the more foreign. A history of fistfights, booze, smoking, cussing, driving trucks, building hot rods; competing in karate matches, motorcycle races, and making money – all evaporated when his part in the prophecy was revealed.

I laughed, said to myself, and then out loud, "How unlikely we are together!"

He answered nothing, but beamed his broad smile, all white teeth and impish eyes.

"How impossible we'd have been at any other time of our lives," I insisted.

"Do you intimidate a lot of men?" he asked me, grinning like he already knew the answer.

I did not intimidate him at all. I felt known. I felt that I knew him too – and loved what I knew.

If there are things rightly called miracles, what God put between 'Iokepa and me on that boat in the sky was a miracle.

We slept together on *Imagine*, high above the ground, but submerged under streaming light. It poured in through the portholes – morning light on my face. "Can you feel it?" 'Iokepa asked. "Feel yourself in the light?"

We'd sleep for two hours, awaken, talk, instruct, listen, sleep again, awaken, touch. He was a healthy, loving male. I was a healthy, loving female. We were well met.

He was shocked when I said after two nights together that I required seven or eight hours sleep.

"Seven or eight hours?!" Apparently, he required much less.

I worried that I would push myself to exhaustion – up half the night talking, listening; half the night making love. By day we toured the ancient, private places: mountains, beaches, canyons, *heiau*.

On New Year's Eve, the night before I left Kaua'i, we danced by the side of the road to old rock and roll from the car radio, on a hilltop under the stars. He said: "You've changed. You are not the same person who came to this Island."

"How did you recognize me before I changed?" I asked him.

He paused only a second. "I was told."

For my entire lifetime I have created pain around goodbyes. Perversely, I have picked fights to ease the separation. I'd turn my vulnerability into a protective wall of anger.

Except when I left Kaua'i and 'Iokepa. He told me that he never wrote letters and he didn't phone. Yet at the airport, there was a deep joy, a single moment of loss, and then a bottomless knowing. It felt easy.

"It's very exciting," 'Iokepa said at the already empty boarding gate. "We don't know what comes next." I didn't yet realize that his words were prophetic – the literal definition of our life together.

We held each other, kissed deeply, and smiled into each other's eyes. I felt a moment of embarrassment at the public affection. He gave me a gentle push in the small of my back and said, "*Aloha*, Inette."

"*Aloha*, 'Iokepa."

I handed my boarding pass to the woman at the entrance door, and quickly turned around for one last look. He was gone.

THE PROPHET

Epiphany

The man and the spirit I missed were naturally entwined.

During that week we were together, 'Iokepa told me his story.

'Iokepa Hanalei 'Īmaikalani was born in Tacoma, Washington. His father was a full-blooded Hawaiian. His mother was from Idaho. The dinner table was bisected. At one end: raw fish, *poi* (boiled, mashed *kalo* root), *laulau* (shredded chicken or pork steamed in *kalo* and *kī* leaf wraps). At the other end: roast beef, mashed potatoes, gravy and green beans. But it was from his mother's end of the table that the Hawaiian of her children's heritage was venerated, celebrated, and insisted upon. In the lily white American Northwest, where brown skin engendered some deep racial hatred and name-calling, Emma Lee took it as her mission to educate.

"My children are Hawaiian," she told her oldest daughter's ignorant teacher. "It's a very special culture they carry." Emma Lee was well-chosen by the ancestors.

"I was glad," she told me when we later met, "that all three girls and 'Iokepa looked like their father – he was a very handsome man."

Tacoma and environs was home to a sizable native Hawaiian community. Music, *Lū'au*, language, and custom were embedded in the household. There were Hawaiian social clubs, and Puanani, the oldest daughter, boarded at Kamehameha School in Honolulu. The family on the Islands and the family in exile in Washington were tight.

'Iokepa never went to college. It wasn't a consideration for the man whose interests were physical rather than academic. He went straight from high school into heavy construction. Over the years he paved extensive stretches of Washington state freeways; he excavated and laid pipe for miles of Seattle's waterlines. He ran enormous work crews, and forests of massive machinery. His rapid-fire judgment calls would cost or save the company hundreds of thousands of dollars for a few minutes lost. He thrived on the pressure. 'Iokepa undertook all things in his life fully. There was but one way to do things: "The right way."

He'd married young, called himself by an English bastardization of his given name – *Joseph* – and divorced after eight years and two children. He had been single since then. I suspected the hurt had been that deep.

Eventually he founded his own company, became his own boss. At forty-six, he was signing a contract to buy four Kenworth Dump Trucks in preparation for excavation work on a third runway at SeaTac Airport near Seattle. His share of the net profit would be nearly two million dollars.

His overriding passion for twenty-seven years had been a 1953 International pickup truck with a small-block, Chevrolet engine – his hot rod. He painted it brown, licensed it *Fudge*, and raced it.

He was a black belt in karate – competing internationally in tournaments for three years, and defining a type of fighting his *sensei* called, "Joseph's War Dance." He raced motorcycles, speed boats, and cars. He loved speed, and he was the insistent defender of the underdog. He was an utterly confident male.

"The only things I used to read," he told me when we met, "were blueprints, Hot Rod magazine, and Playboy."

Little did he know when he assumed his role in the prophecy, that over the next ten years he would devour: Ralph Waldo Emerson, Walt Whitman, Henry James, Thomas Jefferson, Karl Jung; Martin Luther King, Malcolm X, Winston Churchill, and Cornell West – Goethe, Cicero, Leonardo, and Einstein – for starters and for pleasure. The grandmothers called it his *grooming.*

The man and spirit I'd met at Christmas had been transformed in a single breath. He stepped from a conventional American life in Washington into something quite else. He agreed, on Thursday, January 30, 1997, to accept his inheritance. He did it with unshakable faith and unyielding courage.

"I was driving down the road," he said, "in a spanking new Kenworth dump truck. I'd never read the Bible. I didn't go to church. But I always knew I was being watched over – all the high speed things I did, and I was never hurt."

Driving down the freeway in the shadow of the 14,000 foot Mt. Rainier, with the rare Seattle winter sunshine warming his face, he was flooded with gratitude. "I recalled my entire life – how wonderful it had been."

He was moved to offer a prayer. "God, I've gotten to do a lot of things in my life that most men never get to do. I've gone at high speeds, fought national tournaments, traveled in Europe, had homes, cars, wonderful children – my life has been amazing. If anyone in my family has to pass, I ask that you take me."

Later, he explained the impulse to me. "It was about surrender."

He had no idea at the time – nor did I when we met – that the required surrender was unrelenting, and forever.

At the moment he offered himself, he felt an enormous weight settle on his shoulders, unbudging for two days.

On January 30, 1997, in a modest suburban Seattle house, at exactly seven in the evening: 'Iokepa saw and heard his paternal grandmother, great grandmother, and great great grandmother appear before him and hand him his 'destiny' and, not inconsequentially, 'the destiny of the Hawaiian people.'

Two other people were present: his oldest sister Puanani (who he called, 'the foundation of our family') and a Caucasian woman in whose home this took place. Both women saw everything he saw and heard every word. Apparently, the women were there to witness and validate 'Iokepa's experience. The grandmothers spoke only to him.

For an hour and a half, they spoke. "Like I speak to you now," he said. They alluded, first, to his words, "I ask that you take me."

We were waiting for you to say what you said. The timing is perfect.

The weight lifted from his shoulders.

They revealed a thousand-year-old prophecy, and the part he had agreed to play. They catalogued every significant event since childhood that had prepared him for what was then asked.

We remind you of the promises you made to the Creator. You are a voice that will be heard – a voice your people have been waiting to hear. You will help return the land and the culture – the Hawaiian Kingdom – to the people.

In every culture on Earth, God gave keys to survival. Hawaiians will return to theirs. What will happen on the Hawaiian Islands will be an example for all the peoples on Earth – an opportunity for them to emulate.

Much later, 'Iokepa told me and others: "My grandmothers *are* your grandmothers...and yours...and *yours*! People don't know what they're capable of.

"Hawai'i is the place that's been called out in prophecy – not Germany, not Alaska – it's *here*. But my people didn't have a starting line or a finishing line. It goes *out* from here: bringing people together to pray for something larger than self. I encourage a return to Source. Prayer *is* action. We'll see the results."

The grandmothers continued.

Hawai'i will be the first to successfully remove itself from the United States. But it is not about taking anything from anyone. It is about adding to – reminding every soul what they were given at the beginning of time.

Then they spoke of 'Iokepa's personal journey.

We will make you as strong physically as we make you mentally. We are going to remove smoking, drinking, and swearing from you. No one wants to be around you if you have been smoking; no one wants to listen to you if you have been drinking; and you are unprepared to represent the Creator and the Hawaiian people if you need to swear.

Just as we remove smoking, drinking and swearing, we will give you back the authentic language, history and culture. Over the next ten years, you will be given what you need, when you need it – never more and never before.

There would be ten years of preparation – the required readying of the prophet. Afterwards, the ancient prophecy would unfold. "I don't know how it begins," he told me when we met.

The grandmothers continued.

You are being sent as a child, with nothing to unlearn. Once you have heard all the lies, you will know the truth. But you must give up everything you love.

Within two weeks, he had given the house to a girlfriend. To friends and family he gifted the seven cars (including *Fudge*), the tools of his trade, all the mementos (including photographs from childhood to middle age). The multi-million dollar contract, he tore up unsigned. He signed his power of attorney over to his sister Puanani, told her to give away every cent: no savings, no investments, no credit cards, and no secret fall-back stashes.

"What kind of man could say, 'No!' to his grandmothers?" 'Iokepa asked me. He truly could not imagine. Perhaps, only a native Hawaiian could.

On February 1, he awakened and knew he'd never have a drink of alcohol again. On February 2, he awakened and knew he'd had his last cigarette. On February 3, he went to work and didn't know how to speak. He explained, "In heavy construction, every other word is...

"It was," he said, "As though someone had lifted a computer chip from my brain."

On February 12, 1997 he landed on O'ahu. I met him ten months later.

Within hours of my return home from Kaua'i, I called my friend and fellow-writer Lena and asked her to join me for a long walk. From my front door, we hiked along the four-mile loop that circled Council Crest Park, the highest point in Portland.

"I'm going to tell you a story," I said when we were still stretching our legs, "that you may or may not believe or even want to hear. But I'm going to need a friend and I hope you can be her."

Lena is a tall, slender, aristocratic, reserved writer with waist-length hair and a passion for native species, human and plant. She agreed to listen, then and throughout.

She heard my Kaua'i stories. Christmas day: the *heiau*, the word *TRUTH*, my father's message, a Hawaiian with a prophecy. Finally, "If I never see 'Iokepa again, I'm grateful for this week. But there won't be another man in my life – 'Iokepa is it."

'Iokepa and I had no understanding of a future together, I told her. I was to wait to hear from him, he said. Among his parting words were: he never wrote letters, never phoned.

Lena sucked in a slow, deep breath. "I'm in awe of your faith," she said.

I stopped mid-stride, with a view of snow-covered Mt. Hood in our faces, reached over and hugged her.

I had a life in Portland – a very good one – sons to get through adolescence, a serious career, a beautiful home, a place in the community. I was asking only for one good friend to see me though the coming months.

22

"I'm not as brave as you are," Lena told me as we yanked our muddy shoes off in my front hallway. "But I love you, and I know you have some things to teach me."

Three days after I left Kaua'i, 'Iokepa (who didn't make phone calls) called me. A day later, I received a postcard from the man who didn't write. The calls, the cards and letters continued. I was rewarded, I believed, for letting go of expectation, for holding loosely to love.

'Iokepa's first phone message on my answering machine said: "*Aloha.* You are dearly missed." Not dreadfully, but dearly. I missed him the same.

INTERRUPTED SLEEP

January, 1998

When I arrived home from Kaua'i, it was to the deepest loves and most profound concern of my life – Ben and Nathan. Perhaps it was not so surprising that when the grandmothers entered my home: they came to me, first, speaking about my sons.

The setting was perfect. Home was a glass house, like a bird's nest set up into the surrounding fir trees. It had views of the Coastal Range Mountains in the daylight, Portland's city lights at night. It stretched three levels into the hillside at the highest point of the city, across from Council Crest Park where ancient Natives had gathered for ritual purposes. I felt the sanctity of the place.

Three years before, after an intensive search of urban, rural and suburban Portland, I drove past this house that was utterly and peculiarly modern – nothing at all like any other house I'd ever rented or owned. I knew in an instant it would be mine.

So, I drove my little family across the country – away from mother, father, brothers, friends – enrolled Ben in tenth grade, Nathan in fifth, and vowed never to move again, certainly not while the boys were still in school.

The move had been both emotionally and physically draining – the uprooting and then replanting roots – but I came to love Oregon for its mountains, rivers, ocean, and good-hearted, open-minded people. It was a writer's paradise, populated by serious writers and even more serious readers. I placed a wooden *mezuzah* on the front doorpost, *Shabbat* candlesticks on the kitchen window. I'd found home.

I wrote and I reared children in Oregon. But after a series of post-divorce relationships covering almost ten years, I took a sabbatical from men. I'd begun, finally to recognize a pattern in my choices that guaranteed failure – or success, I suppose, if my goal was to live out my years alone. I retrenched, reconsidered, and decided that I could use some time in my own company. Those were the Portland years.

...

I had been a single mother with a vengeance. I laughed and called myself, *Big Mama*. Now Ben was seventeen, a senior in high school and the consummate kid with potential. A genuine intellectual titillated by ideas, articulate, witty, and sensitive – a good kid. He hadn't done an adequate job of running his own life, and I tended to cover his shortfall – intercede where necessary. He came to depend on it. He did almost no homework, lied about completing assignments, swore every semester it would be different, and angered teachers who should have been his natural allies, because he seemed to be so indifferent to the consequences.

This was January of his senior year. Nothing had changed. He wanted college; he wanted a decent college; he needed financial aid. But his high school grade point average was abysmal. It was past time for college applications, he was procrastinating at every step, terrified he'd blown his chances, bailed out only by excellent SAT scores.

I felt like a hitchhiker on his emotional roller coaster. I thought I was going nuts.

"How many economics' chapters did you get done at Dad's?" I asked Ben when he returned from Christmas vacation.

"Uh," he answered and smiled down at me sweetly. Ben stood six feet tall, had soft, curly, brown hair that he loathed and dark eyes you could see his heart in. He was big, but he looked vulnerable.

"Does that mean none?" I accused.

"Well, not *none*," he answered very slowly.

"You promised six back-chapters! You need economics to graduate! Ben...not again."

"Yeah mom. Again."

. . .

The voices began ten days after I'd left Kaua'i, nine since I'd walked with Lena. The night was not recognizably different from any other. The boys were in their bedrooms two stories below me – asleep, or pretending to be. It was quiet.

At nine o'clock, I curled into my overstuffed club chair in the corner, propped my feet on the matching ottoman, and began reading Toni Morrison's *Paradise*. I'd started it before vacation, and I was trying to retrieve the unmarked page where I'd left off.

The top floor – mine – was a giant unbroken space: bedroom, office, library, partitioned bath. It had six skylights and glass walls with no curtains, because the nearest neighbors were trees.

My bed was an antique four-poster covered in a blue and white quilt. It sat under two large skylights, and if there were a moon to be seen through the Portland winter clouds, I would see it.

This night, there was no visible moon. I was in bed by 10:30. Like most writers, I kept a legal pad on my bedside table to capture ideas that might come to me at night. I thought I slept well.

The next morning, I ate breakfast with the boys, saw them off to school and returned to my office for the day's work.

I was settling down at my desk: stretching my neck and shuffling papers. I glanced over my shoulder at the bed – I'd made it before breakfast. My eye caught the legal pad on the night table. The first page looked full. It was empty when I went to bed. I walked over and looked.

That pad may as well have dropped into the room from another planet. It was that foreign. There were pages and pages of writing. Every word was unfamiliar. I had absolutely no recollection of recording them – yet they were undeniably in my hand.

I read the words: alternately astonished, delighted – and thoroughly baffled.

The pages recorded a conversation. Primarily I asked questions – the questions were irrefutably mine. Then another hand (looser, faster, less legible), and another voice (words I'd never imagined) answered. It was bizarre – but unbelievably persuasive.

The words were first and fully about my son Ben – next about my baby, Nathan.

They said:

> *You have held your eldest so close that neither of you can breathe in spirits' truth. Free Ben from your twisted breaths. Send Ben out with faith in his own angels. No more, 'my' sons. They are 'ours.' No more: only Ben, only Nathan. You mother the Earth and its every inhabitant.*
>
> *It is essential to make room for new life. Holding on, you cannot hear the truth – nor can they.*

Even bewildered, I recognized the truth of what I was reading. What sounded to me like a demand that I do the impossible – release my sons – I would come to realize was something quite else. It was simply an admonition to trust: I would not be able to control the direction of their lives. I could not control *them.*

When the voices began that first night, I had no conscious awareness of them. I must have reached automatically for the empty legal pad and pen next to the phone. Mechanically, I must have filled every page with words.

That first morning with pad in hand, I could not have even speculated on the source of the words. I had experienced miracles in 'Iokepa's presence. But that was in *Hawai'i* – and with him. This was different: this was Oregon, my secure home, just the boys and me. What did *there* have to do with here?

But the next night, when the words came, I was wide awake. And on that second night I demanded on the page: "Who speaks these words?" There was absolutely no hesitation between my neatly written question and the almost illegibly scrawled answer.

No one loves you more than your father, but there are many who love you as well as he does. All men and all women are beloved children of mothers, fathers, grandmothers, grandfathers. There is no death. You hear us clearly. We are the continuance of life. We help you to love fearlessly.

The voices continued nightly. And now I was conscious of them. It was always in the dead of night after two or three hours sleep. I'd bolt awake, sometimes turn on the lamp, and frantically write the words that came through me on a legal pad.

I saw nothing but the page. Sometimes in the dark, I didn't even see that. I heard nothing with my ears – and yet I *felt* the cascade of words. As if my gut were able to speak – it was enunciating with perfect clarity. There was no doubt that the soft, sweet, compassionate voices in my gut were 'Iokepa's grandmothers. After the first few nights, there was no doubt at all.

I understood that this wisdom on the page was being offered to me for the taking. But I knew, too, that I was not yet able to absorb it.

I'd transcribe for at least an hour – until the words stopped. (There was never any uncertainty.) The moment I put the pad down, I'd drop instantly back to sleep – soundly.

Sometimes, when I was especially exhausted, I'd refuse: to sit up, to turn on the lamp, to write. But until I submitted, I was not able to sleep again – no matter how tired.

This became our peculiar routine – the grandmothers and me. The words were too powerful to ignore or to resist.

The words ran through me in the dark and spilled undigested onto the yellow legal pads, night after night slicing into my sleep. They were like raw energy. I could see by them, feel the rush of them, but I couldn't hold onto them.

I was there, but I was not there. It was my handwriting on the page, my back up against the pillows of the four-poster bed, my voice that engaged the dialogue. But the understanding came later – years later.

So in those months in Portland, I wrote words and asked questions that seemed completely removed from what was ancient or Hawaiian. Yet they were not. This, I came to know, was my initiation into listening as the aboriginals listened, hearing as the *kanaka maoli* heard. Native Hawaiians heard the ancestors' voices in the wind and waves, the sun and the moon, and in their own hearts.

I came to understand that the teachings from the ancestors marked the trail of my embryonic faith: the pitfalls were my fears and doubts; the peaks were remembering what we all once knew. I didn't yet understand that I was being prepared for a life with 'Iokepa and his people.

I'd written professionally for thirty years, but in truth I'd written since I was a child. I hadn't always known why I wrote. Later I knew and I taught, "I write so that I may understand the world inside me and around me."

I'd written conventionally: journalism for sixteen years (newspapers and magazines); books for twelve years. I'd written at prescribed times: Mondays through Fridays, from the moment the kids slammed the front door heading for school, until the moment they stepped off the school bus in mid-afternoon. If there was spiritual content to my early work, I didn't know it. I knew the writing to be emotionally truthful, and I was proud of that.

What was being given to me and asked of me now was quite different. I was to receive the teachings in a haze of interrupted sleep and transcribe them to the computer during the day, without changing a breath, a comma, or a misspelling. When I typed, I saw them for the first time – and I was in awe. I vowed always to reread them – to *get* them. But I never did, because the next night there was more, and I was exhausted.

. . .

'Iokepa called three nights after the voices began. The moment I lifted the receiver, I poured out an exuberant account of my night-time visits. I stammered through the miraculous story of the grandmothers' dictated wisdom, the night-time writings. Then I read him some of their words.

To 'Iokepa, it made perfect sense. I was a writer: how better to reach a writer's heart? He was thrilled at my affirmation; delighted that I'd been reassured in this way.

"Mail me some pages." And I did. He read and reread them for months and then years afterwards.

But he reminded me immediately. "Say *mahalo*, offer gratitude. What others consider a miracle if it happens once, you get to experience always." He rightly saw the *gift*, where I'd been too stunned and awed to acknowledge it.

I had been given remarkable gifts: 'Iokepa and his grandmothers. But there was another side to these gifts, and embracing that side asked a great deal of me.

I was still a single mom, a homeowner, a feet-on-the-ground woman – driving carpools and living a very familiar life. But by night there cracked open a whole other world and I teetered to maintain a balance.

So from moments of divine inspiration, pure faith and certainty, I plummeted at regular intervals into fear, confusion and despair. I'd find important and unimportant reasons to doubt. Lena reminded me. "Remember, you're still human." But it was the single thing I could never forget. Change, for me, had always been problematic – my acceptance of it slower than I wished. Yet this time, I knew I'd better savor the demanding journey, because the destination was likely to be a formidable one.

First of all, there was my mother. I loved my mother; my mother loved me. But sometimes we didn't like each other so much. I was the youngest of three and the only daughter.

"The boys never gave us as much trouble as you," was her stock phrase.

In my family, *trouble* meant refusing to follow in lock-step the specific gender roles we'd been assigned. She'd prayed hard for a girl and I'd better behave like one.

I had told my mother about 'Iokepa on a phone call to Baltimore soon after I'd returned home. I offered her an edited version of my remarkable vacation. I spoke to her of the man and my feelings for him. I censored the metaphysical – and the physical.

Now my dynamic, eighty-six year old mother called me once a week and dredged up stories of my high school beaus, college sweethearts, and post-divorce years. It all added up to my lack of sound judgment and good sense.

One call began. "You said you loved the doctor."

"Mom, that was twelve years ago. My marriage had just ended…"

"You told me that the professor might be the one."

"Yeah, after two dates, he looked okay. After four, it was a disaster. That was four years ago. I should never have told you.

"Mom, listen. 'Iokepa is my *bashert* – God's choice. I've never had that before."

"You can't know him after one week," she insisted.

"I knew him after one minute."

She was afraid I'd be hurt by 'Iokepa. But more, it was beyond my mother's ability to imagine a Hawaiian – or any man – who'd given up two million dollars to walk the streets in faith.

'Iokepa's mother was proud of her son's choices; my mother believed that they were a sign of indolence and fanaticism. She assumed my attachment to "Joseph" was a dire mistake. 'Iokepa's oldest sister (we'd spoken by phone) listed the acceptable choice of mates who'd pass muster for my Jewish mother: "doctor, lawyer…." Then she laughed and appended, "Indian chief." Puanani was promising to become a good friend.

I knew that my mother wished for me exactly what she had with my Dad – a good, secure, conventional marriage. I loved her for that. At some level it was exactly what I wanted for myself. But I struggled mightily under the yoke of her criticism.

The grandmothers spoke.

You are a grown woman following the path laid out for you. Your mother follows hers. You've each made mistakes confusing your path for the other's, and expecting unanimity of experience. It's a mistake we often make in this life. Remember: The individual path is sacred.

Next, there were my sons. It was hard to watch my youngest child suffer while I felt powerless. Nathan, from sixth grade on, felt the social sting of middle school cruelty – and I didn't have the words or moves to make it better. The school bus was a microcosm of internecine warfare, and Nathan refused to honor the established rules of combat. He didn't accept that he must stand or sit three to a seat, because the back five rows of the bus with many empty places were reserved by unspoken custom for his seniors – the eighth graders. He didn't accept that a boy who was brilliant at math but challenged the teacher's answers should be ridiculed by the teacher. He saw injustices in every corridor of West Sylvan Middle School. He felt it his duty to address them all. He'd bridge no interference from his mother.

On the other hand, his brother Ben and I were at each other's throat. One night, Ben was excitedly setting up his new, long-awaited computer. He'd bought it for himself. After dinner I reminded him to do the dinner dishes – he and Nathan alternated nights.

When my back was turned, he'd escaped down the stairs to his room, to the brand new computer – laughing.

"Ben, you've got ten minutes to get up here."

"But I just started."

I gave him twenty minutes. Then I shouted from the top of the stairs. "Your time's up Ben."

He didn't answer.

"Get upstairs now or the computer goes!"

"You can't! It's mine!"

"I said, 'Now!'"

"I hate you, Mom!"

What was simple had turned nightmarish. I felt worthless. Nothing I did with them was ever perfect.

Perfect is an entirely foreign concept. It allows humans to beat themselves up. To loathe what we love. Stop the self abuse on the kids' behalf – immediately. It saddens

us beyond your knowing. Free yourself from human stan-
dards of perfection.

Trust Ben to make his own mistakes, even as your
parents could not trust you – as your mother still cannot.
You are doing with Ben, exactly as you bemoan your
mother does to you. Exactly!

Money – I had profound doubts about money. I'd seen it, I
think, as the root of selfishness and greed. At some level, I was
more comfortable living in financial uncertainty. I feared that
wealth would corrupt me.

With money, humans have created control, power,
and hierarchy – male versus female. But that is not its
purpose. That is holding on in fear.

Money, like forgiveness, compassion and love are the
currency of God's energy. It is already ours to use – to let
pass through us, and around us.

As we give you these words on this page and you
write them and pass them inevitably out into the world –
so is it with money. Open your hands and it will pass on.

Like these words we give you are yours, but never
only yours, so it is with money – the currency is yours, but
never only yours. It is an energy force for use with grati-
tude always.

Finally, there was the dictated writing. I'd sent those pages
from the nighttime scribbling to 'Iokepa. On the phone
yesterday, he said. "Your words are beautiful. You say the
words come *through* you, but I say that they are your words."

I was defensive: "They aren't mine!"

I asked on the legal pad, "Are the voices I hear just pro-
jections of my own knowing and desire?"

But of course they are both. The voices are heard be-
cause you know and desire. You refuse credit for what you
deserve.

All answers are already on the page. Through your focus and your open heart, there is a selection – yours. So 'Iokepa is right – the words are your choosing. And you are right, too. These are our words.

Like the poets, Rilke and Neruda, you claim and you do not claim. Your name sits on the outside of the book. But you will tell the world how they came – and people will read and understand.

With a grin, I ventured: All is me. All is we.

In those first weeks apart there were times I'd look over my roll-top desk past the Coastal Range to the Pacific Ocean that I could imagine beyond, and I'd send my thoughts and feelings to 'Iokepa in Niumalu, Kaua'i. In return, I'd receive his thoughts in the same way. There were days I felt his joy, days I felt his sorrow.

The 'Iokepa I met carried the pain of his people chiseled into his nervous system.

"God gave the stewardship of the 'āina (land) to the kanaka maoli (the original people)," he said. "We don't own it – only God does – but we were chosen to care for it.

"Yet there are people who believe they need to own it. They destroy the land, the ocean; they level the heiau and then they go home. But we don't have any place to go – this is our home.

"My culture is not for sale."

The man, who had refused to cry for most of his forty-six years, now regularly choked back tears when his people's hurt was articulated. He would beg his grandmothers, "Don't do this to me now!" when he was embarrassed by grief in a public moment.

From his first encounter with them, in January, 1997, 'Iokepa had never stopped speaking to his grandmothers. The flow of words from them to him became over the months and years, a fountain. In mid-sentence he'd grow silent and mutely ask for the words.

"If I rush them, it becomes human," he said. "If I take my time, I open the door for the ancestors' words.

"Word perfect," he called it. "I get a little shot of adrenaline – not much – then I go deeply into the moment of understanding, of explanation. The words – I depend on them. It never occurs to me they won't come."

Exactly like the flood of my nighttime writings – where words on the page alternated between my own recognizable questions and the ancestors' unrecognizable answers – so transparently delineated were 'Iokepa's spoken words from those of his grandmothers. His mouth spoke them, but neither the language nor the ideas were familiar.

The grandmothers words came to him with equanimity and ease; to me the words arrived like a rip into my carefully orchestrated life.

During that long dark Oregon winter, connected only by telephone to 'Iokepa, I paradoxically came to know this man more deeply than during the intense days together in the Hawai'i sunshine. Perhaps it was a combination of the grey days, the isolation, and the chance to savor and digest the experiences of that brief week together.

I recalled that I had witnessed 'Iokepa consistently energized by the challenge of strangers. Contrary opinions seemed to excite him. He seldom tired of one-on-one.

On our third day together that Christmas week, I saw 'Iokepa listen intently while a well-dressed businessman challenged the prophecy. "It's not realistic to expect Hawai'i to go back to what it was."

"If I accept your idea of reality then I've already given up my own," 'Iokepa answered. "*Reality* is a human invention, a human theory. I can't compromise."

Later that same day, 'Iokepa was engaged by a middle aged woman in a grocery store. She asked: "How can one man with no money make a change?"

He laughed. "Nelson Mandela was one man in jail who imagined an end to apartheid."

But more to the point: he *never* felt he was alone.

This Hawaiian, who on a single Seattle winter evening saw his life reshaped like clay in the hands of his grandmothers, insisted. "I *know* that change can happen in a breath. I lived it. I don't want to miss it when it happens."

Afterwards, I told him. "With some people, you are re-markably patient."

He answered: "It's about listening for the hidden words. The grandmothers told me to listen to everyone and everything. They said, *'There are going to be many false prophets.'* They duped the Hawaiians with language. They wrote words my people couldn't understand, couldn't read. I listen for the small print. I won't let it happen again."

Several times during that first week, I heard well-wishers offer 'Iokepa, "Good luck on your journey."

He first thanked them for their prayer. Then he stopped them cold. "Hawaiians didn't believe in 'luck.' That's superstition – something that was brought here. *Kanaka maoli* lived their faith.

"Myth is not fiction. Myth is the reality of an *observed* phenomenon. Unlike science, it only has to happen once. Moses would have had a tough time parting the sea a second time."

For his faith, 'Iokepa had been gradually rewarded with the return of the ancients' gifts: *'ike hānau* – birth knowledge; *'ike pāpālua* – communing with the spirits. Like his ancestors, he could hear his answers in *ka makani* (the wind), in *na nalu* (the waves), in *na pōhaku* (the rocks).

What Iokepa called his 'job' was nominally unpaid. But the return was immeasurable. It was in the light within another soul's eyes – and it was seldom subtle.

Money, however, came in the most miraculous ways.

During that entire Christmas week, I didn't spend one cent of the $800 I carried in travelers' checks. "It's important that you be taken care of now," he said.

Those who recognized him – and knew him as the fulfill-ment of a prophecy, long-dreamed and spoken – wanted to be a part of his journey. They offered: a meal, a room, a $20 bill, a hug.

The grandmothers called him *a proud Hawaiian* and knew that the receiving would be tough. They told him. *You cannot refuse people the right to be part of this.*

He resisted at first, but, inexorably, he surrendered.

I was in awe of 'Iokepa's faith, amazed by his willingness to do without comforts. 'Iokepa accepted the shortfall: days without food, public restrooms for shelter. He never doubted the benevolence of his ancestors.

'Iokepa was a natural magnet for the wounded – the needy looking for a piece of his strength. Just before New Years, I watched one awestruck woman effuse, "You are so filled with...."

He stopped her. "We all are. You already know the answers. Just ask. Then *listen.*"

More than once, he told me. "If in all the words I speak, a single word sparks confidence – I've done my job."

...

In our first week together, 'Iokepa had claimed. "The only things I used to read were blue prints, Hot Rod magazine, and Playboy."

I, on the other hand, had seldom been without a book in my hand; I'd never seen a blueprint up close, never been to a drag race, and I thought Playboy exploited women – reduced them to objects of men's wet dreams.

He dated women who were models and barmaids. I chose men who were intellectuals, gentle, non-combative, 'in touch with their female side.' I'd been with the same man for twenty years – sixteen of them married. When I left him, I continued to choose him (or versions of him) in each relationship that followed. I'd never met a Hawaiian.

Culturally and traditionally, I was Jewish to the bone. Spiritually I'd been, in the years since the divorce, a seeker. The seeking took me from Hindu texts to Buddhism; from Machu Picchu to Bali.

'Iokepa knew one Jew, the tailor in the men's clothing store where he'd been a delivery boy in high school. I was the second.

It is truthful to say that neither of us could have imagined the other. (Though I have a friend who insists we could not have found one another if we had not.)

It is equally truthful to say that I almost immediately loved what I found.

'This is not my choice, it's my destiny,' 'Iokepa was the first to assert.

But I understood at once how remarkable that was in light of our obvious differences.

Now in the depth of Oregon's winter what I loved and admired in 'Iokepa, I was also threatened by. I'd never played second fiddle to anyone else's first. I'd never waited in the wings for my turn. I'd moved mountains with the force of my own personality and competence. Ironically, in the face of 'Iokepa's strength my confidence was flagging.

A great deal has been given to you and a great deal has been asked. We put you back in Portland's winter, alone, among the big-time doubters – mirrors, all, of the remnants of doubt in yourself.

You are separate souls, on separate paths – choosing to weave a life together. Take not what belongs to the other, nor give away what is yours. He will never ask you to relinquish who you are. Who you are is why you are together.

Forgive yourself, your confusion. Forgive yourself, so you may forgive others. In time, even 'Iokepa will require your forgiveness.

Even that?

THE *KANAKA MAOLI*

Dispossessed

In my week with 'Iokepa on Kaua'i, we drove and walked from one end of the Island to the other, but when I returned home and friends reeled off the sites not-to-be-missed in every tour book, I'd seen none of them.

Ironically, what I had seen was an overwhelming majority of Caucasians and a huge percentage of ethnic Japanese and Filipinos. Where were the Native Hawaiians? Almost invisible, it seemed, tucked away in marginal geographic and economic pockets. What the state government called 'Hawaiian Homelands,' 'Iokepa called 'United States reservations for Hawaiians.'

While I was a visitor in those first few days alone – smearing Bain de Soleil on my face and shoulders – the *kanaka maoli* were being herded off to prison, incarcerated in numbers double their meager share of the population. While I was paddling a kayak up the Wailua River, the *kanaka maoli* (once the healthiest people on the planet) were dying much too young at astronomically high rates, of diabetes and cancer. While I was hiking the trails in the Waimea Canyon, 'Iokepa's kin were flunking out of school, beating wives, living on government handout – homeless, hopeless, addicted, and oppressed.

Like the other seven million tourists arriving that year, I saw none of it. The state department of tourism worked hard to make sure we did not. The illusion of paradise was what they were selling. And it required that the indigenous people of the Hawaiian Islands be invisible. To a large degree, they were.

The North Shore of Kaua'i is spectacularly lush – a Hollywood version of verdant Hawai'i. 'Iokepa and I were standing with a local homeowner in a North Shore town – Hanalei. The town shares 'Iokepa's middle name. It was where his grandmother was born. The woman bragged to us. "This is the best part of the Island, because only the *very* rich live here."

'Iokepa quietly asked her: "You love it here? So did my ancestors. Where are they now? Do you see any Hawaiians?"

"Well...sure...," she stammered. She pointed to the gardener across the street.

In fact – 'Iokepa held his tongue – he was Filipino.

It took me time to even recognize the native Hawaiian face in the mix. Like other tourists (and many residents), I imagined that the brown-skin women cleaning hotel rooms were Hawaiian. Overwhelmingly they were Filipino. I imagined that the commercial *Lū'au* featured Hawaiian dancers. More likely, they were Japanese. The *kanaka maoli* – the original people – now make up only twenty percent of the population of Hawai'i.

The *kanaka maoli* trace their lineage back about 13,000 years. They can name their ancestors; trace their genealogies to the beginning.

Within their creation story, the Earth did not begin with just one birthing – one Adam and Eve – a single people. The people of Lāhui – what they called their Islands long before others called them *Hawai'i* – know there were multiple births. One of these, the grandmothers told 'Iokepa: *from the hand and heart of God,* placed five root-families on the Hawaiian Islands. All Hawaiians who trace their lineage to before the arrival of the Europeans are family.

Kanaka maoli do not ask one another: "How much Hawaiian are you?" You either have the blood and carry the lives of your ancestors inscribed in your DNA or you do not.

Being born on the Hawaiian Islands does not make you *kanaka maoli* – nor does dying here. Those who are born on the Islands or immigrate there are still *malihini* – guests. We are blessed however, because for 13,000 years the people of

Lāhui have welcomed guests to their Islands with, the ancestors said: *Open hands, open arms, and open hearts.* They celebrated their connection to every living thing, in every breath – no less so to their fellow man.

Hawai'i is the archipelago on this planet that is farthest away from any other land – the most isolated Islands on Earth. Three thousand miles from any large land mass, the nearest connection was direct: to the Creator, and to the Creator's creation in its infinite manifestation.

Those connections were neither invented nor idealized. The ancients could not imagine *not* being one with their Creator, their ancestors, and all elements of nature. Now, we struggle to imagine that we are.

The ancestors had no Twentieth Century concept of 'I will save that tree.' On the contrary: I *am* that tree, and if it hurts, I hurt. How much more sensitive they'd be to the pain that humans can inflict on one another?

Aloha, then, meant just one thing: *In the presence of God, in every breath.* (*Alo* – in the presence of all of God's creation; *hā* – the divine gift, the breath.) As a greeting, it was an acknowledgment of the soul.

These people carried that singular concept to every place on Earth they voyaged.

They were a people for more than 12,000 years – before the first wave of foreign conquest in 1320 – without warfare or hierarchy, a matriarchal culture. A people without ownership – before the second wave imposed Western missionary law in 1848. For whom even the concept of *charity* was gratuitous, because it implied the impossible: 'I have' and 'You do not.' There was no barter, because that too implied: 'This is mine.' The open-hand was thus: Giving and receiving was a single, inseparable motion – neither more holy. Everyone gives, everyone receives.

Those destined to be fishermen (or women) fished. Those destined to work in the *kalo* fields grew food. Those born to cut timber off the mountain did. Those born to sit under the coconut tree each day and meditate sat – without judgment. Though a child's name (a gift of the ancestors) implied in metaphor his destiny – it was his or her life's work to imagine it, and fulfill it.

When it was time to eat the fish or the *kalo*, or use the wood – every man, woman and child took what he or she needed, and not more. No judgment. *Faith* meant that tomorrow there would be fish, or fruit, or *kalo* – or whatever came. It did not allow for hoarding. It did not allow for insurance policies, freezers, or door locks. Life delivered what God offered – and on the tropical Hawaiian Islands, that was abundance. The emptied hand would always be filled.

That is the culture 'Iokepa and his kindred celebrate. That is *Hūnā* – the pure, authentic religion of Lāhui. His were a people incapable of doing harm – put on Earth, they knew then (and believe still), to teach the rest of the world *aloha*. To teach the rest of us what it is that we have forgotten.

What 'Iokepa had taken me to see and feel that first week had nothing to do with lighthouses, shops, or commercial *Lū'au*, and everything to do with *Ke 'I'oakua* (God Almighty), the *'āina* (land), and the *kahiko* (original language and culture).

We visited a lot of *heiau* – those ancient sanctuaries for ritual and prayer – built always in alignment with the constellations in the night sky, with the migration of the stars and moon. These people knew the sky.

"Do you feel that?" 'Iokepa asked me at the stone remnants of one of these sacred walls. He pointed to the skin on his thick arms, then to his bare legs. Goosebumps stood on end: *'ili 'ōuli* – skin signs. The ancestors were announcing their presence.

Each *heiau* stood at a significant elevation with breathtaking views of the ocean and the horizon – and each was related to the others across the eight inhabited Islands. I learned that lines drawn between different *heiau* across those eight Islands mirrored the constellations as well.

Every single *heiau* spoke its energy to 'Iokepa. None affected me as strongly as the one where we'd met. After that, I responded as much to his reactions as to my own.

We visited, too, his grandmother's grave.

Afterwards, an irreverent friend teased him. "You take your girlfriend on dates to cemeteries?"

The lovely old cemetery was an oasis of green between the only shopping mall on the Island and the smokestacks of the sugar cane mill. 'Iokepa greeted his grandmother with her name in full: "Emilia Maria Haleakala Kunao Lota 'Īmaikalani – *mahalo* for bringing Inette to me."

Then he looked at me for some words of my own. I froze. I shook my head silently, "No."

As we walked barefoot across the cemetery lawn, I said. "I felt shy meeting your family."

He corrected me. "You felt respectful."

I had no idea at the time how intensely and vividly 'Iokepa's ancestors would come to occupy my own life.

When 'Iokepa had returned to the Hawaiian Islands on February 12, 1997, only fourteen days after his life-altering epiphany and full of unrelenting idealism, most of all he looked forward to family. Only his father, among four siblings, had left the Islands. 'Iokepa's relatives were still there, intact and close. There had been visits both ways. For years, aunts, uncles, and cousins (first, second and beyond) had urged him home to the Islands.

"The grandmothers told me that I was kept away from the Islands so my identity wouldn't be compromised," he said. "Here, I would have been undermined by missionary law and teachings at every turn."

It had been fully 185 years since the missionaries' sons discovered wealth in sugar cane – and fenced the *kanaka maoli* off the land that they believed only God could own. That many years since the missionary law forbade the native people to practice *Hūnā*, dance the *kahiko* (the authentic *hula* that was transcendent prayer not entertainment for tourists), name their child a Hawaiian first name (it had to be Christian), or speak the native language in public (without punishment or shame). All remained on the state's law books – and enforced – until 1972.

In these years the native people suffered excruciating losses. But they had not, 'Iokepa insisted, been conquered. "No more than Gandhi and Martin Luther King, Jr. were conquered by their assassins," he said. "They have not forgotten." *Abandoned*, 'Iokepa's grandmothers described the *kanaka maoli* connection to their Source. *But not forgotten*.

When, at last 'Iokepa returned fulfilling the prophecy, some of the family rejected him.

"Why you?! You didn't even grow up on the Islands!"

"Why wasn't it me?!"

"Why not *my* son?"

All were unanswerable. He was undeniably hurt.

"I thought my family would embrace me," he told me. "I thought family was family no matter what."

. . .

The path that 'Iokepa called his 'job' would have been tedious, frustrating, or daunting to any other soul I can imagine. But he saw miracles in every step, every day. It was a rare one when I hadn't heard him say, 'I love my job.'

My mother had a mental picture, I think, that he solicited on street corners, cornered passersby – that he was the ambulance-chasing lawyer of the spiritual world. In fact, 'Iokepa had nothing to sell. What he had to give (it seemed to me), the Earth, the sky, the ocean, and the people of Lāhui had been yearning to embrace for eons. Amidst their rage, bitterness, passivity, despair and confusion – all responses to centuries of oppression – 'Iokepa's was a voice of historical and cultural truth. His was a voice of forgiveness.

Because he'd grown up in Washington and lived a typically American life for forty-six years before his cultural 'grooming,' 'Iokepa owned that rare voice that could speak *to and for* two peoples: both the ancient, ancestral culture and the noisy contemporary one we have created. He was uniquely placed – a kind of middle man – who could speak for both and perhaps be heard by both.

Just a few days after we'd met, I'd listened to 'Iokepa address some raging, young Hawaiians – all tattoos, bulging muscles and swagger. They drew a misguided macho from identification with and idealization of the ruthless, European-puppet King Kamehameha, who – armed by British traders (seventeen years after the arrival of the first white man, Captain James Cook) – killed his own people to 'unify' Islands that had never known separation. From a centralized Honolulu, the sugar cane barons could pass bogus 'laws' to disenfranchise the natives – and they did.

'Iokepa and I both saw in the young warriors' anger, a transparent search for identity.

"My friends," he said. "You haven't gone back far enough."

The old hot rod aficionado found his metaphor in the truly mundane. He told them. "You can't rebuild a Chevrolet engine with Ford parts" and they'd get it. "You have to go back to the *kahiko* – our original culture – not what came after."

The young men were clearly galvanized by 'Iokepa's physical strength, his breadth of knowledge and his confidence. I realized immediately that he was a powerful role model for these young Hawaiian men. I thought of him at the time as 'a man's man.' But that was much too narrow.

It was the first of many such encounters I would witness over the years.

It seemed to me that 'Iokepa loved to engage opposition. He was particularly adept at diffusing youthful rage with an equivalent dose of idealism. "When you turn that anger around," he told me, "you have a passionate ally for the other side."

Still later that first week I heard 'Iokepa correct a group of New Age enthusiasts. 'This is *not* New Age. This is very old wisdom. Accept it as the gift of the ancestors.'

The truth he spoke was of the *Manahune* – an aboriginal people who routinely used the energy of the universe to enact what we now insist are *miracles*. These *kanaka maoli* have been falsely called *Menehune* – tiny leprechauns, magical and marketable. The difference between *mana* (divine energy available to every human) and *mene* is the difference between the true nature of this indigenous people, and a tourist poster. Like the biblical *manna,* the Hawaiian *mana,* fed the people.

Language, among the ancients – Hawaiian, Hebrew, Arabic, Sanskrit and others replicated the sounds that could reach

God's ears – the exact vibrations. It was how they spoke to their Creator.

"You change my word, you change my world," a native Quechua from Ecuador agreed with 'Iokepa.

The *kanaka maoli* were easily overwhelmed because there was nothing in their consciousness that could fathom defiance.

In 1898, the cultural dishonoring was formalized. The American government forcibly turned an independent nation into a U.S. Territory – and turned Queen Lili'uokalani into a prisoner and a martyr for her people. The last reigning Hawaiian monarch (with an army at her disposal) refused to spill her people's blood defending a land that she knew only her Creator owned. She lived and died her faith.

The U.S. government acted at the behest of a dozen American pineapple and sugar cane tycoons – for the purpose of padding the businessmen's bank accounts. American history books uniformly agree on these facts. Hawaiian sovereignty was eradicated at gunpoint. Fully ninety-five percent of all living *kanaka maoli* petitioned their opposition in writing to Washington. It made no difference. The petitions sit still in the National Archives.

I recount a number of specific moments I am calling parables. These are parables in the sense that they convey profound truth, but they are more than that. They are accounts of the most conspicuous miracles I personally experienced on the walk of faith. I was instructed by them.

They were confidence builders. They stoked me and kept me going.

. . .

Once a month, I drove across Portland to the sanctuary of my gifted friend Serge for massage. In January, he offered me a freebie. Would I be the guinea pig for four weekly sessions of advanced bodywork he was developing, involving memory release? I gratefully accepted. We were both amazed by what happened.

The massage itself was profoundly deep. But on the ride home from Serge's, my entire world was transformed. It cracked me open to senses I couldn't have imagined I had. Yet like the grandmothers' words, I had no choice but to accept them.

The familiar streets, office buildings, houses and people changed. All the roads, edifices, and even the plantings of trees, shrubs and flowers looked like a gigantic stage-set – laid out on top of a smothering Earth. I felt the Earth struggling to breathe.

The people walking from work to lunch and back – shopping, talking, gesturing and laughing – had become robots. They were the walking dead – deader in spirit by far than my father who'd passed almost two years before.

I gaped out from the complicity of an automobile traveling across the smothering Earth. When I crossed the Willamette River onto West Burnside Street – skid row – where the homeless were hunched unconscious in doorways near the Rescue Mission – it changed again.

Now the scattered homeless had become the most alive. They alone showed sparks of light and life. I saw their light and I understood that these most defeated of humans were, in fact, among the most intuitive, sensitive and spirited of all.

These were the ones (almost all Native Americans) whose knowing in an unknowing world had overwhelmed and defeated them. These were the people who like 'Iokepa and I had spoken with their ancestors – and it had terrified them. Alcohol and drugs, I understood, were the anesthetics of choice – the way to reconcile what they saw, heard, and *knew* with what the rest of our society told them was true.

Not every homeless soul was alive. But relative to those walking the streets in business suits, dresses, jogging gear and Levi's – they were the shining sparks of visible light in an oppressive darkness.

I had absolutely no idea at the time that this fleeting insight was my foretaste of an almost universal loss – a prelude to my more lasting understanding of what that meant to the native Hawaiian people – and what it would come to mean to me.

For those ten minutes, at least, I'd seen the world without blinders.

February delivered *life* fully – its pleasures, its turmoil. Inevitably I yearned to visit 'Iokepa again. I thought it might be possible during the boys' Spring Break in late March. The grandmothers night-time conversations were increasingly alluding to a time *beyond* a simple visit to the Islands.

'Iokepa and I spoke to one another about once every three days.

For years I'd never picked up a ringing phone when I was working. I let the answering machine take the message and returned the call later.

'Iokepa became the exception. He called at any manner of day or night, and I always listened for his *'Aloha'* and always picked up the phone. He never once forgot to tell me, 'I love you.' But because he avoided predictability and routine, I'd never see it coming and it always took me by surprise. His resonant voice went up on the '....you' and I tingled at the inflection. It revealed vulnerability.

He missed me and told every person he encountered on Kaua'i, how much. He called me 'the smartest, strongest woman I've ever met.' His sister Puanani said. "I've never heard him speak about anyone like he speaks about you."

For my part, his voice and words kept me on track. In the midst of college applications, PTA wrapping sale drives, bills, laundry, and a sit-down, two-vegetable family dinner every night – there were phone calls from 'Iokepa that reminded me that my nightly conversations with God and ancestors were not a dream.

In early February I began teaching my 'Writing to Find Your Voice' workshop, one night a week for six weeks. As always I loved it. For six years it had been the place where I lived my spiritual life most fully.

God had always sent me exactly the right twelve people – each with a lesson to teach me. Then I was given the precise words to encourage, direct and love the written words that were read to me in class. My job was to stay focused – and stay open. The rest was taken care of. I treasured teaching my workshop and because I did it independent of any institution and only when the spirit moved me, I was always fresh.

During this winter, I needed my once-a-week walk with friend and confidante Lena for much more than the simple exercise and fresh air. I needed our walks because we revealed heart and soul to one another on them. Never officially, but informally, one of us would speak for half the walk. The other would speak for the rest. We gave and we received – easily, respectfully – our book projects, our children, our loves.

"When I was single..." I began midway through one of our walks, and then stopped myself. "Was? What does that make me now?!"

"Not so single," Lena answered quietly.

I had definitely become not-so-single. Under the ancestors' gentle tutelage, it became increasingly clear that my future lay with 'Iokepa. More difficult still was the growing understanding that that future must be in Hawai'i. I struggled mightily to leave it in the grandmothers' capable hands.

But one morning I read scribbled across the yellow page that by summer we'd be living in Kaua'i for good. The grandmothers were clear:

Within six months you will have moved to Hawai'i.

I panicked. "It's too soon!"

Check your heart. Do you wish to be with 'Iokepa? Do you trust us with Ben and Nathan's lives? You are ready now. The rest is immaterial.

Within days, the *immaterial* clobbered me.

Ben refused to send off his last three college applications until the absolute last minute; he failed physics; he took an incomplete in economics.

The application for college financial aid that had taken me three weeks to compile and write got lost in the mail. I had one day to reapply. I hadn't kept a copy.

Nathan came home from school in the middle of the financial aid fiasco. When I opened the door to him, his first words to me were: "What's wrong? You're usually full of twinkling when you come to the door."

He was sensitive to my every mood.

During most of January and the first half of February, I had been envisioning a convenient return trip to Kaua'i at the end of March during the kids' Spring Break when they'd be with their father. My workshop would be over then, and I could justify another vacation. I'd been *hoping* that 'Iokepa would visit us before then, but I realized it would take one of his daily miracles – he had no money.

In the middle of a night's sleep, I was prodded by the ancestors to reconsider. *I* was to visit Kaua'i first. Then 'Iokepa would visit Portland at Spring Break when I had planned to go to Hawai'i. It made no sense to me and I was defiant.

All the fears and resistance I'd stuffed inside me under the soothing words of the grandmothers surfaced as explosive despair, most of them about Ben and Nathan.

'Leave my sons alone in the house?! With Ben driving the car?! Abandon my workshop?!

"I'm afraid! Afraid that I will fail! Fail at this relationship. Fail myself, fail 'Iokepa – and now fail even God, ancestors, everyone! I've been given the greatest gift and I'm still who I've always been – not good enough."

> *Seize this opportunity, and forgive your parents for telling you in a million ways – you were not good enough: not pretty, sweet, girl or woman enough. Forgive them – they were only fearful. You were wrong to believe them.*
>
> *Then forgive yourself for picking up the bat the moment they set it down and continuing the beating. Forgive*

*yourself for passing on the teachings of 'not good enough'
to the next generation.*
*It has to stop now. God is forgiving. Can you be less?
Do you dare to challenge the Creator in this way?*

Ben was home from school, sick. He slept on my bed
while I typed the night's writings into the computer.
He looked so sweet-faced to me. I was reminded of him at
birth: the eyebrows, the lips, the cleft, and the shoulders – on a
baby! He'd grown into his baby potential. He'd become a
beautiful young man.

Mothers don't get to study their sons' sleeping faces after
a certain age. But today I was privileged to watch my son sleep.
I was grateful.

Chessie, our sweet cat, slept sprawled on my stomach
while I marked up typed pages. He purred and vibrated
against me and I relaxed. I was grateful then, and I'm grateful
in retrospect too.

*Nothing is beyond gratitude. In human gratitude
there is humility, pride, love, and faith. Gratitude is the
truest art form – alive to the moment – alert to the receiving, the giving, and the One.*

Nathan was feeling excluded. I divorced when he was
two. He'd never had to share me. I anguished about his future
in Hawai'i – his happiness was crucial to mine.

One night we walked together downtown in the slow
drizzle on our way to Borders to just browse. Out of the blue,
he asked me, "Is it wrong for a fourteen-year-old to still love
his mother?"

"No," I answered. "It's wonderful – especially if the
mother is me."

He laughed.

I said, "And it's not wrong for a mother to love her fourteen-year-old when he is you."

"I'm not really a bad fourteen year old."

"You are a fantastic one."

I inhaled a silent prayer. *Let us be alright on Kaua'i.*

All of Nathan's life, he'd led me into conversations about the sacred. He shared his dreams, and God was very present for him. I never discouraged it, but I never promoted it either. I let him lead. We'd dissect the dreams and talk about our larger purpose on Earth. In some ways, God and spirit had always been a part of Nathan's and my conversation.

Now, I had begun to share everything with Nathan: the prophecy, the prophet, the staggering words on the nighttime pages, the skid row vision – the magic as it unfolded. I didn't shelter him from these miracles.

He absorbed every word and he believed them because it was his mother who spoke them – and I had never lied to him. I was thrilled that this was one soul who didn't cringe from the spiritual.

What he might be imagining, I couldn't guess. But with all his heart, he wanted to be part of it. He reiterated what he'd told me a dozen times before. "I never wanted to wait until I was grown up to travel to foreign places!" He yearned for adventure.

. . .

In those first months together – meeting and then sharing by phone – there was such innocence in 'Iokepa, a fresh, raw, wide-eyed innocence.

"I'm glad I began this like a child," he said, echoing his grandmother's earlier words.

"Free of sophistication?" I ventured.

"Free of the intellectual's tools of disbelief."

In the middle of a random phone call, the conversation once turned to theology. 'Iokepa had – since he'd arrived on the Islands – read the Hebrew Bible and the Christian New Testament from beginning to end, three times. ("And I have my opinions about it..." he said.)

Under the direction of the grandmothers, he'd attended a wide variety of Christian church services with family and friends. He explained the purpose: "It was about knowing what they are going to say before they said it."

By now almost all native Hawaiians had adapted to some form of Christianity. For 141 years, from 1831 (eleven years after the arrival of the first Calvinist missionaries) until 1972, Christianity had been legislated. Practicing their ancestral faith and traditions – *Hūnā* – was outlawed.

"Christianity definitely wasn't about building confidence in what the native Hawaiians knew," 'Iokepa said, understating his agonizing emotions on the subject.

"We had our own *kupua* – heroes, like Jesus. They were men *and* women who'd gone beyond what was expected in human life. Our demigods – that's with a little d, little g – were humans who fulfilled their promises to the Creator. The grandmothers said. *The doors won't open until you honor your own heroes.* "

I thought about my own enduring attachment to Judaism. It explained who I am. It was the refracting lens through which I saw the world – the bedrock of my take on family, community, and human responsibility.

'Iokepa and I shared a deep cultural reverence that felt foreign to neither of us. In common we embraced profound and ancient traditions, where ritual, language, and genealogy were central. (I traced mine without interruption to Abraham and Sarah.) We both understood oppression.

No one people have been given the whole of the truth – only pieces of it. Each people were chosen for a different purpose. You already know why: so they can bring the parts to one another and become the One made visible.

Like your Biblical matriarch, Ruth. Accepting the foreigner as yourself – it is a fundamental, redeeming, human virtue.

'Iokepa called us, "Puzzle pieces. What one has lived, the other has not."

Confronting and subduing some of my fears, I acquiesced to the grandmothers' schedule. I would go to Kaua'i now. In the last few days before the flight, I was ironing, packing, painting my toenails, filling the freezer for the kids, teaching the workshop, driving to the bank, post office, grocery – the usual – yet it felt anything but usual.

The kids bought me beautiful yellow and red tulips and a fresh coconut for Valentine's Day. ("To remind you of Kaua'i," Ben wrote on the card, "but we're not *sure* there are coconuts on Kaua'i.") 'Iokepa called and said. "This will be our last Valentine's Day apart." I felt loved and ready.

Nothing awaits you but miracles. Open your heart like your palm and all will drop into it. You will see Kaua'i with different eyes – open eyes, forgiving eyes. Smile at all passing souls. A smile is how 'Iokepa recognized you. That is how the world will.

"*Nothing,*" they told me, "*awaits you but miracles.*" And they weren't kidding.

I stepped off the plane into the boarding area, and scanned the standing crowd for 'Iokepa. He stood, invisible to me behind a narrow wall. He studied me carefully before I ever saw him. Then he appeared, pulled me to him for an embrace that felt both comforting and exhilarating – and he led me to a quiet bench where we sat and talked for a very long time.

His personal magnetism – the voice, the powerful physical presence, and the eyes that lock on whomever he is listening to – were all real. I had not just imagined them.

Our week-long reunion together again on *Imagine*, climbing the mountain trails, sunning on the ubiquitous beaches was without a doubt romantic. This time the Island looked beautiful in a way that seemed to have escaped me on my first visit. On that visit, I saw 'Iokepa – and I saw the encroachment of development. I'd missed the rest.

But this visit was much more than just romantic.

. . .

On the next to the last night of my second visit to Kaua'i, 'Iokepa led me on a trek along the blurred borders of magic. It was the way 'Iokepa traveled. I don't think he so much *expected* magic – I think he just remained open to the possibility.

57

That night, 'Iokepa drove the country roads at a crawl. The pace had a synchronicity with my own slowed Island pulse.

"There," 'Iokepa pointed at some distance, "a *pueo*." I didn't understand at first, or see.

'Iokepa's eyesight was acute; he had the widest peripheral vision I'd ever encountered. There was very little he missed. I, on the other hand, tended to focus inside my own head on the stream of thoughts and miss much of what he considered obvious.

But not this. Fifty feet before us, motionless and regal, was a huge white owl. It stood at the exact edge of the narrow paved roadway and the red dirt field. The owl turned his head to face us as we approached in the car. He held his ground as we passed and stared into our faces with a slow pivot. We stopped in front of him and then crept on. He never budged except to return our attention. Minutes later, he flew over our heads a quarter of a mile after we'd passed him.

"Insight," 'Iokepa said. "*Pueo* convey knowing."

We drove on to a lookout over the ocean where the water erupted into the air like a tall fountain between the reef rocks. The night was formidably black – no lights, no moon – but the sky was completely clear and saturated with stars. Standing, we inclined our faces skywards. 'Iokepa spread his arms wide at the display and said. "This is for us!"

In that split second, a blazing star dropped brilliantly across the sky directly in front of our faces. I gasped. It was the first shooting star I'd seen in my life – and it seemed to last an eternity.

We drove next down the narrowest, darkest path so far – Kipu Road – edged by tall sugar cane plants as far as my eyes could make out. It felt like we were passing through a winding tunnel.

"If anything happens, don't be afraid."

Why would he say that? I was immediately afraid.

He parked where the road petered out into grass and left his headlights on. They bounced off the bronze image of an angular-faced Englishman. His name and image were set inside a stone monument.

'Iokepa climbed out of the car and I followed him. He stood erect facing the 19th century land baron's harsh image. He began to rage in a voice that startled me. It echoed off the stars. "What you have done is wrong! You have lied to my people! You have stolen from the people who welcomed you with open arms. You have murdered! You will never know peace until the wrongs are righted.

"I am 'Iokepa Hanalei 'Īmaikalani, and I have returned to *mālama pono* (make right) the wrongs done to the *'āina* and the *maka'āinana* (people of the land).

I stood to the side, a dozen feet from 'Iokepa and without remotely understanding why, I sobbed my heart out. I held my hand over my mouth so my unrelenting moans wouldn't interfere with 'Iokepa's words. I wept, and as I slowly began to understand why, I recoiled.

"I am the *mo'opuna* (grandchild) returned," 'Iokepa announced in a galactic voice that I felt could drive tidal waves to the shores of ancestors and Creator alike. "I offer you other than what you brought to me and mine. I hold you to the standard of your conscience. You will return to make it *pono*, or your ancestors will."

'Iokepa bellowed and I wailed for perhaps ten minutes. Afterwards, spent, we walked silently to the car, settled in the seats and didn't move from that grassy spot.

I spoke first. "I cried because that man abused me."

'Iokepa hesitated. He was listening for the right words. "You were his wife... and you were mine, too."

None of it made sense to me at all.

After that, we were locked together in silence. We grieved separately in that rental car's bucket seats – and we grieved together.

The next place 'Iokepa parked that night surprised me. After a night traveling from one exquisite natural site to another, this time we stopped in a parking lot behind a restaurant. I was staring at a dumpster.

'Iokepa got out of the car and I walked beside him to the edge of a vacant, five-acre grass field, bordered on three sides by asphalt road. He told me more about the harsh-faced image we had confronted.

"That man killed my great grandfather in 1850," he said. "My grandmothers directed me, a month ago, to his monument.

"They told me then. He had been a missionary. Missionaries were prohibited from owning land. It was the agreement they made for permission to minister Christian faith to the Natives. He broke it. He became a massive landholder. He wasn't the only one.

"The grandmothers told me then that my great grandfather was buried here. But I don't know exactly where."

Then he walked out into the vacant field and prayed. I walked past him until I could no longer see him standing behind with his back to me – and I could no longer hear his powerful voice. Abruptly, I found myself physically riveted to a single spot. Then I felt something try to lift my right foot off the ground and I struggled to prevent it. The result was an awkward shifting of my right foot forward a step, along the grass. I struggled for balance. Then the same contest began over my left foot. Each foot was yanked off the grass and pushed ahead a stride; each time I fought to hold my ground.

I stared in amazement at my sandals being shoved along for ten or more steps. Then it stopped and I felt a tremendous push behind both knees. I fought helplessly to stay rigid, but I was slammed flat, face-down onto the grass: arms splayed out from my sides, eyeglasses and nose pressed into the ground. My chest heaved, my body shook, and I wept uncontrollably. With each inhalation I choked in the damp Earth; with each exhalation I wailed into the pool of my own dirty tears.

I have no idea how long I lay in that position. But I know this: I never wanted to move and I never wanted to stop crying my heart out. I knew, "The only man I ever loved is here." I stretched out and grieved on top of his body. I sobbed wordlessly, "'Imai...'Imai...."

'Iokepa turned around at some point; he saw me exactly like that and he was astonished. He said the first words that I was able to hear: "I would never abandon you."

I tore myself off the ground, crumpled with tears, dirt and grief, and took the short steps into his open arms. 'Iokepa held me tight with one arm and smoothed the matted hair off my face with his other.

I had found the grave of the ancestral 'Īmaikalani. I felt a completion and an exhausted peace. 'Iokepa spoke: "That man killed me because he wanted our land and he wanted you, Lo'ika. You were a great beauty and an exquisite dancer." He had called me by the name of his own great grandmother. "We were very much in love. He told you I'd left you – voyaged, without saying *'aloha.'* You believed him. You thought I'd abandoned you."

It was on this night and in this way that 'Iokepa and I remembered to our very cells, a life before this one. 'Īmaikalani and Lo'ika had two children. 'Iokepa recited the genealogy.

"It had to be almost theatrical," 'Iokepa said of this embodiment, "For us to *feel* what they'd felt."

The genealogy tells this tale: Lo'ika married the Englishman and bore him another two children. He used the marriage to claim the lands, and then he left her.

'Iokepa repeated softly in my ear, "I would never abandon you." I felt the weight of lifetimes lift from my soul. I felt the scars too – still raw to the touch.

But I knew I could never again doubt the truth of eternal life. I had felt it breathe into my chest through the damp, green Earth.

February 28, 1998

We sprawled together on a vacant, pristine Westside beach the next morning – shifting ourselves only as far as the distance from ocean to sand.

Each day 'Iokepa had taken me to a different beach. He'd carefully monitored my exposure to the sun. He allowed only an hour of tropical sun a day, and then we shifted to the shade of a coconut tree. I hadn't burned at all on my way to a deep tan.

I owned only modest one-piece swimsuits; everyone around me wore bikinis. Since Christmas, I'd lost twenty pounds. I had changed neither diet nor exercise regime. The weight – for the first and last time in my life – disappeared effortlessly. 'Iokepa hinted I might consider buying a bikini. I balked – I was much too old. He disagreed.

Our time together was growing short. I felt it acutely.

. . .

On the last night of my second visit to Kaua'i, we marched with the spirits.

"Want to take a walk?" 'Iokepa asked me when he parked the car on an empty country road surrounded by six-foot sugar cane stalks. The moon was new; the night was dark and cold. "I'll get my walking shoes," I answered. I leaned on the trunk and laced my shoes.

"What did you say?" he asked me as I straightened up.

"Nothing," I answered.

Then we both heard the cadence.

"What do you hear?" he asked me this time to be sure.

"Drums," I answered, and I pointed into the miles of empty field. They sounded a slow, deliberate, rhythmic beat.

"Drums," he repeated.

We stood motionless and listened. When the drums stopped just a few minutes later, we stepped forward into our walk. My legs and body pumped with muscle I'd never had, my lungs pushed past old limits. It was nothing short of a vigorous sprint.

Wordlessly, in the pitch black night on the narrow asphalt road (trying hard to hold the center line so I wouldn't fall off the sloping edges), we strode alongside tall cane stalks for company. We marched silently, effortlessly, through the chill. When the road turned steep, we hiked down. I was anticipating: 'The return trip is going to be a struggle.'

Abruptly, the chill air turned balmy as though we'd stepped inside a humid cloud.

"It's warm." I broke the silence.

"Yeah," 'Iokepa answered. "It's warm."

We climbed down to a small wooden bridge over a river. I could hear the water slipping steadily over rocks and stumps below us and I could smell the wet leaves at the water's edge – but it was too dark to see a thing.

"This is as far as I want to go," 'Iokepa said.

He began to chant. He sounded out a steadily patterned cadence, with rhythms punctuated like the earlier drumbeat.

"Eia ala! Eia ala!
Kāua hele hā'upu ka wa mamua.
Kāua hele ho'omaika'i ka wa mahope.
Kāua hele ho'ohanohano ke 'uhane o ka 'āina.
Kāua hele 'ola ke aloha.
Eia ala!"

(Attention!
We come to remember the past.
We come to bless the future.
We come to honor the spirits of the land.
We come to live in the presence of God in every breath.
Attention!)

That night by the river he spoke with a great authority, and paradoxically, with humility as well. He announced himself to his ancestors, recited his remarkable genealogy, and acknowledged their unendurable wait for the return of what had been taken.

Then we began our ascent from the river. But the ascent I'd dreaded went level. There was no climb, no hill at all, and I was filled with enough power to fly. I soared ahead of 'Iokepa, my arms straight out like wings and my fingers spread wide.

I heard.

Let it go. Let it all go. Like the wind through your out-stretched fingers, like water through your hands – let it flow. Hold tight to nothing.

When 'Iokepa said, "Look over there," I did.

By the side of the road, shoulder to shoulder – of different heights and stature – were parade rows of ancestors. There was no mistaking them. They were clusters of mist ("Light," 'Iokepa amended later) gathered into exact human shapes and sizes. They were faceless, but their bodies and heads were precisely defined – there was no ambiguity. The ancestors of Hawai'i stood in lines as crisp as corn rows.

I stopped and I stared: mouth slack, body rigidly attentive. I'd never seen anything like them in my entire life. But there was no doubting what I saw. I felt called to attention by them, summoned to alertness, respectful.

Suddenly, a car barreled up the road with headlights blinding us. It was the only car to pass us that night. We jumped to the outside edge of the road. When the car flew past, the visible ancestors were gone.

We walked on without exchanging a word. I felt an utter sense of well-being. Then 'Iokepa interrupted my reverie. "We're at the car."

I hadn't noticed.

I looked up at the sky. I breathed in the crisp night air. I felt a smile begin on my lips, spread across my eyes, my cheeks and my chin – into every corner of my body, and then beyond even that.

Then I was back in Portland. We began telling our families our plans.

On a long phone call I had with Puanani, she said this: "'Iokepa told me he never asked you to move to Kaua'i."

For a moment, I was stunned – I'd never thought of it. But the answer was obvious.

"No, he couldn't have asked it. It was mine to offer," I said. "But I never for a moment doubted that was exactly what he wanted."

No person could ask of another a surrender of this magnitude. I was expected to relinquish my exhilarating, satisfying, comfortable life – and embrace another, unknown and unknowable. To do this as a simple fact of faith. In 'Iokepa's case, it had been his grandmothers who had asked him. In my case, it couldn't be less than that.

Just over three years ago, I'd sworn never to move again – at the least, not while my sons were still in high school. Nathan hadn't yet begun. Three years ago I'd packed and unpacked too many boxes, said too many goodbyes, dried too many tears of physical and emotional exhaustion to willingly choose to do this to us again.

But in truth, from Christmas morning at the *heiau*, the writing was on the wall: I could struggle against the inevitability – or I could submit. Over the next months (and years) I would do both.

I now faced the reality of parting with a thirty-year collection of diligently acquired and long-prized possessions. Among them were: antique furniture I'd discovered then refinished piece by piece; oriental rugs my parents had given me on special occasions (the birth of each son, the publication of my first book); original paintings by my talented friends.

I began with the books – walls and walls of floor to ceiling bookcases, full to overflowing. I'd never given a book away. Mine was a flourishing library for friends and family.

On the first night I filled boxes with thirty year old college textbooks: psychology, anthropology, philosophy, European history, and more. Then I filled others with: duplicate books of all kinds; well-meant gifts from friends that I'd never read and never would; and every single self-help book that had buttressed me through the divorce years.

I packed up novels I'd read too long ago to care about anymore, but that weren't yet classics or Sixties cultural icons – and I knew I'd only just begun.

The kids carried twenty-eight liquor store cartons downstairs and upstairs and into the Toyota Camry for a half dozen trips to Goodwill that first day.

Then I tackled some obvious parts of my closet: purses that matched high-heeled pumps I hadn't worn in years; my mother's bejeweled belts. (What *had* I been thinking, when I accepted them?)

Within a few days I'd hauled off half my wardrobe. Who said Goodwill customers wouldn't recognize fine silk blouses and Harve Bernard flannel slacks?

I washed the baby clothes I'd been saving for my grandchildren and gave them to my pregnant friend Emily, expecting in May.

Then I took on the storage room: sports equipment, camping gear, old toys. Nathan was incredibly free about letting go. "I want new stuff," he said, packing up a dozen assiduously assembled baseball card albums, forty beloved stuffed animals, three soccer balls, and two baseball bats. He understood instinctively what I struggled to learn: the making room for 'new stuff.'

Ben (my *Benny-boy*) preferred that his room remain a museum to his adolescence forever. Surrounded by empty boxes, he balked.

"Packed up your shelves, Ben?"

"Not yet, Mom."

Change was painful.

The planned logistics: I would fill foot lockers with the boys' prized childhood treasures and ship them to their father's for storage. I'd send a few pieces of my winter clothing – the dressed-for-success suits and one ball gown – to my mother's in Baltimore. I'd find a university repository for my literary papers. And of course I'd ship computer, stereo, linens and more to Ben's college of choice – *if* he were chosen.

There was a house to sell, realtors to line up and a new home for Chessie. The car? Who knew? The ancient bentwood rocker? The silver? The Delft bowls? There was time.

What remained in the sifter when the rest had passed through would go with Nathan and me to Kaua'i.

'Iokepa asked me on the phone. "Do you still want to come along with me on this journey?" Before I could answer him, he heard my lips crackle, "I can hear your smile."

'Iokepa was planning to spend the boys' Spring Break in Portland. He had repeatedly asked *Ke 'I'oakua* (God Almighty) and his grandmothers to make it happen. He felt sure he was on the ancestors' side on this one. He was depending on them to deliver.

"It is right – proper protocol – that I come to Portland," he said. "It's about respecting you and your sons. I need to see the home and the life you're giving up for me."

Days later, he was running at full speed up a long hill under the sweltering afternoon sun. It was part of his daily twelve-mile ritual – feeling the *'āina* through his feet. A car pulled up next to him and a Hawaiian woman he knew handed him a round-trip airplane ticket to Honolulu. "I have an extra," was what she said. Honolulu was the first stop to Oregon.

Ben (who must have *legions* of ancestors sitting on his shoulders) got accepted to his first choice college and another larger university on the same day. Waving his acceptance letters in his right hand, he bounced like a rubber ball – up and down.

"I did it!" he crooned every time his feet left Earth. "I did it!"

I hadn't seen my son bounce since he was half his six-foot height. His head barely cleared the kitchen light. I grabbed his free hand and bounced alongside him.

Beloit College was an extremely fine, progressive, small liberal arts school in Wisconsin that was both intellectually challenging and nurturing to boot. They factored into Ben's awful high school grades, his excellent SAT scores, his candid and heartfelt essay ("The whole is larger than the sum of its parts – I am *not* the sum of my high school grades."), his wonderful references and his extracurricular activities. (He'd taken several college history courses locally, and ironically done very well.) They accepted him on probation.

Additionally, they offered him a financial aid package that covered the entire $28,000 tuition and room and board. Most of that was outright scholarship, a small bit was no interest loans, and a smaller part involved his working at the college for ten hours a week. I felt very blessed. 'Iokepa had never stopped reassuring me. "Do you think God takes care of you, but only *you* take care of your children?"

On the heels of the magic college acceptance day, Gonzaga University (who'd sponsored my own Junior Year Abroad in Italy, thirty years before) called to tell me they were delighted and honored to be the recipient of the Inette Miller literary collection. They would send their curator to hand-sort the papers.

With Ben launched and a lifetime of career and personal papers (diaries, letters, old newspaper and magazine clips) sent out into the world, I could begin to consider what came after the packing, the sorting and the letting go. I could begin to imagine a life after this one. I was less than four months away from Hawai'i.

. . .

'Iokepa had been told by his grandmothers: *Do not forget that you are different.*

The words troubled me. 'Iokepa made no claim that set him apart from the weakest: the addicted, the violent, the poor, the sick.

"If what I do and who I am is never known, I accept that too."

I wasn't at all pleased that he'd been reminded to regard himself as *special* – and I wrote that on my nighttime pages. I was answered promptly.

He is being reminded to honor the gifts he has been given. This is a universal message. Absolutely equality was never the goal – One is. The recognition of one Creator within every soul.

This has nothing in common with the American effort at equality – sameness. That cannot and will not be on Earth or in heaven. Celebrate the differences created within us – the uniqueness – and we celebrate the Creator. Deny that which is special – what makes each of us chosen – and we deny the Creator.

I awakened seven days before 'Iokepa was to arrive weighed down with heaviness. I was anguishing about the money I owed: the airline ticket from my recent trip, the mounting long distance telephone bills, and the necessary house repairs in preparation for sale.

I paid $575 to the carpenter. I was in sore need of a new computer. I required essential dental work.

I awakened four days before 'Iokepa was to arrive, feeling faithless. It seemed that God and ancestors were making it particularly difficult for 'Iokepa to leave the Islands. A $300 airline ticket had almost doubled in price by the time he'd arrived at the travel agent with his friend Albert, and Albert's checkbook. "No," 'Iokepa said to Albert, who'd earlier offered to buy him the $300 ticket. "That wasn't the agreement."

Albert would have written the $550 check without blinking. He was insistent that his business turn-around from near failure to miraculous success was the blessing of 'Iokepa's friendship. 'Iokepa made no such claim on his own behalf. "It's the blessing of *Ke 'I'oakua.*"

Still, 'Iokepa sat on the deck of the boat *Imagine* and waited.

I waited too. But there was a difference. I was full of doubt – and its reactive cousin, anger. It hurt.

> *Keep your hands in your pockets. God can build a world quite well without your meddling.*
>
> *In God's hands you are safe, protected and loved. In your own hands – listening and following the path – you are safe, protected and loved. In your own hands – with eyes, ears, and heart closed – there is confusion, and pain.*
>
> *Men and women are offered choices. In the confusing cacophony of Earth's distractions (sounds, smells, tastes, and sights), you forget to accept what has been freely given. You refuse also to give what has been freely received. You lock up tight in an unforgiving heart, and you hurt.*
>
> *It is your choice. But the Creator, and the ancestors who serve Ke 'I'oakua and serve you too, hope all men and women will choose God.*

On March 17, I awakened early and walked the Fairmount loop, alone. Impulsively, I spoke out loud and offered gratitude to every soul who'd crossed my path this lifetime – every relationship, male and female, names and no-names. Then I heard this: *'Iokepa will be there.*

At that precise moment, 'Iokepa was told: *You can't get there from here – go to the airport.*

He packed a bag, flew to Honolulu with Albert's $300 in his pocket. The cheapest ticket now cost $486. He called his daughter Hokulele, a college sophomore, and took her and her roommate to lunch. Then he waited some more; this time, at the airport.

When 'Iokepa didn't show up on March 18, Ben accused him of "Getting cold feet."

"*Ho'omanawanui,*" I said. "Wait in faith."

Nathan answered Ben: "It means be quiet and quit your griping."

On March 18, I interviewed realtors, set my price and signed a contract for the house sale. "This is not about greed," I told the realtor who wanted to price the house $45,000 more than I deemed right. It felt good to be firm.

On March 19, at 11:00 p.m. 'Iokepa walked off the jumbo jet in shorts, a T-shirt and sandals into the Portland winter. A compassionate airline clerk had *insisted* that he accept a discounted 'family emergency' ticket. He wore a Ni'ihau shell *lei* and the whales tooth hook around his neck. He was browner than any of the returning tourists who poured out of the airplane around him.

He put his arm around Nathan and said, "My voyager." Nathan knew the impressive history of the Hawaiian voyagers. They were the best among the best: physically and spiritually. They navigated the ocean from the top of the Americas to the tip – using stars, wind, and currents. They followed the migration of the whales and they communed with them.

We spent the evening in Ben's room amidst the sports car and sports hero posters – all four of us. Ben leaned back against his antique walnut headboard; his arms crossed against his big chest and haughtily interrogated 'Iokepa. 'Iokepa sat erect in Ben's desk chair, his back to the computer. Nathan and I sat at the foot of Ben's bed.

Afterwards, 'Iokepa told me. "I felt like the boyfriend Ben's daughter would someday bring home to meet him."

Protective of his mother, my eldest son cross-examined my suitor – about, of all things, *theology.*

"What about evil!? The negative nature of man?"

'Iokepa responded. "Ben, I don't give it my energy."

With Ben, 'Iokepa was respectful, kind, honest and direct. Watching, listening to my oldest love – and my new one – I was deeply touched.

Later, together in my four-poster bed for the first time, nestling in each other's arms like the gift we assuredly were, I heard 'Iokepa's words before I dropped off the edge of wakefulness, into a dreamless sleep.

"Forgiveness is a God who will never leave us – even after everything we've done. It's exactly what we're asked to do for one another."

The week together flew by. We shared our days generously with all manner of others. My friends competed mightily to have a look at the esoteric Polynesian who'd turned my head and changed my life so dramatically. My neighbors insisted on meeting the 'attractive Hawaiian...' they saw walking the four-mile Council Crest loop.

We drove to Seattle for an introductory brunch with his sister Puanani, her husband, and their grown sons – and to meet 'Iokepa's eighty-five year old mother. She was wearing a bright red suit and perfect jewelry. I complimented Emma Lee on her outfit and she responded: "I dressed to impress." I found his mother crisply outspoken with a delightful sense of humor. She clearly adored her son.

On our last night together, Puanani, her husband and her son were guests in my home. Together we saw 'Iokepa off at the airport.

RETURNING HOME

April, 1998

In the days after 'Iokepa's visit, my home felt his absence sorely. He had filled the house with vitality from the moment he'd walked down the twenty-three steps through the trees and daffodils to my hillside gate – and offered a chant to the native ancestors of *this* land – before he'd entered my front door.

The next time I would see him, I would have no home at all in Portland and we'd be sharing the cabin of a fifty-five foot sailboat on Kaua'i. The next time I saw him, I'd have left behind: Maya and Emily and Jenny and Perla and Stella – my superbly compatible and gifted writers' group, who read each other's work with compassion and insight, every month. I'd have left behind dear friends: Judy, Neal, Ellen, Bruce, Jan, Ed, Tom, and M.J., for no-friends-at-all on Kaua'i, save 'Iokepa.

Lena, of course, had met 'Iokepa. She'd accepted and enjoyed him. There wasn't a judgmental bone in my friend's body. But on our first walk together after he left, I prodded her with my fears, and she responded.

She predicted, "Glorious times" with 'Iokepa – and, "Difficult ones." She knew me well. "Even though you know his work doesn't exclude you," she said. "I expect you'll be left at times with a great yearning for his attentions."

'Iokepa's concentration on the person he was with at any given moment was total. His wide-set eyes locked onto the other. To be on the receiving end of 'Iokepa's attention was to be inside a pool of warm light. It was, of course, what I'd fallen in love with.

But sharing 'Iokepa pushed a few obsolete buttons inside of me. I wanted to change what, within me at times, felt like

73

deprivation – not jealousy, but a certain lack of my special place in his life. I didn't know how to begin.

> *When he is engaged with others, you can choose to be a part of that engagement – which he loves. Don't deprive yourself of those powerful times: Watching him with others and later sharing your observations with him. He has already come to depend on them.*
> *But don't deprive yourself of your time alone either. You'll need to recharge. If you keep yourself full of the Creator – you will ask less of your mate and appreciate more.*
> *It comes like this: From God to you; from God to 'Iokepa – then, for your co-mingling Your Source never was and never will be 'Iokepa.*

. . .

I'd long contemplated going back to Baltimore for Passover this year. My mother, father and one brother had never lived anywhere else; my other brother moved only so far as the Maryland suburbs of Washington, D.C. I had not gone *home* for *Seder* since I'd moved to Portland.

Passover *Seder* had become ours over the years. My sons and I celebrated the freedom from slavery at the heart of the *Seder* story in our own home surrounded by hand-chosen friends, both Jewish and Christian. With each *Seder*, we'd widened our consciousness of what "Freedom from slavery" meant. No longer was it only Jewish freedom from Egyptian bondage, but freedom for all peoples whose sovereignty had been violated. This year for the first time, I factored in the native Hawaiians.

In early April I made plane reservations for the flight to Baltimore. This *Seder* was important. The life I was entering with 'Iokepa, I already knew, would take me further from my family than the six-thousand air miles.

The boys had no school vacation during the eight days of *Pesach* (Hebrew for 'Passover'). They would stay behind as they'd done when I went to Kaua'i. They'd performed wonderfully then: no wild parties, only discreet small ones.

The Camry was unscratched; the house was moderately clean – with only four days' dishes stacked in the sink. ("We thought you were coming home later.")

On April 5, I co-hosted a baby shower for my girlfriend Ellen. Two other friends did much of the cooking and cleaning so I got to be easy in my own home. I genuinely enjoyed the fifteen women and the fabulous brunch.

"The First Peri-menopausal Baby Shower," Ellen called it, and proposed that it might be worthy of the local news.

We laughed. Every one in attendance was over fifty. Ellen had adopted beautiful Hadley from China.

On April 7, I flew to Baltimore. Throughout the five hour flight, wedged into a tiny airplane seat, I reviewed my life.

Friends had more than once called me an adventurer. Family used less flattering terms – measuring our differences as my deviance from their norms. They might call me 'unpredictable' or even 'irresponsible.'

I'd hitchhiked around Europe for a year at twenty, moved to San Francisco (in that memorable year, 1968), quit the University of Wisconsin one semester shy of graduation (but enrolled in Berkeley six months later), married on four days notice (after a three-year courtship), gone to Vietnam for fourteen months (as a war correspondent), taken flying lessons, and lived in the roughest inner city neighborhood in the District of Columbia and on a farm in backwoods Appalachia.

There were also the things I'd wanted to do, but hadn't quite pulled off. Attending an all-Negro Southern college for my junior year (I went to Florence, Italy instead). Attempting to get incarcerated in Attica, the federal prison, to write the story for my newspaper (I couldn't get clearance).

'Iokepa, of course, had been an adventurer too. I wondered what would happen when two of us merged. Do we fly higher, or fall further?

I was back in Baltimore, where I'd lived until I was eighteen. I went away for college, came home for regular visits but never again to live. Unquestionably, my mother and I loved one another. My brothers were loyal and generous to me and to my family – and we were to them. They loved the idea of a sister and a daughter. But the reality was much more complicated.

My neck and shoulders felt stiff and immobile from the first minutes off the plane.

It'd been my life's path to step out first in uncharted directions. It'd been my family's to find fault with my choices.

The *Seder* at David and Eva's four-bedroom, suburban colonial home set in a forest of trees and shrubs was elegant: English bone china, crystal, silver, white linen – a tulip and iris floral centerpiece. The food was exquisite. My generation was now relieving my mother of her holiday meals – my brothers' wives alternated occasions. I missed *Seder* at my parents' home on the infinitely expandable dining table and I know that my mother did – but it was an exhausting enterprise and I was glad to see my mother relax as a guest. Only three grandchildren were absent: Ben and Nathan in Portland; Rebecca, in the midst of college exams at Michigan.

I suppose I walked into a lion's den with my genuinely radiant smile, my unfeigned happiness, my words about prophecies and ancestors who spoke to me in the night, and the photographs of my handsome Hawaiian. There was not a ripple of interest or enthusiasm for my choices – only one niece deigned to comment kindly on the pictures.

I felt very alone.

My brother Marty, sitting to my left, interrupted the *Seder* to tell me, "I have no feelings for Judaism." My brother David to my right interjected, "I don't believe in God."

Marty, true to character, tried to hold his tongue and be cordial. But he couldn't resist saying gently. "Most people will see it differently than you do."

"You mean," I laughed, "they'll think I'm crazy."

"Yes..." It was exactly what he meant. "...Crazy."

I squeezed his arm affectionately. "If I worried whether people thought me crazy, I wouldn't have done half the things I've done in my life."

'Iokepa loved the challenge of people who disagreed with him. His faith was solid as a rock. But what 'Iokepa saw as 'exciting,' I found draining.

"Civilization," Marty named the life he and the others agreed to live, the life he saw me abandoning.

"Civilization?" I asked as kindly as I could. "Is that what you call it?"

Silently, I asked for freedom from any civilization that mocked faith and God and revered possession.

My brother David, also in character, refused to hold his tongue and spoke his mind without filter.

I asked David whether his daughters were still close to one another now that they were grown. I'd adored his girls all their lives and cared for them since they were babies.

"They don't like each other," he said just out of their earshot.

I was genuinely shocked. "Really!"

"Like I don't like you."

It had the sound of my brother's humor. I thought, "He's kidding, right?" It turned out, he was not.

I spent some wonderful days alone with my mother during *Pesach* week. One afternoon, we sat in her den – a shrine of aging photographs and tourist souvenirs – and we read aloud from her 1937, leather-bound, daily diary. It was the year she'd dated my Dad, gotten engaged, and on December 26, married him. She'd never before shared it with me. Snug, on opposite ends of her orange and brown plaid sofa, we laughed. She told stories about my studly young father; I told stories about my studly not-so-young 'Iokepa. Unlike either of us, we exchanged some very sexy jokes.

Relaxed now, my mother asked me with genuine curiosity: "Daddy and I stayed in one place. Where did you get *that* from?"

I had no answer. But in truth, it was my mother's own aliveness and her engagement with life that I had been given. David got her loyalty, tenacity and sense of responsibility.

Marty got her gift for making people comfortable. Friends vied for her company because she was fun.

I was proud of what I'd taken from my mother. There were differences in our experiences and world views, but there was a core that was very familiar to me. She too, was excited by life; she too, a romantic; she too, a writer and reader. It was time for me to remember who my mother really was. It was not time to abandon my brothers. We'd always cared for one another. I was positive we always would.

On a two-mile walk together around a neighborhood high school track, I told my mother about my parade with the visible ancestors in the cane fields of Kipu. Again, because *I* had spoken the words, she believed me.

There was a lull in the conversation that lasted another half-lap around the track. Then my five-foot-nothing, 105 pound mother looked up at me, and said.

"I wish God had chosen someone else's daughter."

We laughed so hard we had to hold onto one another for support.

The day before I was to fly home, I got a phone call from Ben. He'd been in a car wreck. It was a head-on collision. Ben was at fault, making an illegal left turn. He'd been joy riding, two hours from Portland – during school hours. He was unhurt. The other driver was unhurt, but irate. Her brand new car was totaled. The front end of our Camry was toast.

"*Mazel tov,*" I told Ben. "Everyone has to have one car wreck – now you've had yours."

"Nathan told me you'd say, *"Mazel tov."*

It was nice to be known. It's only a car.

. . .

Back in Portland, Ben, Nathan and I were heading into the home stretch: two months left for the house sale, the visit to Ben's college, the dispersion of possession, a new home for Chessie.

But in the short run, my writing group – the women six – was meeting in my home the morning after I returned (we rotated monthly). In addition to the usual preparations – fresh croissants, scones, and coffee – this month's gathering asked more. We were doing Emily's baby shower (Surprise!) before we got down to business. So, after dark on the day I returned home I bought balloons, a cake for Emily, and wrapped her present.

In the short run: I had to rush across town after the writing group and drop off my beloved, burgundy, '91 Camry with the sunroof, at the body shop – and pick up a rental car. The first new car I'd bought since the divorce was looking pretty pitiful.

And, in the short run: Nathan needed to be driven *back again* across town to Reed College for his computer programming mentorship. Then we headed home to a nice family dinner and some instruction on the use of my new computer from a very patient Ben. (He had selected the computer for me, carried it home, and installed it.) I was exhausted.

Six days after I flew into Portland from Baltimore, I was crammed into another airplane seat, this time with Ben, to Beloit, Wisconsin for three days. Nathan was thrilled to stay behind at his friend Lawton's.

Before I left, 'Iokepa had counseled me, "Have fun!" I didn't think it was possible. But I was having big-time fun. It felt great to be off the emotional roller coaster of the past few months. I'd forgotten what it felt like to just play.

I slept very well, alone and uninterrupted, in a hotel room. Ben was in a College dorm doing his prospective student thing. The parents were entertained separately.

A good proportion of the visiting parents were academics, and I delighted in the level of discourse. My schedule required that I sit in on a writing class – each parent's schedule was attuned to her individual interests. The Dean of Admissions was terrific – he *knew* Ben from two prior interviews in Portland. I was impressed.

Though I'd chosen huge universities when I was a student and I loved them, Beloit fit my idea of the perfect college for Ben – small but diverse. I was at ease with the prospect of

Ben at Beloit, but I hadn't yet seen Ben – and I had no idea of his take on the place.

At Beloit, I was reminded how much things of the mind meant to me. I'd been disparaging things intellectual as roadblocks to the spirit. But in the who-I-am that God gave me there'd been a reliable dose of ideas, and they excited me. I wondered about the balance between head and heart.

> *Mind is a blank canvas for self expression – exactly like your heart. Fear and doubt are your choosing – the false brush strokes. Do not blame the canvas for the artist's strokes.*
>
> *Spirit and mind are allies. They serve one another – they do not compete. The blend is always distinctive – different tools for different paths.*

I had been returned to the home of my childhood. Now I was being reminded to embrace the gifts of that childhood as well.

LETTING GO

May, 1998

Back from Beloit, Portland was lush with the promise of spring. On a series of phone calls with friends, I too felt full of promise. Ed said, "I've never heard you so giddy." Emily said, "You fill me with energy." Tom called me "Radiant."

We had a plan. Next month, my mother would fly out for one last visit to Portland. She'd stay a week. On June 6, Ben would graduate high school (if he made up his incomplete in economics). On June 7, Nathan would graduate middle school with straight-As.

On June 8, we'd borrow massage therapist Serge's pick up truck (and Serge) and haul all our possessions that made the cut, and that didn't exceed one pickup truck load – and have them crated and shipped to Kaua'i. It would cost about $1600. On June 11, I'd drive the Camry to Seattle for its two-week boat trip to Nawiliwili harbor. It would cost $850. I'd take a train back to Portland. On June 12, Lena would give Ben, Nathan and me a lift to the airport – our combined flights were $2000.

On June 12, while we were flying across the Pacific, a woman who conducted estate sales would enter our still fully furnished home and begin pricing every dish, chair, table, bed, quilt, painting, and rug that we'd left behind. Two days later, strangers would pour into our home and leave with Nathan's mineral collection, Ben's poster signed by Sam Snead and my hand needle-pointed, Chippendale dining room chairs.

The boys were scheduled to spend two days alone in Honolulu at a youth hostel. (Ben, passionate about World War II military history, refused to pass up Pearl Harbor.) I'd fly straight to Lihu'e, Kaua'i – relinquishing Pearl Harbor for a couple days alone with 'Iokepa. The boys would have a two week vacation on Kaua'i – then fly as they did every summer, to West Virginia for six weeks with their Dad.

In early August, Nathan would return to Kaua'i. Ben would enroll at Beloit College. The school year would begin again.

On 'Iokepa's end: He'd found us a place to stay with the boys for two weeks. (*Imagine* was too small for even minimal privacy.) He'd located free storage space for our pickup truck load of possessions. The storage unit would hold: our extra clothing, our two computers, a half dozen teacups my mother had since her wedding day, a set of brass *Shabbat* candleholders, a *Chanukah menorah*, one large and rather valuable abstract painting and several smaller ones, five boxes of books between us, one file cabinet filled with my work in progress. It would hold, too: Nathan's boom box, guitar, juggling paraphernalia, and CD collection.

. . .

My birthday was May 12, and for weeks I'd heard 'Iokepa grumbling. What could a man with more faith than money give to his love for her 52nd birthday? This was a man, who had given automobiles to his girlfriends, lavish gifts to friends. He was without a doubt generous – but a year and half ago he had considerably more funds to back that impulse.

I was gratified by his longing. I didn't ask for more.

When the small box arrived, I first read the note. "With cramps and patience, I made this for you. I love you with all my heart. Stay strong in your understanding."

I lifted a strand of opalescent white *puka* shells from the box. No two shells were the same but they were perfectly gradated by size. They draped like pearls to the top of my breasts.

"They were the home to living things," 'Iokepa said. "They're not supposed to leave the Island. But I told the ancestors: 'This one is coming back.'"

'Iokepa had spent nine hours on the scalding sand dunes and under the blazing sun of Queen's Pond at the furthest western edge of Kaua'i, walking the beach and ocean catching the tiny *puka* shells with his toes. There had been a time when the *puka* shells that housed the ocean mussels were plentiful, before chemical run-off from the ubiquitous golf courses, sugar cane pesticides, and developers eroded the *'āina* and killed the off-shore life. The shells were rare now on all the Islands.

Finding the *puka* shells came first; clearing the holes and stringing the tiny shells with thick Hawaiian fingers took twice the patience. 'Iokepa had never before strung a *puka* shell *lei* nor imagined anything of the kind. Neither of us knew that the first birthday *lei* would become a prototype for the way the ancestors spread their message throughout the Islands by means of 'Iokepa.

I held the *lei* in my fingers. Like a tree, their life stories were palpably inscribed on them, in the variation of color, texture, size, and shape.

"This is the best gift you could have given me," I told 'Iokepa. "We've crossed some kind of line. Before, it felt like so many mountains between here and there – but now, it's just a downhill slide."

Time was getting short for the press of business at hand. *Kanaka maoli* – native Hawaiians – insisted that time was like clay – malleable. I remembered a moment when that had been true for me, as well.

On that New Year's Day – my last with 'Iokepa during our first week together – I had been scheduled to catch a 10:00 a.m. flight from Kaua'i to Honolulu, connecting with one to Portland. I had to return my rental car and check in at the airport at least an hour before – the airlines recommended two.

But 'Iokepa wore no watch and mine had stopped dead in the salt air. So we lolled that morning on *Imagine*, loving one another, exchanging last words, and refusing to rush even a moment of our final morning together.

When we eventually noticed the time on the car's clock, it was 9:00. I still had not showered or packed and my impulse was to skip the shower and race to the airport. 'Iokepa did not agree.

"Take your shower, take your time. You'll make the plane."

He lived what his ancestors whispered to him: Time on Earth was a human fabrication. Time, which we imagine to be as solid as a concrete wall, was infinitely expandable. I didn't believe him then, but I deferred.

I showered, applied eyeliner and mascara for the first time in a week, dressed and packed at leisure. We ate breakfast on the boat. We drove with no haste to the airport. 'Iokepa returned the car, met me out front, cut around the snaking, agricultural-inspection line and into the terminal. No one stopped us. We checked my bags, walked to the gate where the last of the passengers had already boarded the plane. It was waiting for me – and it was not yet 10:00.

> *Remember that morning. Time stopped and you made your plane with time to spare. Time, now, is not too short for what you need to do. There is time to write, to walk, and to love your sons. Love – not packing – is what this is about. We will help you pack your boxes, carry them – and take the weight from your shoulders. Just ask.*

. . .

By telephone in May, 'Iokepa asked me for the first time to ask the ancestors a question *for* him. I felt the weight of the request.

"Ask," he said, "About the promises that were made."

I did – and scrawled across the yellow pad the next morning was the conversation that ensued:

> *Survival of the species means remembering who we are: Why we are on Earth. We are on Earth to keep our promise to be faithful to the Creator. This was, and is, the promise we made before populating the Earth.*

*The promise is a two-way street. Humankind prom-
ised faith as our ticket to Earth. But God promised faith,
too – and the Creator will return humans to faith.*

*It will take, it seems, a stripping bare of superficial
distractions. It will take a stripping away of comforts that
seduce, possessions that possess, and addictions to forget.*

*All humankind defines itself as separate – yet craves
always the One we remember. God has always given man
choice. Choice is a component of man's nature. How we
choose is how we relearn faith.*

The promises that were made – are they only this? 'Faith
between man and God.'

"Only." And faith between man and man.
*'Iokepa told you last night. "What you see in me is a mirror
of yourself." Faith between man and man is that – recognition of the One in all. When you see God in all, you cannot
not live faith.*

I asked: "But there are good days and bad days – days
when we get it and days when we don't. All of us have them. I
sure do.

*The ebb and flow you describe is expected. Remem-
bering is a process, not a product – nailed, finished, owned.
God promises compassion for the effort, for the process.*

Is that, 'Stripping bare,' you speak of, apocalyptic?

*There is a loss of nothing of consequence: Not love,
not forgiveness, not compassion – a loss only to the habit of
holding.*

*An exchange is happening here and now. It is this.
Give up a tight fist and inherit an open heart. Give up competing – yours or mine – and welcome One. Give up the
pocketbook – and accept the inexhaustible flow of energy.
Give and you receive.*

*In truth, the choices that have been made do not
work. The old way will perish. It cannot coexist with an*

open hand and heart. When there is change, always, some adapt; always some make way for the new. Some will choose to hold tight to bank accounts and the measure of self against another. Those ways will not survive.

God's promise is eternal. Man's promise to God has been undermined. The change comes to return humans to the gift of faith. It is a tent that welcomes all.

This is the heart of the Hawaiian prophecy – what the kanaka maoli have to offer the peoples of Earth. It is 'Iokepa's work, and it is yours.

I'd asked and I had received. In the midst of my days of distraction and exhaustion, boxes and bubble wrap, had come this incredible teaching.

I now heard an insistent rhythm:

To Hawai'i! Where it begins!
To Hawai'i! Where it begins!

PART TWO

QUESTIONING FAITH: TOGETHER

ARRIVING

June 12, 1998

The plans had gone almost exactly as expected: Ben graduated; Nathan advanced to high school; my mother visited; the burgundy Camry took the boat ride from Seattle; the pick-up truck load was crated and shipped to Kaua'i.

Chessie found a loving home; Ben and Nathan visited Honolulu for two nights, toured Pearl Harbor, and then on to Kaua'i for two-weeks in the incessant rain. They flew to West Virginia for the remainder of the summer. I settled into life on the boat *Imagine*.

There were two glitches. The house didn't sell and the estate sale produced less than a quarter of the promised profit. Very valuable antiques, rugs, jewelry and more went for thrift store prices. Before I left, I had given away Ben's piano to Lena, my best books to any friend who wanted them, a painting to Emily, a full-length black mink coat to Sara, a linen tablecloth to Stella, an heirloom hobby-horse to Ellen – and now I wished, I'd skipped the entire sale, and made gifts of everything. That was the extent of my regret.

I knew, before I stepped foot on Kaua'i for good that the first weeks alone with 'Iokepa on *Imagine* would be the honeymoon. In the glow of our being together, nothing could touch us, save the morning sun shining through portholes on our bare skin.

Maybe I also knew that it would never again be so easy. But I could not have known exactly how hard – or in what ways. Or how I'd respond to what was asked of me.

I believe it was a blessing that I didn't know. Knowing, it would have been unimaginably difficult to submit to it.

The divine in 'Iokepa had been clear to me from the first. Living together, I was asked now to integrate what I found out about the *man* – and, of course, he about me. Spiritually, we recognized each other's soul at first sight, but we were, in fact, human strangers.

For the next year, we would tread water within that paradox. Our mannerisms, attachments, identities, habits, and personalities were foreign soil to each other. We'd struggle for breath and understanding in ugly, unseemly, *angry* human ways.

Only in living that paradox – in fighting one another – would we learn, not just the full truth of the other – but we would learn the weakness of the fight itself (for ourselves, and for the Hawaiian people). We'd fight one another, apologize, and realize the hypocrisy of healing a people's spirit – and not our own. We'd realize, too, the limitation of an apology to heal the wounds.

'Iokepa said years later. "We came, finally, to the place where we wanted to avoid having to make those apologies. So we learned to avoid the behavior that required them."

. . .

Ben and 'Iokepa clashed – almost from the first.

"Mom, this man is not like us," Ben told me two days after arrival. "The guy is totally self-centered and arrogant."

I knew that Ben, Nathan and I formed a formidable triangle. Two of us had an eighteen year history of intimacy; three of us had fourteen. 'Iokepa was the new boy on the block.

At first, Ben didn't say his harsh words for 'Iokepa's ears – only for mine. But 'Iokepa knew what Ben thought of him – and he was profoundly hurt. I didn't know then, how deeply 'Iokepa was capable of being hurt.

Ben treated 'Iokepa exactly as he accused 'Iokepa of treating him: with arrogance and contempt. Ben saw 'Iokepa's spiritual 'ranting' as a threat to the firmament on which he stood proudest – things of the mind.

Ben accused me. "You're going off the deep-end. You're fifty-two and your son is leaving for college and you want someone. But in six months or a year, when this ends – and it *will* end – where will you be?"

'Iokepa wouldn't bend. With Ben, he spoke about the two things Ben had the least desire to hear: God and Prophecy. It felt to Ben (and to me at the time) that he was cramming stuff down an unwilling Ben's throat.

I questioned him: "Why?"

"Because I'm told to."

Four years later, he would say to each boy with a great deal of humility. "I'm sorry. I was younger then. I didn't know."

But at the time, I felt ripped down the middle.

In five days, 'Iokepa had moved out of the house we were sharing for those first weeks with the boys, back onto *Imagine*, alone.

"Mothers hear their sons with different ears," he told me. My sons, he said, "showed no respect." My heart was broken.

Nathan, it turned out, was the mediator. "I miss his energy," Nathan said. He and I drove the ten miles to find 'Iokepa on the boat.

He told 'Iokepa. "You can't give up on people. You *owe* every person as many explanations as they need until they understand.

"Ben's in a hard place: He's scared of college; he said good-bye to his friends and he won't see Mom again until Christmas."

'Iokepa heard Nathan's truth, recognized the wisdom. For years afterwards, he paraphrased my son. "As a wise young man told me..."

The next day, 'Iokepa moved back with us again.

It wasn't easy. I was torn between my love, loyalty and history with Ben, and my love, loyalty and future with 'Iokepa. Without 'Iokepa, it would have been rough letting Ben go off to college – not seeing him for six months. With 'Iokepa, it was excruciating.

The boys left for West Virginia on June 26. I looked down and didn't see a scrap of safety net. When the boys left as planned after two weeks to spend six weeks with their father, 'Iokepa and I moved onto *Imagine*. I wrote: "I am in this boat for life." It wasn't that I didn't want to be there – on the contrary. It's that any choice I may have had seemed to have evaporated under my feet.

After the boys left, 'Iokepa and I gloried in our time together those six weeks, and we literally never left one another's side. The first time I took the car for a couple hours of solo shopping and left 'Iokepa stringing *puka* shell *lei* on the deck of *Imagine,* it was already the second week of July.

When I returned, he hesitantly offered: "You might want to hear this. I missed you when you were gone."

Our days were full and yet never frenzied.

It wasn't so much *what* we did when we were together, or even where we did it. It was that his job went with us wherever we walked and with whomever we talked.

I did a great deal of listening in those early days. 'Iokepa would set me up sometimes. He would begin a story we had shared, then walk away and nod for me to finish it. I went mute the first couple times he did that. It was always a struggle to try to tell his stories – to match what he could do with words and enthusiasm. I was the stranger here. It took a very long time for me to I realize I had stories of my own to tell – still longer until my passion and insights found their own audience.

We were sitting at an outdoor table at 'Iokepa's friends' ice cream parlor, The Endless Summer. We sat in the shadow of the hill where 'Iokepa's great great grandmother was buried. It was the first time I'd found sufficient voice to add words to 'Iokepa's when he engaged the stream of people who his ancestors moved across his path.

'We will send people to you,' 'Iokepa often quoted his grandmothers. 'And we will send you to people. You won't have to look for them – they will find you.'

Bruce was Canadian, open-hearted, wide-eyed, muscular and athletic. He responded to 'Iokepa's words immediately. But when the freshly divorced Bruce spoke of the 'tests' that God puts us to, I found voice enough to disagree.

I repeated what I remembered of the nighttime writing. "There are no such things as tests," I told him, "only opportunities for faith."

When 'Iokepa spoke of forgiving ourselves I added. "The ancestors told me, they are 'saddened' when we criticize ourselves – that which God created."

Afterwards, 'Iokepa let me know that he was thrilled by our collaboration, by "the weave of our paths." He was nothing but supportive.

The last phone call that I'd received at my home in Portland was from my former therapist, Chris. She'd said. "The hardest thing any partner can ask of us is to be fully ourselves in every moment."

First in my head, and then much later in my heart, I understood that was exactly what 'Iokepa was asking me. But I had no idea how hard it could be.

. . .

Always and everywhere in my lifetime, women friends have been central to my happiness and peace of mind. My serious friendships were eclectic. Bringing my oldest and dearest friends together at Ben's *bar mitzvah* in 1993: Merrell, a newspaper editor from Asheville; Garie, an artist from Cleveland; and Sara, a fund-raising environmentalist from Charlottesville – women who'd heard about each other over a twenty year span – was one of the truly exhilarating occasions of my lifetime.

There were always multiple layers of friendship woven into the matrix of my life whenever and wherever I traveled or taught a workshop or lived. In truth, I'd considered my ability to draw wonderfully supportive souls to my heart the most lavish of God's gifts to me.

On Kaua'i however, I was very much alone. At the time, I didn't understand why friendship eluded me. Later I did.

I was with 'Iokepa almost every waking and sleeping hour. That didn't invite men or women to know me apart from him.

But more, 'Iokepa had a world of friends and admirers. It was central to his nature. He was warm, loving, and charismatic. His friends did not become mine.

Nathan noted, much later, the remarkable phenomenon of his mother without friends of her own. "They didn't want to know *you* – only if you were good enough for him, only measured against him." He was right.

I fell short by that standard of measure. First, I was not native Hawaiian. Second, I was conspicuous evidence that he was not celibate (and a surprising number wanted their holy men untouched). Third, with me sitting next to him, they had to share his intense one on one. Finally, I simply was *not* him – not the carrier of this prophecy.

Then there were the *women-ten* as I called them: ten single women who'd taken a shine to 'Iokepa over his months alone on Kaua'i. These were women who well-meaning friends had set up – or who'd been drawn in by his familiar *'Aloha!'* and had asked him to dinner or to the beach. He'd been absolutely clear with me. In his ten months on Kaua'i before me, he'd had no romantic interest in any woman.

But I didn't know the identities of the women-ten (or even that they existed) until they took me on, one by one. 'Iokepa didn't think their place in his life was significant enough to mention.

I became, for them, the momentary excuse to be with 'Iokepa. But I didn't know them, and I responded to each with the warmest interest and consideration as a potential friend. In sum, one by one, they used me to get to him. I'd never experienced anything like it in my life. They were difficult, driven, often obsessed women looking for salvation in 'Iokepa's spiritual and physical being. One of them actually stalked us. Another exposed herself to him.

There was a final reason for my failure at friendship. I didn't much like most of the people who were drawn to 'Iokepa. The neediest of the needy came for the cure. 'Iokepa made no claim to be anyone's guru. On the contrary, he'd turn them back on themselves. "The answers are yours."

Nevertheless, he was strong in important cultural and spiritual ways and that was nectar for the wounded. He was also remarkably tolerant – and always would be. Over the years, he mastered the ability to focus his energies where they best served the prophecy. But at the time, druggies, alcoholics, burned-out aging California hippies, and unquestioning spiritual seekers after anything New Age – what 'Iokepa called 'spiritual dilettantes' – formed the core of acquaintances I had to choose from.

They were fearful escapees from the demands of American middle class life. But in truth, both 'Iokepa and I had flourished in America. Their life experiences were very different from 'Iokepa's and mine. I anguished over my social choices.

Feel compassion for the escapees – not contempt. They need not threaten who you are. They need not force you into reaction. Shine your light. Be who you are without fear of being different.

...

Friendless, I asked more of 'Iokepa. With no ongoing work of my own (the computer was packed away in storage) I expected more of 'Iokepa. Increasingly, I asked less of myself. It wasn't good for either of us.

There was, of course, the question of money. He had lived without an automobile, storage unit, post office box, or predictable source of income for a year and a half. I entered his life with all of them – or at least a savings. My car compromised his hitchhiking and running – how he'd come to be seen and known all over the Island. Plus, it required gas. I crowded *Imagine's* crannies with the contents of four huge suitcases. I still had money in the bank.

The bills poured in from the house in Portland: two mortgages, property taxes, electricity, gas, water and sewage. There were outstanding dental bills, eye doctor bills, and two credit card bills as well. I paid every single one, every single month.

Increasingly, I couldn't imagine how I *could* have money, when 'Iokepa did not. How I could have a paying job, if he did not. I'd thought about teaching my writing workshop but the ancestors vetoed the idea out of hand: the house I'd arranged to teach in disappeared to a rental; the newspaper story announcing the workshop fell through the editorial cracks. Gradually and painfully, I understood: I, too, was in service only to the Creator; I was to support this life, not undermine it. Never again would I work for a paycheck.

For the hard-driven 'Iokepa under what he called the *trance* of his grandmothers' love, it was merely a transfer of energies. He didn't work less hard than he had before – but his labors were freed now from the tyranny of a paycheck. Even the occasional taunt questioning his manhood because he was 'unemployed' rolled off his back.

"Price tags were brought here. Nothing has been too sacred to be packaged and sold – to be trivialized."

For me, the letting go was considerably harder. It was easier for me, by far, to write, to teach, to build a career, to have a steady income – than not.

Inside *Imagine,* crowded next to a single burner hotplate, I continued to write my monthly checks. I paid every bill the day it arrived until I'd emptied my savings account. By mid-September, there wasn't a cent left. I called my creditors and explained the situation. When the house sold, it would all be theirs.

I came to realize that everything material I owned separated me from 'Iokepa; that every dollar in the bank meant that what the grandmothers had required of 'Iokepa would be compromised. Unconsciously, I tried to rid myself of that contradiction by spending my savings down to zero – by refusing to rent out the Portland house.

'Iokepa watched me obsess over the bills. He said. "When you came here, you turned that over to God. Everything you need will be provided."

The ancients didn't fight God for control. "Surrender" is distorted now. Healthy surrender takes you back where you belong.

The more I asked of 'Iokepa, the less he offered. The more I criticized him, the more he withdrew. I didn't yet know how thin-skinned this tough Hawaiian could be. I didn't yet understand that this man, who saw clearly into my soul and recognized my unhappiness in every subtle gesture or facial expression, felt reprimanded for failing to make me happy. For 'Iokepa, who lived to make me happy, the reprimand cut to the core.

I simply did not understand any of that. He said he wanted to take care of me: drive, wash, and fix the car. I'd taken care of myself and two boys for thirteen years. I thought he was controlling.

Whatever he did, he did once, and he did it right. I called him a perfectionist. My competitive edge was sharpened by his extreme competence. My self confidence felt under siege.

In fact I'd forgotten in those first weeks and months *who* 'Iokepa really was. I was trapped into seeing only the man, and I didn't have such an exemplary history of living with men. I'd been known to blame. I'd been known to struggle for control. I'd forgotten, too, who it was *I* am.

We fought. "Sometimes," he told me in the heat of our first fight. "I think you are a ringer. I love you, but...."

He didn't know what damage those words did to me. That he doubted my authenticity split me down the middle. I was already thinking of a life apart. 'Iokepa suffered too: back, hip and shoulder pain. We struggled.

Still the grandmothers spoke to me:

> Remember the Creator, and the rest will take care of itself. Humans forget: They put the relationship at the center. It is what we have been taught – husband and wife first, family next, then a gradation of loyalties.
>
> The danger is at the beginning: Beginning from the ego, not the Source; beginning from a closed heart, not open; beginning from certainty, not questions; beginning from skepticism, not curiosity; beginning with the already-known, not the asking. It closes doors to you.
>
> Remember what came before those societal teachings. Remember what we have known from time immemorial. The lesson is the universally open heart.

After that first fight, 'Iokepa reiterated. "For what is coming in the future, we will need to depend on each other completely."

I vowed to never hurt him again. And yet, I would.

...

In these past nearly thirteen years, I have changed in at least two recognizable ways – ample trade-off, I am certain, for what I'd been asked to relinquish that first year. Male and female, shrunk to opposites and tied to feminist politics for most of my life, grew to embrace what the *kanaka maoli* celebrated within self and other. We are children – all of us – of both mother and father; we each contain the whole. But it was hard times for me before that took root.

The other change was around how I saw my Judaism. I didn't understand that in learning to listen like a native Hawaiian – to value what was traditional there – I would embrace my Jewish *neshamah* (soul) more fundamentally.

That in the Hawaiian *makani* (spirit of the wind), I would feel my Jewish *ruach*. That in the native *mana*, I'd deepen into my own Hebrew name, *Chayah* (divine life force). How could I live his culture, without living my own? But that, too, took root over time.

On a casual afternoon stroll through the lavishly sculpted gardens surrounding the golf course at the Marriott Hotel, I experienced another moment of magic. I was granted, too, some understanding of that moment.

I was drawn to sit on a large, flat stone – placed there, obviously, for ornamental reasons.

Traveling through the ruins of the once-vibrant Inca empire at Machu Picchu years before, I'd felt the life in the Earth's rocks. Likewise at the Mayan ruins in the Yucatan. It was the same at the *heiau* on Kaua'i. I felt the life of the people who'd handled them, moved them, built them into walls, and prayed over them. Perhaps, I felt, too, the energy of the Creator in this simple element of nature.

But never had I felt called by a specific stone. I leaned my chest down to the rock so my heart beat against it and tested the limits of my new-found awareness. I asked silently. "Where are you from? What are you doing here?"

"I am from Lāhui," I heard the authentic name of the Hawaiian Islands plainly within my heart. "I don't know what I'm doing here."

I felt an inexplicable sorrow. Tears burned behind my eyelids – for the displaced rock that spoke for a displaced people.

The Hawaiian language at its most authentic is pure metaphor – every poetic phrase speaks to a deeper symbolic meaning. English speakers struggle with literal translations that need paragraphs to say what takes just a sentence in the *kahiko*. But you need to live the life of the aboriginals to *get* the symbolic meanings – they were written into the way of life.

"In cognitive philosophy," 'Iokepa told me, "the language is the mapping of a culture. To know a people you must know their language."

The words spoken by that displaced stone – shoved to an arbitrary setting as an ornament to draw tourists to the Marriott's commercial interests – were metaphor for the people I now lived among.

After we'd turned our backs and walked away, I repeated the stone's words to 'Iokepa. I told him that I'd felt the desperation.

Abruptly, he stopped. "We have to go back."

We kneeled together next to the rock, our hands resting on top and on the sides. "Don't be afraid," 'Iokepa said. "We will make it *pono* again."

But peace among the displaced people would be harder to realize.

The diseases brought by the first European sailing ships to Hawai'i wiped almost a million healthy *kanaka maoli* off the face of the Earth. Ninety percent of these native Hawaiians were buried by their kindred in unmarked graves along Hawaiian beaches where they remain today. These bones are sacred.

The surviving *kanaka maoli* remained caretakers of the bones of their ancestors. It was quintessentially Hawaiian to accept that responsibility – their continuing gratitude for the gift of life.

Again it is written into the language: *ka wa mamua* is literally translated as *past*. In the original language it meant *the time before* or *in front of* – and *ka wa mahope*, literally translated as *future*, in the *kahiko* meant *the time after* or *behind*.

One of the few native Hawaiian historians Jonathan Kamakawiwo'ole Osorio wrote: "These terms do not merely describe time – but the Hawaiians' orientation to it.

"We face the past, confidently interpreting the present, cautiously backing into the future, guided by what our ancestors know and did."

In 1988, the bones of a thousand native Hawaiian ancestors were unearthed during the construction of the Ritz Carlton Hotel on Maui. *Kanaka maoli* have been locked in emotional warfare with developers ever since – and losing ground. They win one small battle – delay construction a year – but lose the relentless struggle with off-Island investors, speculators, and greed.

Today there are token *native Hawaiian burial councils.* Developers send in archaeologists to locate the graves, find the bones, call in the burial council, shift a roadway a few feet, and then designate some tiny half-acre as a sacred Hawaiian site.

Finding graves has never stopped development. In American culture, where economic prosperity is god, gratitude for the grandparents' gift of life is expendable.

I've heard 'Iokepa tell developers. "Every inch of Hawaiian *'āina* is sacred. It's easy for you to pick and choose what's worth protecting. These aren't your ancestors buried here."

He's told archaeologists. "You're digging holes to find our history – but you're the only ones who need to know. The indigenous people you're digging to find: We already know."

That night on the yellow page, I asked: How is it that I heard a stone speak?

> *The lit path is not just your own sweet way, but the universal way. The light is inside each of us. We teach 'separate paths' and that is truth. But separate paths, only to remembering and reclaiming the One.*
>
> *In each soul there is a single word; within the One, there is the entire story. The rejoined words are the whole of divine history. We ask every human to speak his word, to add her clear voice to the chorus. In singing the universal song with the universal voice, the blaze within all of creation is reborn.*
>
> *So we say: In the beginning there was the word. And the word was God.*

TRAVELING AGAIN

Late July, 1998

For days 'Iokepa had felt the strong tug of the Island of Hawai'i.

At the end of July, an almost-free trip to that Island – which 'Iokepa refused to call colloquially, the Big Island – wondrously fell into our laps.

A friend (who had no hint of 'Iokepa's yearning) got an out-of-the-blue phone call, soliciting his participation in a timeshare presentation in Kona. For $99, it offered airfare for two, a first-class hotel for three nights, and a car rental for four days. He and his wife were tied to a small business – it was the height of tourist season – so he insisted that we go in their place.

It was our first flight together – forty-five minutes from Lihu'e to Kona. We'd been bumped up to first class by one of 'Iokepa's ubiquitous cousins at the gate.

'Iokepa's pull to the Island of Hawai'i was genealogical. It was where the blind chief 'Īmaikalani had prevailed over a quarter of the Island, until the early 17th century. Hawaiian history books were filled with his myth-sized accomplishments. 'Iokepa was his direct descendent, sharing the now-rare last name. Another ancestor, 'Imakakoloa, held sway in an adjacent district one hundred years later. So the pull to the Island of Hawai'i was powerful.

Like most native Hawaiians, 'Iokepa carried his genealogy in writing. But he, like the others, retained almost all of it etched into his soul. To know one's ancestors was to know who you were in this life; to be ignorant of your ancestry was to show contempt for the gifts of the culture. The gifts of this culture resided in the *'āina*. The heart of the people was, and still is, in the land.

So 'Iokepa yearned to go home to Hawai'i – to walk that *'āina*.

The bounty continued. When we arrived at the hotel, the desk clerk bumped our room grade up to top floor, ocean front, best in the house.

All that was required of us was that we submit to three hours of hard-sell – the two of us and two salesmen. But we were escorted out of the timeshare presentation after an unheard of one-hour – because it was 'Iokepa who did the talking.

"Let me tell you about the land you're sitting on. Do you know anything about this culture?"

With neither anger nor disrespect, 'Iokepa told the two excellent salesmen what they'd never heard before, but were hamstrung to avoid listening to.

"Everyone needs to support the Hawaiians," he told the two young men, "because without the Hawaiians there will be no Hawai'i.

"Our Islands are made up of our *kupuna* (ancestors) – and the *mo'opuna* (grandchildren). Without them, the Islands that you cherish disappear."

The salesmen nodded respectfully, asked not a single question, and with increasing awareness that we were not there to buy a timeshare condo sent us quickly on our way. 'Iokepa and I burst out laughing the moment we cleared the door.

Free of the timeshare commitment, we could explore the Island.

All seven of the populated Hawaiian Islands are volcanic. Each Island peeks its mountainous cone above the ocean and reveals only a fraction of the land mass that makes up the Island – the bulk of it lay buried under the sea.

For me, the entire Island of Hawai'i looked and felt exactly like what it (alone, among the Islands) was, an active volcano still spewing. Its *'āina* was uniformly rough, black lava rock; the beaches were spare – black sand or reef. The landscape felt harsh to me on that first trip, the mood oppressive. Within moments of arrival, I suffered a severe headache and exhaustion.

Kaua'i, by contrast, was verdant – green, gentle, and surrounded by miles of spectacular white sand beach.

"Kaua'i is the *Mother Island*, second oldest only to Ni'ihau," 'Iokepa said. "It will hold you and nurture you." It sat at the extreme northwest edge of the Island chain.

The island of Hawai'i – at the extreme eastern end of the chain, was the *Father*. In size, it exceeded the total surface of all the other Islands combined. It was, even now, being birthed.

There was nothing subtle about their differences.

We circled almost every paved road on the Island. We drove from *heiau* to *heiau* – from the volcano to the sea. We walked across crunchy, glistening eight-month-old lava rock, next to steam venting from the molten mountain. We hiked the ancestral district of the ancient chief, 'Imaikalani. We asked – and then followed the ancestors' prodding at every turn.

One of those turns took us to Miloli'i. What composer, musician Israel Kamakawiwo'ole – *Bruddah Iz* – called in song, "The last small fishing village in Hawai'i." We drove eight winding miles through the black rock lava fields before we entered the village. We were met by inhospitable, ice cold stares. It was a town that had felt the threat and encroachment of nearby development.

We turned, prepared for a quick departure; leaving by the road we'd only just arrived on. But 'Iokepa, without a word to me, stopped the car in the middle of the single lane, left the driver's door open, and walked across the street to a radiant, middle-aged Hawaiian woman holding an infant. Momi – of generous heart and spirit – heard the 'Imaikalani name, looked deeply into 'Iokepa's eyes and knew him. "Go down to my house, I'll meet you there."

She offered us fresh cherries, cold soda, and the warmth of herself. We sat outside around a picnic table, on her concrete *lānai* (patio) in the shade of an enormous mango tree. She was a powerhouse Hawaiian spirit like none I'd encountered since 'Iokepa, comporting herself with utter humility, in order to properly welcome 'Iokepa and me. She chose to listen, rather than to speak her own story. But it shone, vividly transparent anyway.

"Prophecy," 'Iokepa told Momi, "is a living, breathing thing – like the *'āina*, like the *koholā* – the whale."

"When we say: '*They* oppress us or they must be persuaded to release us,' we've already given our power away. *They* gives it away. *We* empowers.

"We possess the *mana* to live our freedom. We have ancestors who speak to us in every breath. We are responsible for the care of the *'āina*. We are responsible for one another. We are connected to, and draw strength from, every living thing. We have a 13,000 year culture whose truths can, and will, illumine the world.

"We come from the hand of the Creator. We ask in prayer and hear our answers in every *hā* – breath. We live our faith. We are the *kanaka maoli*, the original people of this land.

"The answers to our freedom lie inside our individual souls – and our cultural one. When we live what our ancestors lived, the land will follow. We will have earned our place as God's stewards of this *'āina.*"

Momi looked intently into 'Iokepa's eyes. Then, she looked into mine.

"I'm grateful and honored that *Ke 'I'oakua* – God Almighty – sent 'Iokepa to my home," she said. "We've been waiting for you."

But 'Iokepa and I knew. The honor of this encounter was entirely ours.

She asked 'Iokepa to offer a *pule* (prayer).

We stood – Momi, her friend, her husband, 'Iokepa and I – under the mango tree and we held hands. 'Iokepa offered his gratitude, and then he intoned an ancient chant: "*He kahakū wau no kēia 'āina, ia'u o uka ia'u o kai!* I may go where I please on this land: Inland is mine, seaward is mine!"

When we left, driving the narrow black rock road through the string of fishermen's modest homes, the villagers, without exception, were luminous with smiles.

We were able to extend our stay on the Island of Hawai'i for two days because the owner of the most spectacular Bed and Breakfast on the Island insisted that we stay in one of her architect-designed cottages for free. The glass-walled, B&B clung to a precipice over the ocean, at the edge of the breathtaking Waipi'o Valley.

Again, the universe delivered the favor. Standing in a gift shop, I mentioned our need for a place to stay. The shop owner phoned a friend who owned the B&B and handed the phone to 'Iokepa.

'Iokepa told our story. The owner hesitated a moment and then she said, "Come on over. We'll see what we can do." This perfect stranger wanted to hear what 'Iokepa had to say.

She and her husband brought us dinner and we sat up half the night talking. She was full of questions that began with, "Should I?" 'Iokepa insisted, "Trust yourself. You know." She asked us to stay another night but we demurred. 'Iokepa left her one of his beautiful shell *lei*.

In that glass room overlooking the waterfall at the mouth of the legendary Waipi'o Valley, I was awakened at 3:15 a.m. and told to write. I crawled quietly out of our bed so as not to awaken 'Iokepa; then I stood on the *lānai* and stared up at the most spectacular night sky I'd ever seen. Were there really that many stars in the heavens?

I got cold, came inside and turned on a small light over the kitchen table. 'Iokepa stirred, saw me bent over the yellow legal pad, and smiled.

Yours is a different message than 'Iokepa's. He lives his truth, and anyone in his presence hears it – in the confidence of his words.

But it is your very process that illumines lives. Others hear your words, your search for truth, louder for the humanness of it: for the fact that it is a search.

'Iokepa's path is unwavering. Your way is volatile. You excite with your passions, your emotions. His is un-flagging commitment to the one truth. Yours is unflagging commitment to the search. Together, you touch different souls in different ways.

All of our children – I know for a fact – were put on Earth, first of all, to instruct their parents. Even this I learned from my sons.

Nathan had been my teacher since the day he was born. At eight days old, a number of observers at his Jewish ritual *bris* remarked that my baby had, "Old man's eyes." As a toddler, with few words to describe his world – but a world of imagery – Nathan told me he had a sore throat, in this way. "Mom, there's an X in my throat." At six years old, staring at his own reflection in my pupils, he said: "What you see is in your eyes."

He was, from the first, a sweet spirit for whom the stream of life seemed easier than for most. His gifts were pronounced, both spiritual and human. He was a gentle, quiet observer of life with a huge non-judgmental heart, to whom other children were immediately drawn.

Nathan returned to Kaua'i on August 12.

We had given two weeks notice to the owners of *Imagine* ('Iokepa's benefactors). The sailboat would be much too small for an amorous couple and a fourteen year old boy. There would be no privacy for any of us. Then one week later, the owners told 'Iokepa, they'd intended to refurbish and sell it anyway. So *Imagine* was no longer an option.

On the morning of the day that Nathan was scheduled to arrive, we packed up what had been 'Iokepa's home for the past year. An extension cord, a tiny fan, a miniature reading lamp went into storage. Old socks, T-shirts, and two rusty bicycles went to the Salvation Army's thrift shop. What we'd need for the next couple of days went into the Camry's trunk. With affection, gratitude and nostalgia we offered a farewell prayer on the bow of *Imagine.*

For me, that was the beginning of my walk of faith. Until then it had been summer camp: the adventure of foreign travel, romance with a handsome voyager, a cozy love nest aboard *Imagine.*

But if 'Iokepa's path required daily, public demonstration of faith – and it did, and he did – then it was time now for me to put up or shut up.

There was my child support, halved when Ben turned eighteen in early September and I simultaneously agreed to put $100 of Nathan's monthly child support towards Ben's remaining tuition. It was now $230 a month. There was the rapidly diminishing bank account that would be gone in a month. I was hoarding that for Portland bills alone. There was whatever the Creator sent 'Iokepa's way.

'Iokepa consistently regarded the Creator's gifts as 'abundant – more than we can even imagine.'

With Nathan's arrival, there would be three to feed, clothe, and house on that promise.

We packed in the morning and picked Nathan up at the airport in the early afternoon. He was full of smiles (just two months out of braces). His thick, straight hair was pulled back into a jet black ponytail that skimmed his shoulder blades. He was about five feet seven, lean and fourteen.

"Mom," he said after a big hug and kiss. "You're so tan and skinny!" Nathan never missed a trick. He'd always noticed every new pair of earrings or shoes I'd ever worn.

We went first to The Endless Summer. Owners Louisa and Albert treated us to double scoops of the richest ice cream I'd ever known (and I *knew* ice cream) – from Lappert's, a local creamery. Nathan fell in love with Albert and Louisa – drawn to their youth, their rapid fire wit and intelligence. Albert was a surfer – he promised to teach Nathan. Louisa was the indulgent, outrageous auntie, who genuinely remembered being fourteen. It was an auspicious beginning.

At nightfall, it was the three of us in the burgundy Camry – with nowhere to go. 'Iokepa suggested – to celebrate Nathan's first night – we splurge on a hotel room. We did. *Kama'āina* had come to mean anyone with an address in Hawai'i. It guaranteed any resident half the going tourist rate. We stayed at the Holiday Inn.

The second night we slept in the car by the side of a road. "Hotel Camry," 'Iokepa called it, and then he laughed. Nathan and I laughed with him, trying to fit three full-grown bodies into sleep positions in a moderate sized sedan. Nathan was curled up in the back, pinned flat in his seat by our reclining seats.

In the morning, each one of us was stiff in a different place, but uncomplaining. It was a lark, a temporary situation until the ancestors noticed their oversight. We showered at the public park near the small boat harbor and stopped in a convenience store for breakfast. We were uniformly grateful for the impressive sunrise, the vibrant rainbow across the horizon, the lucent ocean, the sharply-etched mountains, and the birds.

On the third and fourth nights, Veronica (who had rented the vacation house to me at Christmas) offered *her* home (next door to where we'd gathered for Christmas dinner), while she went camping for the weekend. We settled into comfort.

On the fifth night, we slept in the car. After an Island-wide search for a place to park – a place where the police wouldn't chase us away – we settled on Ahukini Landing, at the edge of an aging ocean fishing pier behind the airport. We fell asleep to the roar of the last plane of the night lifting off just a couple hundred feet over our sunroof at 9:30 p.m. – and awakened to the first one in the morning at 6:00 a.m.

On the sixth, seventh, and eighth nights, we accepted the hospitality of Louisa and Albert. But after three days, we realized that guests crowding their small apartment to capacity were the last thing they needed after their twelve-hour days scooping ice cream and smiling at tourists – and we moved on. *Where* would we live when Nathan started school on day fourteen? The answer soon came clear.

On the ninth, tenth, eleventh, twelfth, thirteenth, four-teenth, fifteenth, sixteenth, seventeenth, and eighteenth nights, we were back at Ahukini Landing, cramped into pretzels inside the Toyota Camry. I'd taken the backseat. I was changing tampax over a plastic bag at the dirt edge of the parking lot. No one was laughing anymore.

Ben had begun college, but at this distance I could do no more than wish him well. His dad drove him to Beloit – doing what I never imagined I'd *not* be doing. I felt empty and impotent.

. . .

In the weeks before Nathan arrived, I had scouted the school situation.

My kids had always been in public schools for financial reasons less than for principled ones. I believed in public education, but I had investigated the most selective private school on the Island because I'd heard abysmal reports, all the way to Portland, about the Hawaiian public school system. I didn't want Nathan to suffer for my decision to move.

I had done the legwork and paperwork necessary to get him a full-blown scholarship to Island School. Even in his absence, on paper alone, he'd made his way. He'd just completed a novel; he'd topped out on the Johns Hopkins' talent search; he'd been a straight A student forever; he'd completed algebra, geometry, and two years of Japanese in middle school; he'd been in a rigorous gifted program since third grade; he'd had ecstatic teacher recommendations.

Island School was small, academically challenging, and they wanted him enough to waive $9000 in tuition to make it happen. But it would be Nathan's decision.

I had also researched the three public high schools, easily eliminating two – one for not being academically rigorous, the other for being a hotbed of student rage – in favor of Kaua'i High. 'Iokepa and I had interviewed the principal. She handpicked teachers and classes that would meet Nathan's needs.

When Nathan arrived one week before school started, he faced a decision: Island School or Kaua'i High?

"I assumed I would go to Kaua'i High," he said, right off the plane.

Then the well-meaning, barrage from friends and strangers began.

"Island School for free? You *can't* turn it down."

"There's no choice at all. Kaua'i High stinks!"

Nathan, 'Iokepa, and I heard a dozen versions of the same chorus.

Then we listened to the insistent racial refrain. During a tour of the school, a Kaua'i High *teacher* warned Nathan.

"If you come here, you'll get beaten up. All *haoles* get roughed up. If you fight back, you'll be suspended."

Daily, we heard it. Students, parents, and even childless adults repeated what was the conventional wisdom: white skin and Kaua'i High School didn't mix.

Nathan was scared. Fear was now his greatest motivator. "I don't want to fight every day."

Nathan had always thrived in small academic settings. At Island School, I assumed, he'd feel known – at Kaua'i High, I worried, he'd be lost. I didn't press my point. It was clearly his decision.

When the time grew short, with the unanimous community opinion lined up against the public school, 'Iokepa weighed in.

"You can't make this decision from fear," he told Nathan. "Kaua'i High sits on what was once one of the oldest *heiau* on the Island. It was my family land.

"Do you think the ancestors would let you be harmed there?"

Nathan listened to 'Iokepa as he listened to everyone – reasonable or not – who came at him. He was quiet and attentive. It was hard to tell what he was thinking.

But on the day before school began, Nathan told us his decision. "I didn't come to Hawai'i to hang around with kids like me. I came to live what's here. I want a *real* high school."

He called the Island School, thanked them for their offer, and refused it. The admissions director gave him a safety net. If he changed his mind within a few weeks, the scholarship would still be his. He thanked them again and registered at Kaua'i High.

. . .

Nathan started high school on Thursday, August 27. It was utterly unlike the elaborate send-off for Ben four years before: new clothes, new backpack, expensive running shoes, an Eggs Benedict breakfast, balloons over the breakfast table, PTA involvement – the works. The discrepancy ate at my heart. I said nothing.

We drove Nathan to the Niumalu Park for a cold shower in the morning, then to the convenience store for orange juice and a muffin, and then to school. I had made him a peanut butter and jelly sandwich for lunch on the hood of the car.

After one day, he came home relieved – not yet comfortable but plainly calmed. He said, "People don't know what they're talking about. Nobody even called me '*haole*.'"

He did his homework that afternoon at a sidewalk table outside The Endless Summer before dark.

That became our routine. Nathan accepted it; I struggled on his behalf.

We drove him to school each morning – always expecting that there'd be a home to return to when we picked him up in the afternoon.

The days while he was at school were alive for 'Iokepa and me. They were full of prayer and people and beautiful places. But after dinner, the increasing probability that we'd be sleeping in the car again weighed heavily.

Nathan was forced by circumstances to spend more time with his mother than most fourteen year old boys would have agreed to. He wanted a place to invite friends. He wanted friends. I wanted that for him. 'Iokepa felt enormous responsibility for Nathan's homelessness. I felt excruciating guilt. My *baby* – what was I putting him through?

> *When the time is ripe, you will not be in the car. This is not about deprivation. You are, each of you, full of life and love.*

The place you seek – a nest, a home – is already within each of us. A building – you believe – represents security and comfort, but that is illusory. All security, all comfort, resides within us.

You told Nathan. "You'll look back tenderly on the smells and sights of the harbor at sunset and sunrise: the rainbows, the cruise ships, and the peanut butter and jelly sandwiches – later." It is like that for you and 'Iokepa. You will look back, and remember sending your son to school fresh from the public shower. You will remember questioning, "Why us? We are faithful."

But because you live this, you will in time, be uniquely armed with compassion for dislocated others. Trust that we offer you nothing you cannot grow from. What looks like deprivation is not. It is nourishment. It builds muscle, mana, and faith.

CRUMBLING

September, 1998

I had no home, no middle class quotient of security for my son, very little money, and no work of my own. On an absolutely superficial level, I had three months worth of grey roots and split ends, and I yearned for a good haircut and color.

From my lengthy wish list, the ancestors directed me to find an office space first – a place to write. I had no money for rent, but I shopped around as though I did. Then Louisa and Albert stepped in. They opened their home to me during the hours that they were not there. I accepted.

'Iokepa removed my computer from storage, and we rearranged the living room furniture to create a niche. I absolutely delighted in unpacking my manuscripts, dictionary, staple gun, and familiar file cabinet full of office supplies. I lifted 'Iokepa's little fan and lamp from its cardboard box. I sat in a borrowed chair, at a borrowed table, in a borrowed room, and I wrote (what I'd prematurely hoped would be the start of this book) from 10:00 a.m. until Nathan's school bus arrived 'home' at 3:00. Soon after, 'Iokepa picked us up.

It was my safe haven – a tiny space to fill my soul. It was also the place that my oldest son could phone us. That alone was a miracle. We'd been without a telephone for three months. I had called Ben from noisy public pay phones – much too infrequently – with scarce calling cards. My calls missed him as often as they caught him in.

Ben's transition to Beloit College had been uncomplicated. He loved the students, professors, classes, all of it. I could not remember when I'd last heard him so alive.

In the middle of Nathan's first full week of school, 'Iokepa bartered one of his *puka* shell *lei* for a cozy hotel suite for three nights. The Inn sat at the foot of the hill that climbed up to Nathan's school. We had separate rooms – finally. Nathan could walk to school. We were inordinately grateful.

But when the three days ended and we were again sleeping in the car, my faith dwindled, Nathan's complaints intensified, and 'Iokepa was increasingly annoyed with both of us. Nerve endings were frayed.

My mother-heart begged the ancestors for relief for my child. I heard instead.

> *We want more for this child than mere comfort. We want him to feel the confidence that he can make his own comfort. For Nathan, this is about making his own way.*
>
> *You have loved Nathan so that he will love himself. When he loves himself, he can trust himself to take risks – as you have done in your life.*

...

'Iokepa and I had been joined together by an authority that was both mystical and inevitable – at sunrise prayers, by a sacred *heiau,* on that Christmas morning. Eight months later – in absolute darkness, under a cloud-covered night at Ahukini Landing, standing next to the Camry on a decrepit fishing pier – it all fell apart. What had felt like destiny, now felt impossible.

This time, there were three of us – and each of us played a part in the destruction.

For my part, I used Nathan. I made him my ally; I cut 'Iokepa out. I'm not proud of that.

For Nathan's part, he wanted what he'd always taken for granted – a home. And though Nathan was generally speaking a quiet kid, he'd never stinted on telling me exactly what he wanted – loud and clear.

For 'Iokepa's part, he cut Nathan very little slack for being fourteen, in a new place, and scared. He cut me even less around the issue of faith.

We'd been heading toward a blow-up for days. At the tail end of August, standing on that rotting fishing pier in the dead of night – just the three of us – it happened.

The specifics are a blur of inconsequentiality. Earlier in the afternoon, 'Iokepa didn't like the way Nathan spoke to me: 'Disrespectfully.' He dove in head first to defend me. I dove in head first to defend Nathan. Maybe it was the classic paradox of step-parenting – maybe what happened to us wasn't even original.

That afternoon, I sent Nathan into the ring. I had him hand deliver 'Iokepa's Laundromat-dried laundry in a clump (ours, I'd neatly folded). 'Iokepa, in turn, goaded Nathan with adolescent taunts and ridicule. Nathan shouted an obscenity at 'Iokepa – and even worse, sneered: "*You* were the one who was supposed to find us a home – and you *didn't.*" It was a well-placed knife into a man who took his caretaking responsibilities more seriously than most.

I put my arm around Nathan and walked away. We left 'Iokepa alone in the car for the night. Nathan stretched out, head in my lap, on a disintegrating wooden bench built into the pier.

"I will come to think of love as fighting," he told me. My heart broke.

The lines were drawn. Three loving souls were locked into hurt, rage, and immediate remorse. All the words that could have been spoken had been spoken. Words felt used up. I had none left to offer.

"Last night was a nightmare," I told 'Iokepa after we dropped Nathan off at school the next day.

"No," he said. "You awaken from a nightmare." Resolutely and wordlessly, he drove toward *Poli'ahu heiau*, where we first met.

"Don't!" I said, when I realized where he was going, and why. He was going to the place where our lives intersected – to offer the ancestors our separation. I started sobbing.

We walked our separate paths around the rocks, and offered our solitary words. I heard. *With 'Iokepa or without him, you are where you are.*

I understood. Kaua'i, the nighttime writings, all of it – they were mine, regardless.

"Everything for a purpose," 'Iokepa said when we returned to the car.

I dropped him off, as he'd asked me to, at The Endless Summer. He transferred each of his possessions – cane knife, beach chair, duffel bag – from the trunk of the Camry to the sidewalk.

"I will always love you," he said. But he never looked back.

. . .

I drove to my office in Louisa and Albert's home. I studied the newspaper classified ads: $750 a month, plus utilities, for the least of the rentals. I'd already paid September's house mortgage and utility bills. I had $150 left in the bank.

I was staring into another brick wall. I had no friends of my own. Louisa and Albert were 'Iokepa's. They would offer him their place to stay. I phoned the only person I knew in Hawai'i independent of 'Iokepa – Veronica, whose vacation home I'd rented at Christmas. I left a message, full of heartache and slurred grief. "Do you know anyone who needs a house sitter?"

She called me right back. A German tourist, scheduled to lease the oceanfront vacation-rental house for September, had fallen ill. She'd cancelled the night before.

Veronica had been sitting at her desk for the past couple hours thinking, "Inette and Nathan...." She had no idea why. Then I called.

"This happened so you could get on your feet," she said. The two-story, two-bedroom, lavishly furnished, oceanfront home was ours – gratis, for the entire month. "I'd always pictured someone writing a book in that house," she said. "It was you!"

I felt cradled in the palm of the Creator – never safer.

That first night *alone* in a king-sized bed, under a fluffy comforter, in a lavish room – the only time in three months –

was bliss. Nathan had his own room and bathroom. He had his own TV, too. The Nintendo that he'd inadvertently left at his Dad's arrived that day by UPS. He was a happy boy indeed.

We were in the town of Kapaʻa on a very quiet street facing the ocean. But we were also a short walk from every major fast food restaurant, video rental store, supermarket, and bookstore on the Island. It was Nathan's idea of heaven and – alone again with my son – maybe it was mine too. We ate that night at Taco Bell.

By morning my gratitude had dimmed and the bliss had turned to something else. My whole self yearned for 'Iokepa. My heart floated on a sea of emptiness. But I could not visualize a path back to him. How could we get past our deadly words, our mutual betrayal?

> *There is a physical withdrawal. This way, you get to understand what you have – and what you do not have – when you share a life with a powerful man. What you have – and what you do not have – when you share a life only with your sons.*
>
> *Life isn't about contracts, certainty, control. Life is breath to breath. You and 'Iokepa are together only as long as you both agree it serves you. Relationship is renewed with every breath. 'Do we agree now? Now?' Yesterday you no longer agreed. It no longer served you.*
>
> *But you never once asked. 'How do I love all three, and protect all three?' We would have told you that in loving One – in seeing One in all – you love all. You don't dole it out in little boxes: To family, but not to strangers; to Nathan, but not to 'Iokepa.*

After three days and nights of self imposed solitude – weeping intermittently through the ancestors' nonstop instruction that spilled across a half dozen legal pads – I surrendered all that I had held so certain: 'Iokepa and I had no future. It was time to get on with my own.

I let go – with profound heartache – of the future that brought me to Kauaʻi: fulfillment of the Hawaiian prophecy by

'Iokepa's side. Eight months of ancestors' coaching had shriveled to unfulfilled promises. I had failed.

Then like a baseball thrown at the side of my head when I was looking elsewhere, this.

> *You are who you are – with or without 'Iokepa. But you have agreed to live your paths together. Find the words he can hear – and he will hear them.*

> . . .

I immediately wrote the words that he might hear, stuck them into an envelope and put the envelope into the car. I wrote, because I didn't think I had the guts to see him. Nevertheless, our coming together was divinely synchronized and made my letter irrelevant.

Two days later on a Saturday, Nathan and I were hauling my computer and office equipment out of Louisa and Albert's home in Kalaheo. It was a forty-five minute one-way trip back to Veronica's in Kapa'a. It took us three round trips in the loaded Camry – each time, unavoidably passing The Endless Summer. I'd look over, see no 'Iokepa, and continue on relieved.

On the final trip there remained just a folding table to move, so I left Nathan behind at Veronica's. Because I had room in the car this trip, and because 'Iokepa was nowhere to be seen, I planned to stop by The Endless Summer on the return trip and pick up a treasured oil painting that been, oddly enough, left unsold at the estate sale in Portland.

I had decided that the huge self-portrait by the Balinese artist Madi Kertenegoro that I'd bought from the artist while visiting Bali years before – did not want to stay in Portland. It seemed that Madi wanted to return to Polynesia. I'd told the estate sale manager to send it on to The Endless Summer – and it had arrived and taken up valuable store space there for three days.

I greeted Louisa and Albert behind their ice cream counter, "*Aloha!*" with huge hugs and kisses. "I'm here to collect Madi."

The painting, in its richly carved Balinese frame, was impossible to lift. I was dragging it backwards across the floor of the store, inch by inch. I was halfway to the sidewalk when I heard the rumble of the unmistakable voice that would rouse the Hawaiian people.

"Do you need some help?"

He reached out for a hug and I stiffened. I accepted his help, but not his hug and he loaded the painting and tied the trunk down with bungee cords.

"All we've been together," he said sadly. "And not even a hug."

I handed him my letter. He set it aside.

He asked me. "Would you mind giving me a lift to Louisa and Albert's?"

I was headed in the opposite direction; I hesitated. I had followed the grandmothers' directive and written the letter. But the hurt remained.

During the next few hours alone at Louisa's and Albert's, we pieced together an awkward reconciliation. I kept studying his eyes. His words were flawless.

"I've always loved you. I never grieved as you tell me you did, because I never believed we wouldn't be together."

He said he missed my face, my voice, and my smiles.

I was full of ambivalent feelings. That I loved him was never a question. That this unfathomable life was somehow my peculiar destiny was the given – it had been since last Christmas. That Nathan, 'Iokepa, and I would find peace together was far less certain – and that terrified me.

He stayed on at Louisa and Albert's for the next few days, visiting me – then Nathan and me – when I invited him. As before, he walked miles effortlessly, and he hitchhiked.

On one of these visits, 'Iokepa told me we were being prepared for a lengthy separation – we would be out of communication. He was leaving for Moloka'i soon. It was his grandmothers' directive. Exactly when, how, or where were a matter of faith. He'd go exactly when he was told, not before, not after.

He didn't know a soul on that Island. In our days apart, he'd been instructed to walk the 'āina – the land – of *every*

Island – or, as he now said, "All parts of *the* Island" – seeing them undeniably (both, geologically and genealogically) as one.

With his departure imminent, it seemed foolish to live apart. He moved into our home, into my bed. We had family breakfasts and dinners again. I prodded Nathan to forgive the litany of wrongs.

"I won't do it for you," he said in no uncertain terms. "It just has to *happen*."

In those few days, I felt the walls of my resistance to sharing a life with 'Iokepa crumble.

On our next to the last day together, 'Iokepa received this. He was in the shower when the words were peeled off, one after another, with large spaces between them.

He shouted them out to me, one by one, as I was making the bed. He was listening to his ancestors speak them while he showered.

> "*Manifest*....
> Then, "*Manifest illusion*....
> "*Manifest illusion with mana*...."
> Then "*Manifest illusion with mana and faith.*
> Finally, "*Manifest your magic with mana and faith.*"

We discussed it. Every soul, we agreed, had within them the ability (the absolute necessity) to claim his own magic by tapping into the energy of the universe that's available to each of us at all times – with faith.

'Iokepa explained. "Can we agree that *mana* is divine power – the energy of the universe? That *Hūnā* is harnessing that energy of the universe? The *kahuna*, then, is the man or woman, who finds the key to harnessing the energy of the universe. But the key is only for that particular person – at that particular moment. It won't work for everyone, and it's for use only when absolutely necessary – often, only once.

"You don't need to know – until you *need* to know. The *kahuna* doesn't need to know all the stars in the sky – until he's asked. Potentially, the *kahuna* is the jack-of-all-trades and the master of all."

He continued.

"A person, who calls himself a *kahuna,* is definitely *not.* It was never about naming yourself. He can tell you who he thinks he is, but you'll know the truth. You'll know it the minute you look into his or her eyes."

His grandmothers had promised him from the first. *You will have what you need when you need it – but never more than you need.*

He said. "I don't have to know everything. I just have to feel confident that I *can* know everything. It's about taking down barriers and limitations to what I can know, or can do. Increasing human confidence is at the heart of the prophecy."

'Iokepa left the day after Labor Day. I dropped him at the airport with $20 in his pocket and no ticket to Moloka'i. In the last days together we'd been our closest – to one another, and to the grandmothers. We were about to be separated, but we were undoubtedly together again.

He dissolved the heaviness inside both our chests at the looming separation with a joke about his incredible hair.

"Remember! All the other men wear wigs, and they're liars!" While I was laughing through my tears, I heard him say.

"When I get back, it'll be better."

. . .

I went directly from the airport to the post office. I was standing in line waiting for stamps when I looked into the pitying, black eyes of a younger acquaintance.

"How *are* you?" he asked. His voice was oozing concern. "Are you returning to the Mainland?"

His concern was understandable. Publicly, 'Iokepa and I were apart. Only close friends knew we had reconciled. The community's perception was that I'd been dumped.

I didn't like being pitied – had never thought of myself as someone who'd elicit it.

"I'm terrific," I laughed and I meant it. "Of course I'm staying."

"Well at least you're still laughing."

What could I have answered?

"Step back, Mom, and listen," my fourteen year old son advised me. "Wait for the words."

'Iokepa called Veronica collect – briefly. I had no phone card and I could accept no collect call on my phone; he had no calling card. He left me this message: He had sat in the Kaua'i airport for more than three hours, then a woman came up to him, asked if he was going to Moloka'i, and handed him a one way ticket. Just like that, he was there.

Moloka'i – he told Veronica – was a tiny population of 7,000 spread over an undeveloped *'āina*. There were few roads, a couple of general stores and two gas stations in the single town. He told her to tell me he was fine.

Veronica related every word he'd said. But no matter how many questions I asked her, I couldn't get enough. It was the first of too many second-hand accounts of 'Iokepa – and the beginning of my resentment.

That first week he was gone, 'Iokepa placed a collect call to The Endless Summer. I heard an account of it from Louisa, then later, from Albert. I heard another account from his sister Puanani. She had a toll-free number and 'Iokepa called her often. But all 'Iokepa's words were filtered through the screen of other people's version, and I hated it.

'Iokepa left me expecting he'd be gone a month. Now Puanani told me he'd be gone for six.

I charged a telephone calling card to my Visa, and gave the number to Puanani. I told her to read the pin number to 'Iokepa the next time he phoned. Then, he could call me directly.

I asked the ancestors for the truth: one month or six?

Live these months fully. We know nothing of the future. 'Iokepa is on Moloka'i because that is where he remembers. The separation makes him stronger. It makes you stronger too. Outside of the considerable shadow of 'Iokepa, you flower. There is a need to grow in confidence –

*apart. Then, you will bring your powers together again –
magnified.*

"This separation isn't just for 'Iokepa," Nathan said, echoing the ancestors' words without having heard any of them.
"It's for you to find your own Kaua'i, to make it yours.

"You *have* changed. You need to tell your own story. You
tell it very well."

But it took me much longer than the separation on Moloka'i to make Nathan's words – and the grandmothers – mine.

By the time 'Iokepa called me, he'd been away for two weeks,
and I'd built up a fair head of steam. I resented that after six
months of living on phone calls between Portland and Kaua'i –
and just two and a half months of flesh to flesh – we were
again reduced to phone chatter.

I spent a fair amount of that first call scolding 'Iokepa: I
was sick of second-hand accounts; pissed that he couldn't
remember if he'd told *me* what he had, in fact, told Puanani or
her son, and that I didn't think I wanted to speak with him on
the phone again.

It wasn't good.

"The one left behind has it harder," Nathan said. "Flush it
through you, Mom. Let God come in."

It was another week before I heard from 'Iokepa again.
My resentment had not abated.

"Do you *want* to talk to me?" 'Iokepa asked first thing, on
the second call. I softened. I told him about this miracle:
Nathan was wearing the *puka* shell *lei* that 'Iokepa had given
him. It was out of his backpack and around his neck again.

"That's the best thing I've heard on either call."

On the third phone call, 'Iokepa said, "I don't have the
words to tell you all you mean to me. Our last phone call was
the fix I needed."

Later, he asked. "Would you like me to come for the
weekend?" (On the outside chance that he would have money
for a round trip ticket.)

I hung back. "If you're supposed to...." But I feared going through a withdrawal again, afterwards.

> *Fearing you might be abandoned, you protect. But fears protect us from the very things we want: Love, compassion, forgiveness. Fearing we might be left alone, we insure that we will be left alone. No one can get through: Not 'Iokepa, not God, not your loving ancestors. Closed, you are alone.*
>
> *Would you burn yourself, so that you would not be burned? It is foolish. Take your chances; risk abandonment; love 'Iokepa.*

My weeks alone with Nathan were delightful – surprisingly lighthearted and fun. The day 'Iokepa left – the first day of the third week of school – I asked Nathan the same question I'd never stopped asking him and Ben, since kindergarten.

"How was school today?"

I realized early on, it was probably not the best way to elicit more than an, "Okay" from Ben. But Nathan was usually more forthcoming. Every day, for his first two weeks at Kaua'i High, Nathan had come home depressed – he hadn't made a single friend. Throughout his first two weeks of high school, Nathan had been stuck inside his head observing, frozen in silence, and hating himself for it. Teachers and other adults were Ben's key to self worth. Peers were Nathan's.

On the day 'Iokepa left, I routinely asked the question that had evoked grief for two weeks. "How was school?"

But this time Nathan answered, "Great!!!" He'd broken loose. "Eleven!" he'd counted the significant conversations he had engaged with other kids. It was the turning point.

We lived outside of the school district's borders, so Nathan was not served by a school bus. I'd been driving him to and from school and it was cutting almost an hour and a half from my writing day. It was at the point of "Great!" that I stopped picking him up after school.

"Hitchhike," I recommended with copious backing from others. With only a single sporadic bus line, kids hitchhiked here. It was something I would never have allowed my children in any former life – let alone suggested. But Kaua'i was a safe, small place – not by a long stretch the United

States. (The word, *Mainland*, was an oxymoron to an independent Hawai'i – conscious *kanaka maoli* didn't use it.)

Nathan learned to choose the spots where a car could stop easily. He learned to make eye contact from the side of the road, and conversation once inside. "You remembered your seatbelt?" I needlessly nagged. Every day he came home (sometimes sooner, sometimes later) with a fabulous story of some colorful Island character he met on his ride. My little boy was growing up.

Nathan and I had wonderful home-cooked dinners, and afterwards shared nightly walks along the beach in front of our house. We walked for miles under the moon and stars, and we had incredible conversations.

One dark night, weeks into our time alone, Nathan told me this. "After the last fight with 'Iokepa, I carried so much hate – even when it seemed we were talking.

"But now I'm getting close to saying, 'I'm sorry.'"

I caught my breath in gratitude and hugged him.

On another walk, I was praying out loud. "*Mahalo Ke 'I'oakua*, grandmothers, Daddy, spirits of the land. *Mahalo* for the stars, the moon, the ocean, the beach, the mountains. *Mahalo* for our dinner, our strong bodies, Veronica's generosity. Send our love to our family and...."

Nathan interjected. "...to 'Iokepa across the water. We pray that he is well and cared for."

With God's grace, the thaw had begun.

. . .

'Iokepa had been no less embraced by miracles in his weeks on Moloka'i. His $20 bought him a room for one night. The next day, with one penny and an apple in his pocket, he hitchhiked to a county park. He'd been told he could sleep inside a picnic pavilion.

When he arrived, it was pouring rain. A sprawling extended family was packing up from their weekend reunion. 'Iokepa kept out of the way, reading Joseph Campbell's *The Power of Myth* under cover.

A large, middle aged native Hawaiian woman moved across the grass in his direction. He told me: "She looked like she was floating on white light – like she wasn't touching the ground."

"*Aloha,*" he said to her. "I'm 'Iokepa.

"'Iokepa," she said, repeating the name in the unique way he pronounced it. "You're an 'Īmaikalani, aren't you?"

"Yes, I am." He laughed.

"Well," she said. "I am Leilani – your great great grandfather raised my great grandmother."

Then Leilani burrowed her wise, kind gaze into 'Iokepa.

"You have no money?" She asked, but knew it for a fact.

"No I don't," he answered with a grin.

"And you have no place to stay?"

"I have no place to stay."

"Well," Leilani said. "Now you do. You'll come home with us. We've been waiting for you."

'Iokepa went home with Leilani, her husband Daniel, and their seven children. He slept for a month on an army cot set up for him in their living room. It was the room where four sleeping boys sprawled on couches, chairs and the floor.

It was a humble rented house with no phone. The meals that were stretched to barely feed nine, now fed 'Iokepa too. There were absolutely no conditions to their generosity. "*Kahiau,*" 'Iokepa told me later, "means giving with no expectation of return." When the children asked who 'Iokepa was, Leilani told them. "Don't worry who Uncle is – he was sent to us by God."

'Iokepa grew very close to those seven children. They filled his plate and never allowed him to wash a dish. They were unselfish, well-mannered, and engaging. They each savored his individual attention.

Leilani and Daniel were perhaps the most remarkable native couple 'Iokepa had encountered since he'd accepted his mission. Leilani was a powerful woman. She saw beyond our usual human limitations – but she didn't have a scrap of patience for what she saw as other people's self-deceit. She had the gift of lucid dreams. But more, she acquiesced to and lived the gift of her prophetic dreams.

Daniel gave authentic meaning to the commonplace, local expression – 'talk story.' Unself-conscious metaphors spilled off Daniel's tongue. A most unpretentious man spoke from unbelievable depths and insight.

They each lived the uncorrupted gifts of the Creator. They had not yet forgotten what the rest of us struggled to reclaim.

From Leilani and Daniel's home at the far north end of the Island, 'Iokepa ran and walked over two hundred miles on Moloka'i roadways. Every day, at the hottest part of the day, to the outermost edges of the Island – without a shirt – 'Iokepa ran. He was brown and he was strong.

To phone me 'Iokepa had to run almost three miles from the house that had no phone service to the nearest public phone. If I wasn't home or the line was long-busy, he'd run back again.

On Moloka'i, without exception, those few cars on the road stopped and offered a pedestrian a ride – even if he were headed the other way. 'Iokepa typically refused the ride, but he seized the opportunity for conversation.

For 'Iokepa, running had been a God-given part of his job. Running regularly, he was public, visible, known in ways that otherwise would have taken him years. People saw the silver-haired, forty-eight year old Hawaiian running like a steam locomotive up the long hills. They saw him daily, and they came to feel they knew him. The good folk of Moloka'i – overwhelmingly populated by *kanaka maoli* – smiled, waved, and hailed him.

Moloka'i was friendly – as small places sometimes are. But Moloka'i also had the heart of a warrior. Moloka'i was governed by Maui County – and it had successfully and consistently fought off every assault by the commercial development that had enveloped the Island of Maui. As a result: there were no large hotels, no fast food restaurants, no supermarkets, no chain stores, no car dealerships – no signs of economic prosperity. This was at great odds with the ambitions of the County Council, on Maui – where the lure of the tourist dollar ruled.

To outsiders, the people of Moloka'i looked poor. But that wasn't at all how they saw themselves. They knew they lived on one of the last pieces of authentic Hawai'i. They spoke with, listened to, and lived as allies of the spirits of their *'āina*. They were impervious – fiercely resistant is closer – to the plans of others to make them rich. They knew better.

. . .

Nathan and I were enjoying *Shabbat* dinners again each Friday night. I'd fished my heavy brass *Shabbat* candlesticks out of storage. We'd set the table with cloth and flowers each week, made do with a bread other than *challah,* and followed the ancient rituals Jews have observed forever – for our first time on Kaua'i.

I'd circle my hands three times over the flame and bless the candlelight.

"*Baruch atah adonai elohenu melech ho'olum, asher kidushanu b'mitvotov vitzivanu, l'hadlich n'er shel Shabbat.* Blessed art thou O Lord our God, King of the Universe, who commanded us to kindle the Sabbath lights."

Nathan would offer prayers over the bread and over our not-quite-wine. I'd lay my hands on his head for the blessing of my last child still at home. "May the Lord bless you and keep you. May the Lord shine light upon you, and grant you *shalom* – peace." I missed Ben profoundly, at those times.

Rosh Hashanah, the Jewish lunar New Year, began that year on a Sunday in September. For weeks, I'd anguished over spending the High Holy Days outside of the heart of a Jewish community. If one existed on Kaua'i, I had not unearthed it. I'd heard only about a man named Aaron and his orthodox Jewish friend, Samuel – who Aaron affectionately called, *The Rabbi.*

I felt desolate that Nathan and I would be alone for the holidays.

"It would be nice," Nathan said, "For 'Iokepa to be here for the New Year."

The day 'Iokepa left for Moloka'i, he had removed the whale's tooth hook on *hau* (lowland tree) twine from around his neck and put it around mine. "*Ke 'I'oakua,* may this hook help Inette find Samuel for *Rosh Hashanah.*"

The one of a kind hook – which held solemn significance in native Hawaiian culture – had been crafted by Aaron, and gifted to 'Iokepa, as a testimonial of respect and support. I'd never met Aaron – and neither 'Iokepa nor I knew Samuel.

Four days before *Rosh Hashanah*, Nathan and I were down to our last $25. I filled the Camry's gas tank with most of it. I spent the remainder on priority postage, sending early chapters of my manuscript to a potential literary agent. I smiled when I'd spent the last of it. I felt that sure of God's gifts.

I put the key in my post office box and extracted the usual bills and junk mail. But there was one envelope on the stationary of my now-deceased literary agent. I opened the envelope and a $610 royalty check from Germany slipped out – for a book ten years out of print in America.

I picked up Nathan, thrilled to share the news, and excited to treat him to the book he'd ordered two weeks before. I dropped him at Waldenbooks.

"I'm going to run into Safeway for butter. I'll be done before you are. Meet me at the car."

I ran through the floral department to the dairy aisle, grabbed the butter, turned to leave, and stopped myself short of colliding with a full grocery cart.

"I'm so sorry...."

The man pushing the cart had a full, black beard and a little blond girl at his side. On the top of his curly hair was the unmistakable signature of an Orthodox Jewish male, a *kipah*, or skullcap.

I didn't blink. "Excuse me. Is your name Samuel? Do you know Aaron?" I pulled the whales tooth hook to the fore and waved it.

The answer to both was, "Yes."

He was slightly startled by my assault. "I'm Inette Miller...I'm Jewish...I'm new on Kaua'i...I don't want to spend *Rosh Hashanah* without other Jews."

He laughed, gave me his phone number, took mine and assured me that there was indeed a Jewish congregation on Kaua'i and that a rabbi had been hired from California to officiate at *Rosh Hashanah* and *Yom Kippur* services. The rest, he assured me, he'd tell me on the phone. He, too, was hurrying home before sundown for *Shabbat* dinner.

We would not be alone for *Rosh Hashanah*.

...

A week later, a few days after our *Rosh Hashanah* in the heart
of a small and welcoming Jewish congregation and a few days
before *Yom Kippur* – the holiest day on the Jewish calendar –
Nathan offered me $100 from his savings to buy a round trip
ticket to see 'Iokepa. "I *want* you to go."

He was acting on the impulse bred of these High Holy
Days. *Rosh Hashanah*, and ten days later *Yom Kippur*,
bracketed a time for healing wounds, making amends, entering
the New Year cleansed of our worst behavior.

Nathan's offer was sincere and generous. He'd come from
Portland with a $600 savings account of his own. It was down
to $400. I was grateful for his kindness, but I had never
touched my sons' money – and I didn't intend to now.

On Saturday, September 26, I was on the phone with
'Iokepa. I found myself saying words I didn't recognize as my
own – let alone premeditate. "I'll come to Moloka'i." I shocked
myself.

"Is that what you want?" 'Iokepa asked.

"Well," I stumbled now. "It seems like it." I felt a will
other than my own at work here. Before that moment, I'd not
once considered leaving Nathan *or* going to Moloka'i.

"Why don't you think about it?" he said. "I'll call you back."

Nathan repeated the offer. "Take $200 if you need it."

I called the travel agency one hour before they closed at
noon. "The canoe races are in Moloka'i this weekend –
nothing's available today. But I can get you there first thing
tomorrow morning."

'Iokepa called back.

"I'm coming!" I would spend two nights and three days
on Moloka'i and then rejoin Nathan for Yom Kippur on
Tuesday. Veronica would keep a watchful eye on my son from
next door.

Then it was 'Iokepa's turn to astonish me. "It's time for
me to come home. I'll return with you to Kaua'i on Tuesday."

Yom Kippur would begin at sundown. I would spend it
with Nathan in synagogue. Like most Jews, I took *Yom Kippur*

very seriously. I needed to be home for our twenty-four hour fast.

"Two things are really wonderful about 'Iokepa," Nathan said, anticipating his return. "He's loyal. And his faith, it doesn't change."

Then he said. "We need to live being okay with whatever happens. So much has been given to me. I've never said *thank you* so much in my life. Poor people get hung up because they think they're poor."

It never occurred to Nathan that we too might be poor.

Leilani and Daniel were everything that 'Iokepa had intimated. Moloka'i was more. Like the other Islands, there was a stark dry end, and a lush wet one. Like the others, it was physically breathtaking. But this one had a *heart* that I recognized the minute I stepped foot on the land. Moloka'i seduced me from the first.

'Each Island has its own spirit,' 'Iokepa said, when asked – as he often was – his favorite. 'The *'āina* breathes.'

Moloka'i was the place where the ancient *kahuna* – those destined to fulfill their spiritual gifts – traveled to study the harnessing and use of *mana*. Among their remarkable and varied skills: when they harnessed the *mana,* they could move heavy *heiau* rocks into place without touching them.

It was impossible not to feel the magic of Moloka'i. On our third morning together, I awakened before sunrise, rolled over, and expected to see 'Iokepa smiling at me. My slightest move invariably awakened him. I thought he was feigning sleep when I touched his lips with my finger and he didn't budge.

I escalated my affection, kissed his forehead and ran my fingers down his chest. He was more than asleep – from the sound of his breathing now, he was almost unconscious.

We'd been staying at the Pauhana Inn, an aged, community-run hotel on the southern edge of the Island. We were in a plain but clean, double room for $19.99 a night.

I gave up trying to rouse 'Iokepa, climbed out of bed and into Ben's old grey knit athletic shorts and a T-shirt. I had my hand on the doorknob; then I pulled it back and turned towards the dresser. I'd forgotten something, and I felt the reminder.

I slipped the *puka* shell *lei* around my neck. I tied the braided *hau* rope 'Iokepa had made from tree bark (and wound around his own calf during his first months on Kaua'i) around my waist.

He'd given it to me at Christmas. "These *hau* trees grow at the edge of Pele's forest," he said. (She was the Hawaiian deity who created land from volcano.) Months later, he explained the oft-misunderstood concept of Hawaiian deities. "What we call *deities* – or *kupua* – are what Christians call *saints*. They are human beings who grow into their purpose on Earth – fulfill their promises to the Creator. And they do it for *others* – not for themselves."

I had tied the *hau* braid around the headboard of my four-poster in Portland for six months. But I'd worn it for the very first time when I flew to Moloka'i. I didn't know why I tied it around my waist when I boarded the plane, but it felt important.

I slipped out of the room – key in pocket. I had no plan.

The sun was barely cresting the horizon as I wandered the two-hundred foot path down to the ocean.

When I first met Daniel, he told me, "Where you're staying, the ocean is low in the early morning. You can walk out a long way." The most recent time I saw him, he asked. "Have you walked the water yet?" I hadn't. But he'd made it sound important. In Hawaiian, *wai* is water, but it is more. It signifies abundance, the substance of life itself.

This southern tip of the Island was marked by a mammoth banyan tree that sat at the water's edge. It faced the Island of Lana'i, less than five miles away.

I climbed through a couple of trees and over a few rocks to a small scraggly beach. I slipped off my shoes. I looked across at Lana'i. It looked like a mountainous stage-set in the distance. The water seemed calm enough for the vigorous Hawaiian ocean. I stepped in and stumbled over slippery reef rocks and muck.

I had no intention of getting my clothes wet. My bathing suit was in our room.

I took one step, then another, tentatively, from one mucky slick rock to another. I made my way for about forty feet, and then the bottom turned to firm sand. The water hadn't yet passed my knees.

I would walk, I thought, until the water hit the hem of my shorts. I placed one foot after another, slowly – a walking meditation into the middle of the ocean. Lana'i felt like the Holy Grail.

I saw the fishing pier off of Moloka'i in the distance to my right: first ahead, then beside me, and then well behind. I turned around now, frightened that I was so far out I'd be lost. How would I find my way home?

At this distance, it wasn't obvious. Hills, trees, beaches and houses sprawled across the perimeter of Moloka'i with very little definition. I committed the landscape to memory, the shape of this hill and that one; I strained to make out the banyan tree in the distance. I assured myself I would be able to find my way back; then I turned to face Lana'i again and continued the walk.

My legs pulled through the deepening water; each step took increasing effort. The going was slow, but I was in no hurry. I had no strategy but submission. There was absolutely no question now, but that I was being led.

Lana'i got closer; I didn't look back again. I rolled the bottom of my shorts, but they didn't hold the roll. I stopped caring about the shorts.

I took step after balanced step. It was something like a dance with the ocean. The water was at my waist, then, my breasts. The ocean bottom turned to rock again, and each step became precarious. It never occurred to me to swim, though I love to swim. I was still wearing my glasses.

Lana'i advanced. It came so close that I could no longer imagine not completing my trek. Or, for that matter, what I'd do once I scurried up the rocky cliff that now faced me. I watched the large yachts pass between me and Lana'i – crossing the deep boat channel around the perimeter of the Island.

But when the sand bottom changed to rock again, the forward impetus that had propelled me since I stepped foot out of our room, slowed dramatically. It was like a hand that prodded me along, now let up pressure. I felt myself being stopped short of what I assumed was completion – Lana'i – and all I could do was obey.

I heard: *Turn now and face Moloka'i.* It had been a couple miles since I last peeked. I turned and Moloka'i looked incredibly beautiful at this distance, hovering in the morning mist and in the spirits' arms. The glow off Moloka'i felt holy.

I walked a few steps back to the sand bottom; the water was less than chest high. My arms reached wide and high above my head embracing the grace of Moloka'i.

I could hear the guidance clearly now.

Dunk yourself in the water completely.
And again.
And once again.

I did as I was told – three times. Each time arising with my arms stretched to the heavens.

On the final emergence – out of my chest at unmuted volume, with full breath – there arose these deep bellows from my chest.

"I...am...One...

"I...am...love...

"I...am...life...eternal..."

Each syllable lingered like a chord on a harp. The vibrations passed from my body into the water and up into the sky that surrounded Moloka'i.

I was what I spoke. I was one with the vibration of all that was around me. I touched the *hau* braid knotted tightly around my waist and I knew that in the hallowed waters of Moloka'i, at the hands of the spirits of this land and this ocean, I was being blessed.

I didn't want to move at all, but I was impelled. Glowing, I had no doubt, from the touch of the ancestors; I walked the return steps as slowly and as deliberately as I had entered the ocean.

When I finally approached the tiny beach, I looked up into the utterly astonished faces of two women staring out at me from the *lānai* of their cabin. They were basking in my glow, I could see the reflection.

"That was beautiful! Do you do that every morning?" one asked.

"No...," I laughed, startled and embarrassed that there were witnesses. "It was unplanned. I was guided."

"Like a meditation?" she asked her mouth still wide open in amazement.

"Uh huh, like that," I said.

I was shining like an incandescent light and I could feel its warmth. I looked up at them, God's witnesses, and I said, "*Aloha.*"

I returned to the room. 'Iokepa awakened now to the noise of my key in the doorknob. I sat down on the floor next to him, dripping ocean water, and while he stroked my sopping head and shoulders, I told him this story.

I had been gone for two hours.

Honor ritual.

'Iokepa heard these words from the grandmothers loud and clear when we arrived home together for *Yom Kippur.* Nathan and I were preparing to begin our twenty-four hour fast at synagogue.

I had no expectation of 'Iokepa's participation in the observance of the Jewish day of atonement. It was the single day of the year that we ritually made amends for violating our promises to God and man. It was a time to ask forgiveness of those we have wronged – before we entered the New Year. For me, and for most Jews, *Yom Kippur* was profound.

But 'Iokepa was Hawaiian. He knew nothing of Judaism, except what I'd shared. In some ways, I regretted that 'Iokepa's first exposure to Judaism was *Yom Kippur* – it was a particularly somber holiday.

In following his grandmother's edict to *Honor ritual,* 'Iokepa honored me and my son. We three fasted – no food and no water – from sunset to sunset, twenty-four hours. We spent Tuesday evening and most of Wednesday in synagogue.

Nathan and I were honored as new members of the Kaua'i congregation, with an *aliyah* – we were called to the open *Torah* to chant our prayers.

Nathan had celebrated his *bar mitzvah* almost two years before. He had ritually entered Jewish manhood on his thirteenth birthday with the responsibilities and privileges that bestowed. One was: he was permitted to read Torah from the *bima* (altar).

141

'Iokepa was visibly moved by the sound of Nathan's deep melodic voice and my higher, more erratic one chanting the blessings in Hebrew from the pulpit.

At the close of the final service, when the sacred *shofar* – ram's horn – resounded at the lips of both Samuel and Aaron, 'Iokepa was invited (perhaps for the first time in the history of *Yom Kippur* on Hawai'i or elsewhere on the planet) to join in. 'Iokepa put the hallowed Hawaiian conch shell to his lips, and together with the two *shofarot*, sounded the heart-rending cry of the people to our God. I wasn't the only one near tears.

We broke fast with the Jewish community afterwards.

LANDING

October, 1998

Veronica had offered us two more weeks in her vacation rental. But on October 14, she needed the house for her paying guests.

We packed up: *Shabbat* candlesticks, computer, family photos; Nathan's juggling equipment, guitar and Nintendo; the huge oil painting of Madi. It all went back into storage – joining two dozen other boxes that had been taped up tight since Portland.

We three stood at the ocean's edge in front of Veronica's house facing the cloudless sky and sent up a heartfelt prayer. "*Ke 'I'oakua* give us a place to live on the beach again. *Mahalo.*"

We drove away.

And *then* after seven crowded nights sleeping in the Hotel Camry on the asphalt parking lot of the not-so-lovely Ahukini Landing, listening to the howl of jet engines overhead, and eating peanut butter and jelly sandwiches – that is exactly what we got. But not necessarily in the form we expected.

The grandmothers, who directed our decisions daily ('Iokepa would insist it was 'breath by breath.'), now presented an alternative plan. We were to buy two good-sized tents, one air mattress, and a pump. Walking through Kmart, 'Iokepa ventured a wild guess at the cost: "Two hundred dollars." The math was irrelevant; we didn't have $200.

From the moment Nathan heard "tent," he became an enthusiastic advocate. He wanted out of the car and into camping. Camping had been a cherished part of our family vacations since Nathan had been three. He said. "Take the money from my savings."

I anguished. 'Iokepa resisted. But the prayers yielded this.

> *You cannot deny Nathan the opportunity to live his faith as you live yours.*

I went to the bank with Nathan, withdrew $200, and looked down at the withdrawal slip the teller had handed us. "Rose," I asked, "is this the figure *after* withdrawal?"

She assured me it was. Nathan had been rewarded – phenomenally and immediately – for his generosity and faith. There had been $250 in his savings before the withdrawal; there remained $250 afterwards. It was no bank error. It was very simply a miracle for Nathan's heart. No future bank statement refuted or explained the difference.

We ran through Kmart grabbing tents, air mattress and pump – never stopping to calculate the prices. When the cashier rang up the total, not one of us was surprised. It came to $198.49. We were abundantly confirmed: We were to live (for a very short time, we assumed) in tents.

From the storage unit, we pried loose 'Iokepa's sheets and blankets, foam mat, single burner gas stove, two forks, two spoons and an army can opener. Nathan had a sleeping bag. I had two flashlights.

There were four county parks and three state parks open to camping. The state parks were transcendently beautiful – but at extreme ends of the Island. Nathan's school was dead center forty miles away. There was a single county park within the school district, but it was inhabited largely by transient drug addicts and alcoholics from the United States.

The next nearest park was *Kaheka* – the Salt Pans. It had been misnamed in English – Salt *Pond* – and every road sign attested to the error. But there was no pond. The park sat next to a unique geological phenomenon. Ocean water seeped under the soil and left a residue of salt on the surface red dirt. The *kanaka maoli* had ritually harvested that sea salt since the beginning of human habitation on the Island. The methods –

their sacred rituals – had been handed down through the generations. They were practiced still. Salt was a necessity of life. *Kaheka* was a gift of the Creator.

So the beachfront home we'd prayed for when we stood in front of Veronica's house was manifest. It would be two tents in the sand, at the ocean's edge, at the Salt Pans. From the door of our oceanfront home, without budging an inch, we could watch the sunset paint the sky and ocean vibrant orange and neon red. Then, we could turn our heads and follow the golden moon rise behind us. Every morning, we could watch the sun burst into a ball of enchanted light across the threshold of the horizon.

That there could be any barrier at all to beach use by native Hawaiians – or to anyone who understood the *kanaka maoli* reverence for the *'āina* – was unconscionable to 'Iokepa.

"Imagine what it felt like the first time a *malihini* – guest – told a native Hawaiian he was forbidden to walk the land he'd walked forever," he said. "They had to teach my ancestors the English language so we could read the "No Trespassing" signs."

I was only beginning to imagine. Those signs were everywhere. Living in tents, we began to realize exactly how restricted the people's access to their land had become. Legendary Hawaiian songwriter Bruddah Iz sang. "Cry for the gods, cry for the people, cry for the land that was taken away, and then...you'll find Hawai'i."

On Kaua'i, poignantly, every scrap of public space was savored and used. Postage stamp sized patches of public parks with open pavilions perched by the ocean were occupied day and night, weekday and weekend with: *hula hālau* (dance instruction), birthday parties, family reunions, canoe clubs, fishermen, endless streams of outdoor cooking – and *always* music.

Typically, the native people felt hemmed in by the four unbending walls of their homes. The land, the beaches, the out-of-doors was how they breathed. Without it, they were, as a people, dead.

By imported Western law, all Hawaiian beaches (to the high water mark plus twenty feet) were public. But even that imposed law had only superficial meaning. Huge stretches of pristine beach had been turned into harbors to facilitate the transport of sugar cane from mill to market – to profit the entrepreneurial and foreign few.

The concept of all beaches for all people became even more elusive when Sheraton, Marriott, Hyatt, and others gobbled up huge expanses of beachfront property for their palaces to tourism – and their accompanying golf courses.

Most hotels had a tiny, legally mandated sign at the entrance, "Beach Access." These were the legislated paths, rock ledges, or driveways that led the *local* populace to the scrap of beach they might use – at a distance from hotel amenities such as beach chairs, towels, or snack bars.

'Public,' it seemed, increasingly meant that someone, somewhere – with no claim to indigenous ancestry – called the shots.

"It is about borders, fences, separation," 'Iokepa said. "None of that is Hawaiian."

Annually, tourists outnumber native Hawaiians by thirty to one. It is a brand of tourism that has nothing whatsoever to do with traveling to a foreign place, savoring the differences, and honoring the host culture. The chain hotel brand of tourism (with the restaurants, car rentals, and dress shops that grow up around it) has everything to do with replicating American life intact. In its way, it is as authentic a reproduction as Colonial Williamsburg – a perfect re-creation of what the traveler refused to leave behind. It is a form of travel that precludes surprise.

. . .

In the face of this cultural invasion, the ancestors of the Hawaiian Islands were not without recourse.

There has been a great deal of misunderstanding about the Nightmarchers. That they were ancient spirits – marching only at night, always en masse, with torches and drums – was agreed. That they'd been visible to humans for thousands of years, and were visible still, was widely accepted.

What I'd seen and heard in the cane fields of Kipu last February was not unprecedented. Most Hawaiians (and innumerable *malihini*) had stories.

The grandmothers told 'Iokepa. *They are most visible to those who believe the least.*

Some superstitious and fearful people insist they must throw themselves to the ground and cover their faces to avoid the Nightmarchers' menace.

But the grandmothers were insistent. *Spirits do not hurt humans, only humans hurt humans. It is what a person brings in his heart.*

Every Island had its resident band of Nightmarchers. They serve to remind us of our responsibility to the *'āina* – the land. In the spring 1997, before the dedication of the newly reopened Holiday Inn at the mouth of Wailua River, a throng of Nightmarchers filled the hotel lobby with their visible essences, torches and drums.

'Iokepa heard a first-hand account from the front-desk clerk who had witnessed the gathering and had been awestruck. I spoke to the president of the county historical society, who'd been summoned instantly to the scene. The newspaper recorded the event.

The hotel had been built carelessly between two sacred *heiau*. There had been neither prayer asking for spirits' acquiescence, nor ritual recognizing the presence of those ancestors. The Nightmarchers came to redress this wrong – to remind us.

Soon after, the Holiday Inn's management invited what they hoped were heavyweight spiritual *kahuna* to offer prayer and ritual to mollify the Nightmarchers – because, in Lāhui, even corporate America isn't free to overlook the land they defile. There are – even for Fortune 500 companies – sometimes spiritual consequences.

We knew that camping in the county parks was free to *any* resident of the Island. It was three dollars a night per person for tourists. What we didn't know were the hoops 'Iokepa Hanalei 'Īmaikalani would be put through to prove he is a resident. For me (a Caucasian, who'd been on the Island four months), it was a piece of cake. I had a car registration.

When 'Iokepa had undertaken the terms of the prophecy, he was asked to relinquish all remnants of American citizenship – and reclaim allegiance only to his native nation. The name he'd adopted to blend into American society – Joseph – (and the one his father had adopted for the same reason) was simply not his name.

He was to go through no legal maneuver to resume his rightful name. He owed obeisance only to *Ke 'I'oakua*, God Almighty. He was who he was – without the imprimatur of any state or federal government. He carried no driver's license – not a single scrap of governmental identification.

The *malihini* behind the County Parks' camping permit desk was rude, bureaucratic, and inhospitable from the moment we entered. She listed the only acceptable possibilities. "A driver's license, a bill addressed to your home, a car registration...."

"I have no bills, no car, and no need for a driver's license. I've lived here almost two years, and my family has been here for thirteen thousand."

"Well," she said, "*if* I knew you – or if there were *someone* who knew you."

She was a brick wall. We had tents now, but no place to put them. We left the office.

148

Directly outside the door 'Iokepa saw Moki, an old family friend, and hailed him. Moki happened also to be a distinguished and popular county councilman.

'Iokepa asked, "Would you mind telling the woman behind that desk that you know me?"

Moki laughed. "Of course I will."

The woman behind the desk did a very slow burn. She couldn't refuse the logic. "I know 'Iokepa well. His father was born here, his uncle is...." She couldn't refuse to honor Moki's council position. But she didn't have to like it, and she didn't make it easy.

"I must speak to my manager," she said, and she disappeared for a full fifteen minutes. When she returned, "We'll give you a pass for one week only. Next week you have to have identification."

'Iokepa laughed. "You mean by next week, a native Hawaiian will no longer qualify even as a resident?" Moki shrugged at the silliness.

"Just a reminder," I heard 'Iokepa pronounce to the bureaucrat for the first but not the last time. "This is Hawai'i. And that is not Hawaiian behavior."

. . .

The Salt Pans – "Salt Pond Park" at the permit office – became our home. The roofs over our three heads were nylon. Our dining room was a picnic table, sun or rain. Our meals were public and almost always shared. Our living room was the beach and the ocean. Our neighbors were every soul who walked that Park, in the daytime or at night.

We understood dimly at first – clearly, as time passed – that the *'āina* was our home so that we could learn what the *kanaka maoli* had always known, had lost to theft, but had never forgotten.

From their never-forgetting came 'Iokepa, and all that was prophesized.

"And now," "Iokepa said, "Even when the *kanaka maoli* speak of sovereignty, they mistakenly believe it means a transfer of ownership – from the takers to themselves!

"Sovereignty was never about owning the land. It is about remembering and returning to our unique relationship with all of God's creation. Then we will be free. The land will follow."

The Salt Pans – the Park – was a week by week proposition. Each seven day permit granted us the right to set up our tent within the boundaries of the waterfront county park. With that privilege, came three women's toilets, two sinks, and an ice cold outdoor shower. I never saw the interior of the men's restroom.

For the duration of our stay at the Salt Pans, I never took a warm shower and I never took a naked one. I was always in a swimsuit, furtively soaping my more intimate body parts under the surreptitious attentions of nearby picnickers or sunbathers.

Nathan took his shower at six in the morning in the dark. I'd make him oatmeal, orange juice and tea on school mornings, on the single burner and by flashlight. Weekends, if there was money, I'd make banana pancakes and feed everyone in sight.

School lunch was just seventy-five cents.

Because money was only just enough; because gasoline was always at least fifty cents more a gallon than any place in the United States; and because his school was twenty miles away – I'd drive Nathan a mile only, to the main road. He'd hitchhike the rest of the way to Kaua'i High. On a good day, it'd take him forty-five minutes. On that good day, if he timed it right, he'd be picked up by one of his regulars and make the trip in two quick rides. On a bad day, he'd be late for school. I wasn't thrilled with the arrangement. I felt impotent to change it. Nathan didn't complain.

He hitchhiked home as well, then stripped off his school clothes, grabbed his boogie board, and jumped into the ocean with 'Iokepa or with me. Those were the compensations.

Dinner almost always included other campers. We served up hefty amounts of pasta, great quantities of rice and veggie stir fry, lots of canned tuna, occasionally macaroni and cheese. What we had, we shared; what others had, they shared.

'When your hand is emptied, it will always be refilled,' 'Iokepa reminded me. Scarcity was about fear – a human invention. God, the *kanaka maoli* knew, was unending abundance.

Bananas, papayas, coconuts, mangos, avocados were plentiful, and often free. 'Iokepa was good with his machete and he knew how to bring home the fruit. Louisa and Albert's ice cream parlor doubled as an organic produce market, and they were exceedingly generous. 'Iokepa and I occasionally gave them a day off and minded the shop for fun and friendship.

On very special occasions, when there was money, 'Iokepa insisted on the quintessential Hawaiian meal: *'ahi poke* (raw tuna cut into seasoned cubes) and *poi* (a brown, sticky mush from the *kalo* plant's root). Nathan was the only Caucasian he'd met who loved both from his very first taste. For most of us, *poi* was an acquired taste at best. But 'Iokepa and Nathan shared that passion.

Nathan had his own tent, and inside it was as chaotic as his room had been in Portland: dirty clothes and clean ones heaped together; school work scattered alongside uncased CDs and used up batteries for his Discman. Nathan's organizational skills had never been honed. "Mom....I can't find...." was the wail of his childhood.

'Iokepa and my larger tent, on the other hand, was scrupulously organized. The air mattress sheets were tucked and straightened every morning. Our clothing was folded in duffels; our towels were in their own bag. Books, flashlights, and yellow legal pads for nighttime writing were stacked at hand. 'Iokepa was painstakingly tidy. I was his near match.

After seven nights camping on County Parks' land, there was a mandated, "Breakdown day" to discourage the natives from permanent residence. We were required to roll up our tents, the clothesline, and the sleeping bag; pack our food and kitchen into boxes; fold the clothing, sheets, and blankets. We deflated the air mattress, and flattened the folding chairs. We loaded every item that constituted our home into the car, filled the trunk and the back seat to capacity – saving just enough room for Nathan to sit.

We spent our breakdown night at Ahukini Landing – emptying the contents of the backseat onto the asphalt, to sleep. The next morning we went to the County Parks' office for a second week's permit.

I chose to sidestep the 'Iokepa ID card issue entirely this time. I went into the office alone, asking for a permit in Nathan and my names only.

"*Aloha*!" I smiled at the bureaucrat. She glowered at me. She'd been laying in wait. Clearly she remembered me and didn't like what she remembered. She grilled me about the absent 'Iokepa before she granted me the permit.

We were setting up our tents for the second time when the County Parks' ranger greeted me amiably. We had gotten to know him during that first week, and up until then he'd been nothing but cordial. I didn't yet know he'd been phoned by the bureaucrat and enlisted into the persecution of 'Iokepa.

"You know you'll need a permit," he said with a big grin.

"How are you? I've already got one."

"You do? Mind if I see it?"

I handed it over to him. He took my permit and, sight unseen, stuffed it into his shirt pocket. "It's invalid," he said. "'Iokepa is not on it."

Infuriated, I reached into his pocket and grabbed it back.

"You lied to me," I said. "This is mine. It's a valid permit for Nathan and me."

He looked a bit ashamed of himself.

'Iokepa stepped in to educate him. He did it far more gently than I would have at that moment.

"This," 'Iokepa said, "is Hawaiian land.

"It is not about permits and it's not about *enforcers*," he pointed to that word emblazoned on the man's uniform shirt.

"I've lived here my whole life," the ranger sputtered his defense.

"Then you have no excuse for not knowing the culture."

'Iokepa began teaching what was, and was not, Hawaiian. He refrained from mentioning that the man was Caucasian – he saw that as irrelevant. It had only to do with the ranger as an instrument of the oppression of a people.

It had to do, 'Iokepa said to him, "With taking a stand *for* this culture – and accepting responsibility for your actions."

The enforcer backed off. He told us. "Get this straightened out by tomorrow."

"Tomorrow" we drove up to the county building without a plan. When we arrived, the grandmothers directed 'Iokepa to the office of the Mayor of Kaua'i.

The receptionist heard 'Iokepa's story. She disappeared and returned with a senior staff member.

This woman knew and deeply respected 'Iokepa's now ninety-year-old Uncle Gideon – his father's youngest brother – who'd been honored many times over on several Islands, as a "Hawaiian Living Treasure."

"Please," she begged him. "Don't say another word. Can I get you coffee – or juice? The Mayor will be here in half an hour."

The Mayor arrived.

She was at the bitter end of a hotly contested re-election campaign – just days shy of the voting. Yet she sat with us for more than an hour, listened to our tale of camping woe, and never implied that there might be anything more important on her calendar. We were without homes, jobs, clout – or voter registration cards – but it made no difference to her.

'Iokepa told her the story of the grandmothers, the prophecy, and the part he played. The Mayor's top-ranking advisor sat to her right. He was everything the Mayor was not: inattentive, filled with self importance, the quintessential political lackey. At one point, he interjected an irrelevant account of the politics of golf courses on the Island, and ended with, "This isn't spiritual."

'Iokepa cut him off mid sentence. "My friend," he said in a voice that would stop a raging bull. "*Everything* is spiritual."

The Mayor agreed. "This Island is a magical place. Things happen here that *only* have spiritual explanations." She sent her advisor out of the room.

She cut to the chase. "I'm going to behave like your mother," she told 'Iokepa. "Shouldn't you have identification in case of an emergency?"

'Iokepa laughed. "There are no emergencies the Creator can't handle."

Then she turned to me. "I can get you a low-rent apartment. Your son shouldn't have to live in a tent."

"*Mahalo*," I said. "That isn't what this is about. We don't accept government assistance. It's a walk of faith."

"If you knew this young man," 'Iokepa bragged, "you'd understand. He's strong and he knows what this is about."

"Okay," she said. "Who can I call to verify how long you've been here?"

"I stayed with my cousin Bertha when I first arrived," he said. Cousin Bertha, it turned out, was the Mayor's close friend. But when the Mayor called her, there was no answer.

"Who else?" she asked.

She called the County Historical Museum, headed by another relative. We heard the Mayor's end of the conversation.

"I have your cousin 'Iokepa here, he wants a camping permit. Can you vouch for how long he's been on Kaua'i?"

There was a silence, then laughter.

"Thanks Susan, I'll tell him you send your regards."

The Mayor called downstairs to the head of the Parks' Office – the boss of the boss of the surly bureaucrat at the front desk.

"I have a man here who wants a camping permit. He does not have identification, but I will vouch that he is who he says he is."

Then, in response to her employee's rebuttal, "Yes, I suggested he get an identification card too, but he has his reasons."

After considerable silence while the Mayor listened, she issued this gentle edict. "I'd like you to arrange it so that 'Iokepa will be given a camping permit whenever he requires one – and that the Mayor's office will not have to hear about this again. Can you do that?

"...Good."

A few days later, she won her re-election campaign.

On all occasions after that meeting, the Mayor – and years later, the ex-Mayor – rushed to embrace 'Iokepa whenever we'd chance to meet. Her face would light up at the sight of him across a room. Their relationship was something outside of politics.

After hugs, we returned to the permit office. The hostile woman was no less hostile – and just as obstructive.

"Name?" she asked 'Iokepa.

"Spell that," she insisted after she'd already copied it off of last week's permit. Our new permit was marked, "By order of the Mayor's office."

We left full of good feeling and gratitude.

Each week that we set up our tents at the Salt Pans, we expected would be our last. We never stopped thinking of tents as provisional – camping, only until the spirits provided a *real* home.

Nathan spent Halloween weekend at his friend Erik's. Erik's family had an extra room for Nathan – and a swimming pool. Erik drove his own late model convertible. He had an extra surf board for Nathan's use. The family was generous.

After six years as a fish-only vegetarian, Nathan now ate steaks, roast beef and pork chops at his friend's house. I'd relinquished seven years of strict vegetarianism on Moloka'i. When Leilani and Daniel, with very little money and seven children to feed, had offered me their best – a stew – I knew in my heart that it was morally reprehensible to refuse. Being a vegetarian was a luxury I could no longer afford.

We were delighted for Nathan's comforts, and for his growing friendship. We liked Erik very much.

Coming into that Halloween weekend, 'Iokepa and I put our last five dollars in the gas tank. We'd eaten peanut butter and jelly on bread for breakfast, lunch, and dinner for three days. We were out of bread. On Friday night, we walked into the town of Hanapepe for two reasons: we could use the walk, and the art gallery openings might provide dinner. Cheese and crackers sounded just right, but we settled for half dozen chocolate cookies, while we chatted art with the gallery owner. We walked home.

In late October, I stopped hoarding every bill that came to me from Portland – stopped pouring useless energy into lamenting my debts. I did what 'Iokepa suggested. I tore them up unopened.

"You have no money," he said. "Trash the bills."

"It feels irresponsible."

"Your greater responsibility is doing what you are doing here."

"I've never screwed people out of their money – ever."

Again: "You handed it over to the Creator when your came to Kaua'i. It isn't about money."

Perhaps the most remarkable thing about that October and November was how little I asked of the ancestors on the yellow page – and how little I received.

The prayers 'Iokepa and I shared in his words or mine sometimes a dozen times a day – dwindled. He still prayed aloud, but out of my earshot. I prayed far less.

I asked little because, still in tents and still waiting for the Portland house to sell, I was on hold – waiting for my life to begin. I was neither in the breath nor living the definition of the word *Kaua'i* – "Come and be."

The grandmothers told me. *No more doing.*

In sum, my faith in all that we had lived and spoken wavered. My doubts took their toll on 'Iokepa. He called it, "Your negativity." Near the end of November, we began to fight in earnest.

"You're a spoiled brat," he said. That was the warm-up. I focused the warm spotlight on my hurts and nurtured them: no real home, meals, or work – the price of all of it on my *son*? I could remember every angry syllable 'Iokepa aimed at me. I could remember none that I'd directed at him. That was the remarkable truth.

Nathan tried to mediate. He bravely dove in to the middle of the fray and with fourteen year old innocence offered sage advice that neither of us heard. Most of all, I cringed that the proximity of our lives allowed Nathan to witness the fights. I felt doubly impotent.

One morning when I heard 'Iokepa begin a thought with "When you are *around* me..." then quickly amend it to "When you are *with* me..." I realized how far I'd fallen. I had become an appendage to him. Increasingly, it was exactly how I saw myself.

On November 19 Nathan turned fifteen. An ancient tax refund reached 'Iokepa out of the blue, and we blew it to make Nathan's day exceptional. We both thought this kid deserved some celebration of the person he'd become. We got Nathan a used surfboard and rack for the car roof, his own beach chair, snorkel and fins, a subscription to *Rolling Stone*, and the state manual for his driver's permit. I made his favorite dinner, tortellini alfredo. I bought a chocolate cake. We celebrated at a friend's home. It was the lull before the storm.

The storm broke on the last days of November.

'Iokepa announced to Nathan that the grandmothers were sending him to Maui. Later that evening, sitting in beach chairs in front of our tent, he told me.

I accused him of running from our problems – abandoning me when the going got tough. He said: "It's my job. It's time."

The week's camping permit expired the next day. Nathan and 'Iokepa broke camp – packed, rolled and folded all our belongings and piled them on a picnic table. I went to the Laundromat, three miles away, to wash our clothes. When I returned, we would pack the car for our night at Ahukini Landing.

With 'Iokepa, there was one way to do things large or small – the right way. Rolling tents, folding laundry, washing the car, they were strictly a one man show. On the other hand, I too had been independent and competent – forever. Our differences were nothing more high-minded than a struggle for control. But they played out *only* over the most trivial matters. On the crucial Earth-shaking questions – cultural, social, political, or intellectual – we were at ease and in harmony.

Packing the car was the perfect example. "My Dad taught me how to pack," I'd interposed the last time – apparently impugning 'Iokepa's expertise. Now one week later, he remembered. "Do it yourself; you know how."

"Don't be so defensive," I retorted.

With very few words between us, 'Iokepa separated his possessions and refused my offer to drive him to the airport. He sat at a distant picnic table surrounded by his fishing spear, snorkel and fins, duffel bag, roll of duct tape, beach chair, towel, spoon, knife and fork. Perhaps more. It felt like he'd piled things around himself as a protective wall against me. He left us the tents, the cooking stove, the pots and pans, the sheets, the rest. People were staring.

Of all the pain and hurt that first year: I believe that the worst of it was the absence of four walls around our fights. Everything we said or did was acted out in public. Until then, I'd lived the extremely private life of a writer – most days and nights inside my own home. Family fights stayed at home, invisible to outsider's eyes. What I lived now was mortifying.

I stood in the parking lot of the Park, bereft. In just five minutes, all was gone. 'Iokepa could not be budged.

"This relationship has been the best – and the worst – of my life," he said. That was all he was prepared to give.

We left him sitting there.

Nathan and I spent the night alone at pitch black Ahukini Landing. I felt certain that 'Iokepa was on the last airplane vibrating over our heads that night, to Maui.

It was a hard night. I prayed with fervor that we'd be watched over, mother and son, exposed and sleeping alone in the Camry.

In answer to my prayers, we were. We both slept effortlessly. When I awakened at dawn, I heard this Beatles' lyric inside my head.

"And in the end….

"The love you take,

"Is equal to the love,

"You make."

For two straight days, I sang those lines aloud. I couldn't clear them from my head.

With our bit of child support, Nathan got his long hair cut and colored that next day. From shoulder-length black hair, it was now short, spiky, and streaked blonde.

We had a permit and we could have returned to the Salt Pans the next night, but we didn't. It had something to do with not wanting to return to the scene of the recent crime. We spent a second night at Ahukini. Then it was Sunday, and we drove very slowly back to the Park.

"Don't look at the shower," Nathan said when we pulled into the parking lot. I did. I was genuinely shocked – somewhat paralyzed. 'Iokepa was there – in his red swim shorts, washing his hair at the public shower. With my heart in my throat, I could only croak syllables. We unloaded our tents, and staked out our campsite before I walked over to him in the pavilion.

"The ancestors wouldn't let me go," he said. "Something was keeping me here. I suppose I was waiting for you."

We sat in the middle of the Park at the most public table. Tentatively and gently we talked. "It takes more than an hour to heal," he said. He spoke for both of us.

'Iokepa helped set up my tent and he told me a story:

A man he'd never seen before came up to him just hours after I'd left and gave him a small two-person tent. "It leaks," the man explained.

'Iokepa accepted it sight unseen, and then realized that the random tent rain-cover he'd been carrying around for no known reason fit the leaking tent like a glove. It even matched the color. 'Iokepa slept those two nights inside his new tent, on his beach chair.

After he told me the story, he hesitated, and asked to spend the night in my tent – formerly *ours* – and I said, "Of course."

His plans had not changed. The grandmothers' directives were clear – he was headed to Maui the next morning. His departure had been delayed until we'd had this time together – until we'd at least begun the healing.

The next morning I drove him to the airport. He had a ticket this time, the gift of a supportive friend. He had no money, and I had none. He had fanny pack full of his beautiful, distinctive *puka* shell *lei*.

I had no telephone where he could call me. He had no idea where he'd be on Maui. In the hands of God and his ancestors, 'Iokepa stepped onto an airplane headed for Maui.

In the hands of God and ancestors, I got into the Camry and drove the familiar road back to the Park.

Summer evaporated the moment 'Iokepa stepped onto the airplane.

The days became cooler – the nights, colder. The winds blew the tent flat over my face, and I more than once wondered if Nathan and I would survive the night. Then the rains began.

It was my first winter on Kaua'i, and even if the seasonal shifts were subtler than Portland or Virginia or any place else I'd ever lived – in a tent, we experienced them to the extreme. There was no place to hide from the weather.

Or from the people.

Inside almost every park on Hawai'i, there were the sad excesses born of oppression. At least one pavilion was filled morning, noon and all night long with addicts, alcoholics and gamblers. Their behavior – to me, who never drank more than a glass of wine at dinner or an occasional beer (I'd quit both at forty) – was pitifully self-destructive. It was hard for me to witness.

Harder still was the spousal abuse and child abuse that went hand in hand. With 'Iokepa, there were daily decisions: when to intervene, when not. It was never about stirring further violence. It was never an easy call. But alone, for a *malihini* with Nathan, it was impossible.

'Iokepa's shame ran deep. Tourists visited the parks, saw the inebriated brown people and heard them rambling incoherent words to ingratiate themselves to twenty-one year old Californians. The visitors returned home, he feared (and he was not far wrong) repeating what they've seen of the 'Hawaiians.'

He confronted the participants when they were sober. "These tourists go home and *laugh* at you. Is that what you want?" They listened to him sadly, but they had no answers.

There was yet another painful phenomenon that I could not have foreseen. Hawai'i was the dumping ground for end-of-the-road folks on the social welfare rosters of a half dozen states. When these homeless, unstable, addicted, mentally-ill men and women hit the end of their state's willingness to care for them, they were given a one-way ticket to the Hawaiian Islands. Within a month, they were promised, they could collect government subsidy here – and there would be no winter.

'Iokepa, Nathan and I watched the parade of America's cast-offs wander, stagger, and falter into the Park over the years.

There was skinny, strung-out Rosa who from the solitude of her tiny tent screamed in agony. "Get off of me! Get off of me! I don't want to go to Hollywood!"

There was tall, lanky, grease-slicked-hair Robert. He stalked around the campgrounds dressed only in a long black trench coat – and terrified everyone but Nathan and 'Iokepa, who befriended the man. He'd been raised by his brother on the streets of Chicago.

There was Pete from New York who traced his decline to his military days on an aircraft carrier doing air traffic control, to a wife on drugs, and to an infant who died. These – and so many others – became a part of our lives. In the world of this host culture, community is responsible for all of its parts.

The rainy, gusty, lonely days at the Salt Pans were long and sometimes hard for me to fill. My body finally caught up with my spirit, and I was sick. I ached, my throat hurt, I was bone tired. I'd bottomed out.

"I don't think I can do this," I told Louisa, our proprietor friend from The Endless Summer. I was choking back tears. 'This' was living without money, home, or 'Iokepa. 'This,' I suppose, was living in faith.

Still the grandmothers answered when I asked.

I asked on the yellow pad. "How long am I to live hand to mouth?"

> *You are to demonstrate the faith that you will be cared for – forever. Transitions are hard. You have been removed from the material, tangible world – to the invisible, trusting one.*
>
> *Change brings emotion – sometimes doubt. Doubt brings pain. Soon you will not doubt. Soon you will feel peace.*

How soon was "Soon"?

Lono was a ten year old *kanaka maoli* who'd attached himself to teenage Nathan. He spent weekends vying for my son's attentions. He camped out at our dinner table and, as often as not, ate with us.

"Are you homeless?" he asked. It was a question he'd undoubtedly heard the grown ups say.

"No," Nathan answered. "This is our home."

"But do you have a house?"

"We don't need a house," I said. "Where our family lives is our home."

The Ranger was after us for not taking down our tent on his day off. We had not. Our breakdown day had finally fallen on a Saturday – he was off weekends. There was no way he could have known if we'd broken down, then reset, per our permit. But even in his absence he was determined to enforce.

Nathan called him, "The kind of kid who kissed up to his teachers."

Earlier 'Iokepa had said "There is no commitment there. Men like him can go either way – they take whichever is the easiest course. When it's convenient, they'll say, 'I've been here all my life.' When it's not, they'll say, 'But I'm not Hawaiian.'

"They are the people who can't stand it when I tell them, 'This is Hawaiian culture; this is Lāhui.' They want so badly to belong – without any responsibility for knowing what the culture is. These people fear it's going to *take* something from them.

"The only way you – Inette – have felt included is because you gave up what you no longer needed."

When I called my mother collect from the single pay phone at the Park, she would ask me with great regularity and much emotion, "Why can't you live a *normal* life?"

I'd typically laugh and ask her what in the world she meant by 'normal,' and she'd say, "Like mine."

It was during this long stretch alone with Nathan at the Park that I actually found myself spouting her words.

"All I want," I told Nathan over Friday night dinner, "is to live like a normal married couple."

"No you don't!" He stopped my dissembling. "You walked feet first onto a path you knew was anything but normal." He didn't judge me – only held me to the truth.

To acquaintances at the Park – who'd witnessed our public parting, our reconciliation, and 'Iokepa's subsequent departure – I behaved as though 'Iokepa had gone on a short business trip. I pretended more cheer and equilibrium than I felt.

The head of park maintenance was one of the most heart-felt Hawaiian men I'd met on Kaua'i. Like so many natives of the Island of Ni'ihau, Joseph lived his culture. He personally welcomed every soul to that Park by name and with laughter.

By starlight, he and his buddies played exquisitely tender music on slack key guitar and ukulele – and they sang. We'd fall asleep at night to the gentle Hawaiian guitar riffs of Joseph and his band, *Home Grown Hawaiians*. I counted them among my blessings.

Joseph alone acknowledged my loss. "I know you miss 'Iokepa," he said words that matched the compassion in his black eyes. "You were together all the time."

'Iokepa loved and admired Joseph. The feelings were reciprocated.

When I walked across the Park in a bikini that 'Iokepa insisted I was not too old to wear, Joseph laughed and said. "I thought you were a twenty-four year old girl." He knew my confidence needed a kick start.

Because of his gentle ministrations, I felt safe alone with Nathan at the Salt Pans.

. . .

As soon as 'Iokepa left, I turned back to the yellow legal pads with passion. Weathering the wind and the rain in tents, I returned again to Source and throughout December I filled a half-dozen pads.

I asked *again* and again about our fights.

> *Your fights are teachings in no-separation, because the pain we inflict cuts into our own hearts. We cannot harm the other without harm to ourselves.*
>
> *Slowly we learn, as humans learn. There are no shortcuts. People change. You must be an instrument for that change – a reason for it. To judge people – or yourself – is to lock them into where they were at any given moment. Don't do it.*

One night I *heard* for the first time the soft sweet Hawaiian voice. "Grandmother...?"

> *Inette ....*

It was she. It was time to soften my own.

> *Choose. The gift of alone and the gift of married are different. Choose. Alone you see and hear unencumbered by another's eyes or opinions. Married to 'Iokepa, there will be a powerful in-between, not always without hurt. The gifts are different.*
>
> *Separation has become god on Earth. Humans have come to glorify separation.*

> *Surrender the fear of losing your own soul in mating with another. That loss is not possible. The divine resides in re-membering – reassembling what is already whole. Marriage of hearts is God on this planet.*

As always, the grandmother's words rang absolutely true. My digestion of those words was another matter entirely.

. . .

Outside the Big Save supermarket near the Salt Pans, I was stopped by a woman I'd met picnicking with her family on Sundays at the Park. We'd shared conversation too sitting on hard plastic chairs at the Laundromat while watching the dryers spin. Nani, like Joseph from the Park, was from Ni'ihau.

Ni'ihau was a tiny Hawaiian Island to the west of Kaua'i that had been privately owned by a sugar-cane and ranching family for a century. The Robinsons held the Island still. It was considered by many the last stronghold of native Hawaiian culture.

On Ni'ihau, supposedly, only ethnic *kanaka maoli* (excepting the Caucasian land owners) could walk that land; only Hawaiian was spoken; fish was plentiful and the beaches were immaculate. There were those who celebrated the Robinsons for preserving the Hawaiian culture that they found there when the Robinson ancestors bought the land from a weak, dissipated Hawaiian king – and for allowing the native people of the Island to remain on their Island.

In fact, that benevolence was fiction. The Robinson family had simply inherited a labor force. They used the native people in their pursuit of profit. Like a medieval fiefdom, the property owners set every rule of behavior. They determined where and how the people lived – when and how they worked. They prayed (by edict) at the Robinson's church; their children were taught to read from a Bible – and their original language had been sorely anglicized and compromised. If a Ni'ihau native objected to any point of the Robinson rules, he was exiled. The slow, miserable Robinson barge removed people or brought food, as necessary. The Robinson helicopter was used to transport the white people.

At its paternalistic peak there were 200 natives on the Island – all of them close family. But as the Robinson's sugar cane operation on the west side of nearby Kaua'i sprawled, they moved their labor force here.

The truth now: most Ni'ihau natives live on Kaua'i; only seventy-five permanent native residents remain on the Island; and a ranch full of imported African animals is marketed to rich Americans for hunting. The remaining natives have become hunting guides.

But there is another truth. The Ni'ihau natives remain exceptional among modern Hawaiians. For a century their lifestyle was simple, rustic, and captive – but their smiles, their hearts, their peace, their *aloha* – as yet uncontaminated from the faster, crueler world – are genuine. Their connection to the *'āina* – and through it to *Ke 'I'oakua* – literally shines from their wide, brown, very recognizable faces. Their relation to one another and to all of God's creation remains intact.

I'd watch them, at the Salt Pans, pass an infant from hand to hand, woman to man. It was quite impossible to distinguish whose baby it was. When the baby needed a diaper change, it was changed, as often as not, by an unrelated male. It was like that with care of the *kupuna* – the elders. Because, in fact, *ohana* – shrunk in modern translation to mean only 'family' – always meant (and means still to the Ni'ihau natives): 'Everything you can see that you can wrap your heart around is your responsibility to take care of.'

I was leaving the Big Save with a loaf of bread when one of Nani's children hailed me.

"Auntie, Auntie!" Her five year old with eyes as big as the moon over the Salt Pans ran up to me for a hug. "My mother wants to see you."

We walked hand in hand through the parking lot to their pickup truck.

"*Aloha Nani. Pehea 'oe?* (How are you?)"

"*Maika'i no.* (Fine)"

Nani thrust a bag of groceries towards me. While the bag teetered in my arms, she kept filling it. My immediate reaction was a firm, "No thank you." This woman had seven children

from two marriages and like most Ni'ihau families removed to
Kaua'i she had nothing to spare. How could I accept food from
Nani?

How can you not? Can you refuse Nani what you live?

I could not. I returned to the car with boxes of Nathan's
favorite macaroni and cheese, our rice staple, canned soup,
and much more. We had more than two weeks worth of food –
and we needed it.

. . .

I was being bombarded, once again nightly, with profound
answers to sometimes unasked questions.

*The moon is the reflected light of the sun, but the
moon doesn't feel second best. Understand the metaphor.
Understand male and female form: Separate, equal, but not
the same – and always essential to one another.*

*Again – 'Iokepa is the sun, a powerful heat off the
Creator. He is a charismatic soul – a magnet to others.*

*You are the moon – heat off of the Creator, and heat
off the Sun too. Your attraction to others is that they feel
less alone because there is an empathetic soul who knows
them. They are slower to idealize you.*

*You and 'Iokepa began last Christmas from a respect
for each other's differences. Hold onto that – and you'll
have something to offer one another.*

Every night in the tent, I scribbled a different challenge
from the ancestors.

*We send many messengers, many voices – many
ways. Remember to respect the other ways. You do not
need to embrace their ways – just them. If you do not hear
the truth, embrace them still – but distance their way.*

*It is a fine line: Embracing all, respecting only truth,
not mistaking others' truth for your own, and never embracing lies.*

. . .

I wrote a great deal. I swam a little. I began to engage the other campers on my own. Every day was a new configuration of tourists and locals. I stopped hiding in my tent. I became something new on Kaua'i, my gracious, engaging old self. Nathan complimented me. "You've been warm to everyone since 'Iokepa left. It's time for us to be positive about what's happening."

Then Nathan offered his greatest tribute. He said that he *respected* 'Iokepa and me. We were among 'the few not burned-out or compromised adults' he knew.

My son had become a devotee of the band, Rage Against The Machine – and he ardently opposed compromise. He spoke words these days that resonated less of spirituality than of late Sixties radicalism. I watched his changes in awe.

Nathan was counting down the days to Christmas vacation. He would fly to his father's farm in West Virginia on December 18 for a two week visit. He'd return a few days after New Year's with his brother. Ben had a month's vacation from Beloit: he would spend half of it with his father's family and Nathan; half with Nathan, 'Iokepa and me.

'Iokepa and I had agreed to spend our one year anniversary at the *Poli'ahu heiau*, where we'd met.

I prayed for a genuine rapprochement between 'Iokepa and Ben this visit. I prayed too that I could love them both – but neither at the expense of the other.

It never crossed my mind that 'Iokepa would not come home for Christmas. I checked the post office box every few days for mail from 'Iokepa. It never came. I rationalized. He wasn't a letter writer, he'd once said. But I remembered quite well a time when he wrote anyway.

In anticipation of 'Iokepa's Christmas return, I drove the forty-five minutes to Queen's Pond.

It was the westernmost beach on Kaua'i, the place where the paved road that almost circles the Island expired twenty miles shy of completion. The remaining Na Pali coastline was accessible only by foot, or boat.

To reach Queen's Pond, I left the paved highway and drove fifteen minutes through the sugar cane fields on a rutted, red dirt path next to the spectacular coastal peaks of Polihale.

I parked where I could, so as not to get stuck in the loose soft sand dunes, and climbed the dunes on foot. In the summer, my feet had burned even in my beach slippers. It was that hot. This was the extreme dry edge of Kaua'i – the desert.

Every time I had topped the peak of those dunes in the past and looked down onto the seventeen mile stretch of undefiled white sand beach and the most unusual blue-green ocean I'd seen anywhere – I had to suck in my breath. It was almost too beautiful to be real; too perfect not to be part of a Hollywood movie. Too untouched and unpopulated to be of this Earth.

But the moment I'd thought it, I would immediately re-tract it. Had man so desecrated God's Earth that this tiny slice of undefiled land seemed as false as a movie set?

The shoreline and the dunes of Queen's Pond and Poli-hale were perhaps the last remaining beach in Hawai'i where you could still glean open-ocean *puka* shells. It was where 'Iokepa collected his. Always, he had – as his ancestors had, before they took fish from the sea or shell from the shore –

offered prayer the night before and asked 'Was this was the day?' He prayed again when he walked the beach. He performed his ritual, and the shells came to him, tiny to huge – and in the rare-colored blue, green, grey, pink and yellow.

Each *lei* was different from the last. He labored to create them, but he took no credit at all. "They are the spirits' *lei*."

He loved the *lei*, carried them in his hip pack every step he took, and was extremely reluctant to part with one when someone wanted to buy it. The *lei* bought food and gas for our family when we needed it, but no one ever had to sell them. They did that for themselves.

"They were each made for a particular person and that person always recognized which one was his or hers," 'Iokepa said. "They bring people together to hear the Creator's story."

I was at Queen's Pond that morning intending to collect shells for 'Iokepa for his *Chanukah* present.

I'd left the Salt Pans as soon as Nathan left for school at 6:45. I planned to make a day of it. Collecting shells was long hot work. They were no longer plentiful. A day's picking might fill half a baggie.

I topped the dunes this time and saw what looked like a post office jeep parked down on the beach. I ignored it. Four wheel drive vehicles with surfboards strapped on top sometimes made their way to this invitingly rough surf.

I set up a beach chair, a gallon jug of water, and my back-pack with sunscreen, a baseball cap, and T-shirt – if the sun grew unbearably hot. I took out a plastic cup and started down the shoreline, back bent, scanning the tidal line for shells. There wasn't a person in sight.

When I passed the jeep set against the dunes, a uni-formed figure emerged. He walked towards me. I said, "*Aloha*."

"You can't go there," he answered.

"I'm picking *puka* shells," I said.

"The Pacific Missile Range Facility is testing today. No one's allowed on the beach."

I laughed in his face. "You are mistaken. All Hawaiian beaches are public. This is Hawaiian land."

"On launch days the U.S. Navy has authority," he an-swered.

"I'm afraid you do not. I don't grant you that authority."

His hand went to the pistol on his hip and he caressed the dark handle. He was no taller than me. His eyes and his voice pleaded.

"I'm just doing my job. It's for your own safety. Please go away."

I walked off in the direction I had come and mulled my options. I could oppose him, continue down the beach, and perhaps be shot. I could fight with him and be led off forcibly. I could leave, as he told me. Or I could wait and see what happened.

I waited in the beach chair in the hot sun and I fell fast asleep. I was awakened to the sound of a fast moving object displacing air – it was a squeal. To my left, two missile launchers arched one behind the other over my head over the Queen's Pond dunes, and fell into the blue-green ocean in front of me, sending their missiles further out to sea – beyond the reach of my vision.

It was surreal. The last remaining pristine beach on Kaua'i had American Naval missiles lofting overhead.

The United States military owns or controls more than 200,000 acres of Hawaiian land, including a quarter of all land on the most populous Island, O'ahu. U. S. military personnel and dependents account for fully ten percent of the Islands' population. These strategically placed bases remain the overpowering reason the United States insistently holds onto the Hawaiian nation as a state.

I couldn't leave. Like the attraction of a crowd to a burning building, I needed to witness the unthinkable – to trust to my senses that which my heart could not even imagine. I was forbidden to walk the Hawaiian 'āina at Queen's Pond today because the land belonged to the American military. I wanted to cry.

. . .

Eight days before Nathan was to fly to West Virginia, I went to the weekly farmer's market in Hanapepe. I didn't know why, I had no money. But stepping out of the car, I bumped into Phil.

Phil and Eleanor, his wife of thirty-eight years, were acquaintances.

We'd met Eleanor first, on the beach at the Salt Pans in October. She was walking the sand with a trash bag picking up other people's garbage. It was something 'Iokepa always – and now I too – habitually did: *mālama ka 'āina* – take care of the land.

'Iokepa was particularly adept at instantly snatching up trash that an unthinking soul had dropped, without saying a word to that person – or perhaps only *'aloha.'* It was a form of teaching more powerful than a lecture. The man or woman usually thanked 'Iokepa – occasionally apologized.

So we noticed Eleanor on her garbage run. Blonde, tall, our age – she moved with the grace of a fairy. Phil was her tall, rugged husband, and their home – we'd later found out – was five miles up the road in Kalaheo.

"I knew 'Iokepa the moment I saw his eyes," Eleanor told me.

Though Phil had taken a path to conventional success as a computer software guru of international reputation, he and Eleanor were first and foremost on a spiritual journey.

On that October day at the beach, after an hour of pleasantries and some shared story, Phil and Eleanor left. A couple hours later, they returned.

"You were holding out on us weren't you?" Eleanor had asked 'Iokepa and giggled. Alone, she had asked spirit, and then heard in no uncertain terms the truth of the man. She was that connected.

They had a guest wing in their home and they offered it to us whenever we needed a warm shower or a break. We had taken them up on it for Nathan's birthday dinner. When they knew 'Iokepa was leaving for Maui, Phil was the one who simply handed him the airline ticket he needed to get there. Phil kept a stash of inter-Island airline coupons for his frequent business travel.

I had seen the two of them at the Salt Pans only once since 'Iokepa left. I liked them; I simply didn't yet know them very well. Eleanor's spiritual language was very different from 'Iokepa's. I didn't always understand what she was saying.

At the farmer's market that day in Hanapepe, Phil said to me. "You'll want to go to Maui when Nathan leaves, won't you?"

"I...I don't know," I stammered.

"Well, spirit told us that we were to support the two of you in any way we can.

"You'll need two airline coupons. I've got a couple in the car. Wait here." He handed them to me and then as abruptly as he'd come, he left.

I stuck the tickets inside the driver's side door pocket and I thought. "Iokepa will need these when he comes home for Christmas."

. . .

On the eight days and nights of *Chanukah* – 2,165 years ago – there was the miracle of divine light. Jewish people celebrate it still. In past years, each of my children received eight presents – one commemorating each night that the tiny drop of oil miraculously burned in that long-ago, war-devastated Hebrew temple.

This year, the idea of *Chanukah* weighed heavily against the reality of my pocketbook. I considered myself ahead of the game for having bought each of the boys one present: the National Geographic's new CD Rom, *Maps of the World* for Ben's computer; a replacement Discman (hidden in the Camry's trunk) for Nathan's broken one.

There was no appropriate gift wrap on Kaua'i – and not a *Chanukah* candle to be found. Explaining the size and shape of the candles to the clerks at Safeway was tantamount to describing snow to a Pacific Islander who'd seen neither TV nor magazine. It couldn't be done.

Our *Chanukah menorah* (the nine pronged candle holder) was buried inaccessibly in storage. It made no difference, I rationalized – because there were no candles to fit it. *Chanukah* was looking grim.

It was time to make concessions.

After school, still hours before sunset on the first night of *Chanukah*, I picked up Nathan and suggested an impromptu excursion to Kapa'a (where the stores were) and then out to dinner. He loved both ideas. It had been a while.

We happened past one of the two movie theatres on the Island. The new Star Trek movie was just released. Nathan had been dying to see it.

"Let's go!" I offered.

"Can we?!"

"If the time works."

We were exactly on time for the late afternoon show, still at matinee prices.

Afterwards I ran into Safeway while Nathan waited. Birthday candles and no *menorah* would have to do. The miracle of light came first, I reasoned – the specifics of the celebration came much later.

The plan was to light the candles when we got home. We were an hour east of there. Dinner at a restaurant was first. We agreed on Mexican, fifteen minutes closer to home.

I was barreling toward dinner in the left hand lane of a four lane thoroughfare, when I heard. *Turn right here!* We were smack in the middle of an intersection.

Without as much as checking the rearview mirror or glancing out the window, I cut across the lane to my right, and turned. When I straightened the wheel and realized what I'd just done, I shuddered. But there were no sirens and not a single car on this densely trafficked stretch of highway when I'd brazenly cut over.

As soon as I turned, I knew where we were headed. *Poli'ahu heiau* near Opaeka'a Falls – where 'Iokepa and I had met. This was not part of the evening's itinerary and I apologized to Nathan. "I'll only be a minute."

I got out of the car and walked to the exact spot where I'd first laid eyes on 'Iokepa. I prayed from deep inside of me for all of us – and for more. The black night felt full of response. *Light your candles here.*

"How's that sound?" I asked Nathan. He agreed.

I rooted through the trunk for Nathan's present and an envelope my mother had sent him. I melted the bottom of two birthday candles on the car's lighter and mounted them on a stray college alumni magazine up on the dashboard. The *Shamash*, the lead candle that lit the others, was a bit higher (as tradition dictated) by virtue of a fold in the magazine's page.

We were parked on the side of a dormant volcano. There was no other light, no other person in sight. Nathan and I belted out without a shred of embarrassment: "*Baruch atah adonai elohenu melech ho'olum, asher kidushanu b'mitvotov vitzivanu l'hadlich n'er shel Chanukah.* Blessed art thou O Lord our God, King of the Universe, who commanded us to kindle the Chanukah lights."

I could not remember when my heart felt fuller. I could feel Nathan's bursting against my chest when we hugged tight and wished one another "Good *yom tov!*" (Happy holiday!)

He was thrilled with his present – and his grandmother's check. He offered me a gift of a much-needed haircut. We listened to Rage Against The Machine on his new Discman – rapping the rhythm against the dashboard on our drive to the Mexican restaurant. The doors to La Bamba were still open – we were the very last customers of the night.

On each subsequent night we added a candle to the lid of a cookie tin on top of the picnic table at the Salt Pans. On most nights, other campers gathered when we sang out the Hebrew chants. Some nights, we sat by the candlelight with the others and shared our *Chanukah* stories.

Traditionally, we were to put our *menorah* in the front window of our home so that passer-bys could revel in the celebration of the miracle of divine light. Those nights at the Park were the purest fulfillment of that intention – we shared our lights, our prayers, and some cookies afterwards too.

There were six candles blazing the night that Nathan left for his father's. As he got on the plane, he said. "I loved our first night of Chanukah."

. . .

I left the airport feeling lost and disoriented. Nathan was gone – two weeks stretched ahead of me – and I knew nothing of 'Iokepa.

"I'm in your hands *Ke 'I'oakua*," I said aloud and stretched my arms up and out to their limits in the airport parking lot. I drove slowly, and I was led without calculation to The Endless Summer where Louisa greeted me with a long face.

"'Iokepa won't be at the *heiau* for Christmas," she said. Then she studied my reaction and hugged me. "His sister called. He asked her to call us – and for us to tell you. He won't be home for Christmas."

It felt like the bottom had dropped out. All I managed was, "I was sure he was coming!" And then, "How long ago did Puanani call?"

It had been an hour. I went to the nearby pay phone where 'Iokepa had regularly called me in Portland, and I dialed Puanani's toll free number.

Getting the first news I'd heard of 'Iokepa in three weeks felt like pulling teeth. Whether it was my insatiable appetite for details or Puanani's reticence, I couldn't say.

When he stepped off the plane at the airport in Maui, she told me, 'Iokepa had been approached by a man who admired the *lei* he wore and wanted one. From penniless to eighty dollars before he picked up his luggage – he went to the Salvation Army's thrift shop for a warm quilt and a cheap air mattress.

He hitchhiked to the only beach park on Maui where it was legal to camp – Baldwin Park.

There, a few days later, 'Iokepa was attacked.

She told the story. He had spread his assorted *lei* on a picnic table at the park and asked a friend to keep an eye on them when he went to the restroom. The friend had been distracted. When 'Iokepa returned, three were gone. One was around the brazen, belligerent neck of a notorious local drug dealer.

"What's with the *lei*? 'Iokepa asked the hulking youth.

"What *lei*?" the smirking delinquent answered.

At that moment, an even larger (just released from prison) brother came up behind 'Iokepa and with the full weight of his ignorance and rage punched 'Iokepa dead center in the back.

While 'Iokepa sustained the shock and pain, the first man came at 'Iokepa from the front.

For three years, 'Iokepa had fought in (and consistently won) international karate matches. He had, when asked in recent months, demonstrated his moves to Nathan. To both our eyes he was incredibly fast, strong, and seemingly invincible. What's more, he knew it – and that was without factoring in the grandmothers.

But when he was being pummeled, 'Iokepa had the presence of mind to ask his grandmothers, and he heard. *You are not to fight.*

"Do I have to keep getting hurt?" *You do not.*

With that, he began what his sensei had called his 'dance.' Kicks sliced the air next to each man's head. Jabs that chose to miss the mark but deliver the message. The men were stunned by the turn of events and they disappeared quickly – with the *lei.*

While I pressed Puanani for details, I knew in my heart that 'Iokepa had passed with flying colors the greatest challenge to his integrity in two years. He took the punches, rather than fight. I was immeasurably proud.

Later I learned. The grandmothers told him.

> *It starts with a fist. Then someone picks up a rock. Someone else picks up a stick. Then someone pulls out a knife – then, a gun. It is how wars start. Fights do not stop until someone stops fighting.*

'Iokepa was also told to remind the angry young locals what they didn't remember. He was to say: 'My ancestors took care of your ancestors when they arrived on the Island.'

For 12,300 years on these Islands, there was no war. It was this matriarchal, ancestral culture that 'Iokepa now lived to revive. "The women didn't think that God needed help in taking the lives of the children they birthed," he said. "And the men respected that." Within that ancient culture are modern answers for a warring world.

Puanani didn't know where 'Iokepa was now. When she'd spoken to him last, he'd moved to the south end of Maui on La

Perouse Bay. "He was camped illegally near a lighthouse 'that's not really a lighthouse,'" she puzzled. He didn't know how long he'd be there.

When I hung up the pay phone next to The Endless Summer every muscle and bone in my body yearned to be with 'Iokepa on Maui. But I was cautious. I knew that missing him wasn't reason enough. He hadn't asked me to come. Perhaps he didn't want me to.

That night I asked the ancestors, "Am I to go to Maui?"

It was no accident, they answered, that I'd been given a round trip ticket to Maui. It was no accident that I had money (because I had not yet paid off Ben and Nathan's flights on my American Express card with their father's check for half).

But they were specific. I was not to leave the next day. I was to wait until Sunday. I was not to take the morning flight. I was to wait until the one that left at 1:15 in the afternoon. They would tell me what to bring.

I asked: "Why isn't he here for our anniversary?"

Because he asked, and we told him: 'Stay. You are not done on Maui.'

I had assumed I'd hitchhike on Maui until a friend told me that hitchhiking was illegal there. I called the car rental companies. *Exactly* like last year at Christmas the first seven companies said. 'No way, Christmas week has been booked for a month.' And just like last year, the eighth company – this time, Alamo – said. "Sure, we've got a compact."

On Sunday morning I broke camp and put two peanut butter and jelly sandwiches, a bottle of water, and a banana in my daypack. I packed two small duffels, strapped Nathan's tent to the top of one with bungee cords and Nathan's sleeping bag to the other.

Everything else went inside the car. I parked the car on 'Iokepa's friend's beautiful ten acres. He gave me a ride to the airport.

He was full of fear for me.

"What will you do if you don't find 'Iokepa?"

"Camp out myself."

"Suppose you find him right before you have to come home?"

"It's in God's hands."

"Do you have any money?"

"Forty dollars after the car rental."

I was on a pilgrimage. I'd always been a sucker for the unknown.

You will meet 'Iokepa at four o'clock.

It was the first thing I heard when I awakened in the tent at the Salt Pans on Sunday, December 20. I'd heard it – I knew I heard it – but I doubted. Maui was a far bigger Island than Kaua'i. I'd never been there. 'Iokepa could be anywhere – and wherever he was, camped illegally, he'd be invisible.

My plane arrived in Kahului at 1:45 p.m. When I picked up my car at Alamo, the woman peered into her computer and told me. "It says here you rented this car yesterday – but that's not possible. We haven't had a car available Christmas week for more than a month."

I smiled. Obviously, someone other than Alamo management had pulled some strings.

I asked for a map. The Alamo map forbade taking rental cars into La Perouse Bay, where the paved road disappeared into lava rock. I asked, instead, how long it would take to get to Makena Beach – the last resort town before La Perouse.

"A half an hour," she said.

I fumbled out of the airport and took a fair number of wrong turns in urban Kahului. I took another one fifteen minutes later that brought me back full circle to where I'd started. It was discouraging, but my adrenaline was pumping and I heard it again. *Four o'clock.*

It had become the whispered mantra: repeated on the plane, at the Alamo counter, and now in the car.

I knew I wanted to head south. The ocean stayed pretty much to my right. I drove though the towns of Kihei, then

181

Wailea, and finally Makena. I stopped occasionally and asked. "La Perouse Bay?" Strangers kept pointing me down the road.

The paved road narrowed. It became one slender lane through treacherous curves, with no view whatsoever of what might be coming at me. I kept driving.

All signs of human intrusion on the *'āina* ended. I was surrounded by lava fields: sharp-edged, massive, black boulders tumbling as far as I could see in all directions up to the ocean's edge – impressive and alive. Truly, it felt like the end of the world – or the beginning of one.

I drove until there was no place left to drive. The paved road turned to dirt then to rock then to ocean. I stopped and asked some locals with fishing rods. "Where's La Perouse Bay?"

They waved at the many miles of lava and ocean stretched in front of me in all directions.

"Can I drive out there?"

"Not in that you can't." They looked askance at my Ford Escort.

"Can I walk in there?"

"Yeah, you can find paths through the lava."

"Do people camp out there?"

"Some."

I pulled my daypack from the trunk, strapped it on my back and began picking my way in *slippers* – flip-flops – through the sharp rocks. I figured that the furthest point I could see at the end of the bay was four miles distant. Maybe it was the site of a lighthouse that Puanani told me 'isn't really a lighthouse.'

I walked. It was hot and slow going. I stopped at the first encampment I came across right next to the water.

"*Aloha.* Have you seen a Hawaiian man with white hair called, 'Iokepa?

"Nope."

"Are there campers further in?"

"Yes."

"*Mahalo.*"

I walked another mile, I guess. It was hard to estimate because nothing was straight, smooth, or easy. I was focusing each step to keep from twisting my ankle, or slicing my exposed feet on the lava. I wished I'd had the foresight to wear my walking shoes.

There was another group of tents ahead – four.

"Have you seen....?"

"No, but that name sounds familiar."

"Is there anyone else camped further down the rocks?"

"No, we're the last of it."

"*Mahalo.*"

I continued to walk – mostly because I didn't know what else to do. I passed a large clump of trees to my left and I peered inside of them from the trail. I was tempted to explore, but I did not. I knew it was pretty unlikely that 'Iokepa would be camped on the trail itself; far more likely he'd be tucked somewhere out of sight. But I realized if I wandered off what passed for a trail, I'd be lost forever in this barren and enchanted place.

I made a deal with myself. I would not leave the trail, regardless of inducement. I began negotiating with God.

"*Ke 'I'oakua*, I understand if I am not to be with 'Iokepa. I know you'll take care of me.

"But I'm aiming to walk all the way to the farthest point, the 'lighthouse' – unless you tell me otherwise. And I'd be grateful if you'd see to it that I get back to the car before dark."

I was hungry, thirsty and I had to pee. I pulled the water bottle from the daypack and took a deep swallow. I grabbed a peanut butter and jelly sandwich and ate it as I walked, albeit considerably slower. Then I looked in all directions for signs of another human; there were none, so I squatted on the rocks out in the open and relieved that pressure.

I walked.

My plan began to feel pretty hollow. *If* Puanani had gotten the names and the details right, it had been four days since she'd last spoken to 'Iokepa. *If* he'd been here then, what was to say he'd be here still?

And this, I'd never seen his new tent. If I found a tent standing in the lava fields and if he'd gone to town, or swimming, or fishing – I'd have no way of recognizing it as his. My doubts multiplied, but I walked.

I approached a stand of thorny *kiawe* – mesquite – trees to my right, about two miles now from the car. I'd long since lost sight of the ocean. I walked past the trees – holding fast to the trail consistent with my deal – when I felt a pressure against my shoulders turn me right and push me back into the trees.

My brain was racing. "Why am I leaving the path? Why?!"

I stooped down and climbed deeper into the wood without answer or reason. I felt like a puppet.

I saw nothing. I asked under my breath, "Iokepa?" Twice. No one heard my whisper.

. . .

Later, 'Iokepa gave me his account.

He was camped behind those *kiawe* (mesquite) trees, on the other side of a twenty-foot high boulder, invisible from the path. Every day he had hiked out next to the ocean; then hitchhiked to town. This Sunday he'd stayed put – and he wondered why. He had every intention of walking out, but he couldn't make himself move.

At some point he heard the ancestors. They directed him to stand in front of the massive rock, twenty feet high and fifteen feet wide – at the back of his campsite. He knew that *La Perouse Bay* was the colonizer's bogus name for these hallowed lava fields. They were actually *Keone'o'io* – the altar of God. He stood briefly staring up at the venerable boulder, and he asked. "Why am I here?"

At that exact moment, he heard a crunching of branches and leaves underfoot herald movement from the upper path. He looked up and glimpsed the 51st birthday *lei* around my neck. He thought, "That looks like one of mine."

A breath later, he recognized my snug canary yellow knit top with the scooped neck and cap sleeves. "I *know* that shirt."

As usual, 'Iokepa saw me before I saw him. "Your head was bent down; you were coming under a branch."

Just as he saw me, I looked up stunned. Thirty feet away, but blurred through tree limbs and leaves, I saw red shorts, white hair, and a brown face looking up at me in the woods. I thought, "Iokepa?' But I wasn't sure.

His first words were: "I'd hoped you would come."

He walked up to me. His face looked innocent, like a beautiful woman scrubbed clean of make-up – young and fresh. He was Adam standing almost naked in the magical woods. I was his Eve in navy walking shorts, yellow knit top, *puka* shell *lei*, and slippers.

"What time *is* it?" I asked him after we'd reached up for one another, stumbled on the uneven ground, leaned against a rock to steady ourselves, and gently kissed. Neither one of us wore watches. He glanced up at the sun and answered. "Four o'clock."

That night we lit the eight candles I'd brought with me and the lead candle I'd brought too. We stood them tall on a rock in front of our tent. It was the last night of *Chanukah* and I sang out into the dark night our *barucha* – blessing. Then together in Hawaiian, we said. *"Mahalo Ke 'I'oakua."*

On the New Year's Eve that had welcomed 1998 a year before, 'Iokepa and I had discovered quite by chance, that we both loved to dance and we were both pretty good at it. We'd danced for the first time, at midnight, to old rock and roll on the rental car radio under the stars on a hilltop overlooking the Kaua'i harbor. It would be a hard act to follow.

'Iokepa and I left his campsite at Keone'o'io the morning of the last day of 1998, with Nathan's tent and sleeping bag in the trunk, a little food, and a clear picture in 'Iokepa's head and heart of the spot where we'd welcome our second New Year together – though he'd never in his life been there.

We drove the rental car around the dry, stark, dramatic southern edge of Maui, where Haleakala, the dormant volcano that shared the name of 'Iokepa's grandmother, met the ocean. The rocky cliffs, the remnants of ancient volcanic flow, stretched for fifty, slow-going, unpopulated coastal miles.

Other parts of Maui were pure jungle: lush, luxuriantly green, etched with the unstinting colors of tropical flora and riveting waterfalls. That was certainly what visitors imagined when they dreamed of Hawai'i. But this southern coast was, like *poi*, an acquired taste – for many, I suspect, never acquired.

We drove, stopped at hidden coves, climbed rocks to inaccessible places, trying to reconcile the vision that 'Iokepa had been given by the grandmothers with the physical reality of our campsite. Late in the afternoon we found it.

"This is the place," 'Iokepa said. No doubt, no question.

We parked the car out of sight of the road, on the side of a hill, and climbed in the rest of the way. 'Iokepa – absolutely certain of his unseen destination – marched us over precarious rocks in a direction that was entirely concealed from view.

It was the site of a *heiau* – aboriginal constructs evident in the stacked stone, nine-foot walls opening to the sea. When we walked through the gateway of the first set of walls, I gasped for breath. I felt an enormous pressure on my chest, and chills up and down my arms and neck – *'ailona* – signs of the presence of the spirits.

"Do you feel that?" 'Iokepa asked me.

We prayed.

We welcomed the New Year in that small steep bay encircled on three sides by sixty foot rock cliff walls. Within the circle of walls, the ground was flat for 100 feet wide and just as deep. We placed our tent in the center of the cove, facing the ocean.

We welcomed midnight, 1999 under a swollen moon – *mahina poepoe* – full and luminous against a black sky and ocean, without another person in sight. But we were not alone. We felt pressed snugly against the walls of that holy place by a palpable and congenial assembly of ancestors. New Year's 1999, we figured, was the spirits' turn to dance.

. . .

"This relationship has softened," 'Iokepa said at the end of my two weeks on Maui.

I prepared to leave on January 2 to meet Ben and Nathan's plane the next day on Kaua'i – and I assumed (as on Moloka'i) that 'Iokepa would come with me. But what I expected was not what 'Iokepa intended.

> *Expectation leads to disappointment. No expectation leads to surprise.*

I would be alone with both sons again. I yearned to hold them.

I flew into Kaua'i – after a long day waiting for stand-by flights in Honolulu – with seventy cents in my pocket, twenty-five dollars in the bank, and no place to spend the night. I called the man on whose land I'd parked the Camry. There was no answer. I called Louisa and Albert at The Endless Summer for a ride to my car – but they'd already left for home. After the two calls, I was out of change, out of energy and, it seemed, out of options.

At the luggage carousel, I asked my former airplane seatmate for thirty-five cents, and called a couple that I knew. I'd known them separately before they knew one another. They'd met camping – both single – at the Salt Pans. Greg picked me up. Anne had dinner waiting for me. They were dying to hear about 'Iokepa and Maui. I was eager to share, but I was exhausted.

Anne tucked me into their extra room under a satin comforter and in the morning she made me pancakes, eggs, and tea. We ate outside on the *lānai*: talking, staring at the green mountains, and listening to the roosters next door. I felt nurtured. They drove me the forty-five miles to the Camry.

I headed west to the Salt Pans, but I didn't yet have a permit. I surprised myself at the last minute and veered left towards Phil and Eleanor's. I remembered I was to deliver 'Iokepa's *aloha*. They'd want to hear the stories.

At an intersection just two blocks from their home, my Camry met their massive Lincoln SUV – they were returning their visiting children and grandchildren to the airport.

"Your timing," Eleanor said out the passenger window, "is impeccable. Stay here with the boys until the ninth." I agreed. We'd meet at their home in a few hours.

At the Salt Pans, I saw a half dozen people I knew, all eager to find out if – or how – I'd found 'Iokepa on Maui. I was glowing. "Your smile! Your smile!" one man marveled. I was being hugged from all sides, human and spirit. Every step of my return felt orchestrated.

It was Joseph's day off, but magically he was there anyway – Nani, too. These natives of the Island of Ni'ihau studied me with their serious Hawaiian eyes. "You grow stronger," Nani said.

Without 'Iokepa – as with him – I felt guidance in every step. But when we were together, I attributed those divine favors to 'Iokepa's connections. Alone, I knew they were mine.

'Anyone would give his life,' 'Iokepa had reminded me, 'to receive just a paragraph – one time – of what you receive always.'

I had accepted Phil and Eleanor's generosity, but the boys' flight had been cancelled.

"Why!?!" I asked the airline's voice-on-the-phone.

"Where have *you* been?" she answered. "The largest snowstorm of the century shut down half the country."

"Oh," I laughed, "I've been on Maui." But I realized that I'd been a great deal further than that. I couldn't remember the last time I'd read a newspaper.

I'd been a news junkie since I became a reporter at twenty-two. As recently as Portland, I'd read every page of the Oregonian every day – plus a morning dose of National Public Radio.

Of course I wondered why my life now precluded a daily fix of news. I imagined it to be part of the general letting go, but I was embarrassed by my ignorance. All I now knew of public events was transmitted by hearsay, often inaccurately.

The next day, the American airports were still closed. Now, two days less with Ben, and Nathan would miss his first days of school. I was aching for them. But they were safely with their Dad, and I was at Phil and Eleanor's.

I went to the post office to retrieve the two week pile of mail. In the heap of advertisements and out-of-date Christmas catalogues were: a surprise *Chanukah* gift from my mother – $200; a larger by $100 child support check because of some tuition error. I couldn't stop laughing – the gifts poured in.

I piled the rest of the mail onto the front seat unopened. I walked to the County Parks' office for a camping permit to begin on January 9. For the first time since mid-October, the surly woman at the front desk cracked a grin when I asked for a permit.

"This is your *last* permit." She practically leapt across the counter with pleasure. "Your sixty days are up!"

I had no idea there was a county camping limit for any twelve month period. Now I did. I would have exactly what I needed while Ben was here; the rest was in God's hands.

I tackled the mail. There were two certified letters from Beloit College: one for Ben, one for me. I opened mine. It was the blow I had not seen coming. Ben had been kicked out of college for the coming semester – he hadn't made the minimum grade point average that was the condition of his acceptance on probation. He would be offered another chance the following fall.

He could appeal the decision, but the appeal deadline on this two and a half week old letter was the next morning.

I was shocked. On all phone calls with Ben from Beloit, he'd sounded happier than I'd heard him in his life. He loved his professors, his classes, his fellow students. He had an active social life. It seemed, now, perhaps too active.

I was trembling. The thought of calling Ben and delivering the news was nightmarish. Should I protect him until he arrived? I turned it over to the Creator.

I heard, loud and clear. *Call him, tell him. It is his, not yours.*

With a twenty minute calling card Lena had sent me for *Chanukah*, I called Ben from a pay phone near the post office. "I got a letter from Beloit, Ben," I said. "I think it's best if I read it to you."

Ben was sometimes foolish, but he had never been stupid – so he'd known, of course, before I did. He'd done no work, handed in no papers, had a great first semester freed of the obligation of doing more than attending classes (which he loved), reading his texts, and partying.

"I thought they'd wait until I got back and issue me a warning," he said. Life had finally caught with Ben.

He was crying when we hung up, but I felt clear.

"I love you Ben. I know this hurts. We all screw up in life. The measure of our worth is how we respond afterwards. I have complete faith in you."

Ben walked off the plane with a sardonic half-grin. At the luggage counter he said, "I'd forgotten how oppressive you were."

"What!?!" I choked back my reaction and tried to joke. "I'm sure you meant *impressive* – right?"

It was like that. His too-little-too-late appeal to the Dean had failed. The suspension held. The Dean called him 'immoral' for disregarding all the people who had invested in his admission to Beloit. His airplane ticket from Kaua'i would take him back to college where he was no longer a student, his friends would discover his shame, and his future looked pretty uncertain. I became his scapegoat. I was grateful at least that 'Iokepa was not there.

It was a rugged visit. Ben hid out behind science fiction books, one after another – first in Phil and Eleanor's guest wing, next in Nathan's tent at the Park. He refused the sun, he refused the ocean, and he refused the food. He was sullen to every unsuspecting person who dared to ask him, how he liked Kaua'i.

"It's hot. It's boring. There's nothing to do."

He started to bad-mouth the absent 'Iokepa on a drive up the spectacular Waimea Canyon. I slammed on the brakes, pulled over and bridged no answer.

"You will *never* criticize 'Iokepa in my presence – and out of his – ever!"

He took the fight. I called his bluff. "You want to leave before next week? Okay, I'll drive you to the airport and pay the difference myself." He chose to stay.

It was during that week that Nathan decided to bleach his beautiful black hair. He planned on blonde – and only on the ends. Instead, it went clown orange, root to tip.

"It's ugly!" I blurted out without thinking.

"It's not so bad," Ben said. He had been – paradoxically – reliably kind to his little brother throughout the trip.

Nathan, in any case, was exceedingly pleased with himself.

He had, since he'd returned, taken first prize and fifty dollars in an Island wide art competition. He was particularly proud because the poster was outspokenly radical. He hadn't compromised his politics to win.

I was proud too, but the kids were wearing me out.

Look at your sons sleeping. Just love them.
Being their mother does not give you the right to judge them. These are growing adults. The anger that you

have chosen in the past – exactly as Ben has chosen – you will each un-choose when you are secure in yourselves and in Source.

When he insults you, respond simply. "Would you like to be with someone who insults you?" Then quickly change the subject.

I looked at Ben sleeping. He looked, again, so sweet and vulnerable. I remembered him asleep in my four-poster bed, under the skylights, on his last sick day in Portland. It felt like only yesterday – and it felt, simultaneously, like an entirely other lifetime. We'd been through a lot – together, and apart.

I'd spoken often since I'd returned about 'Iokepa's visibly growing authority. After the attack when he'd refused to engage – *Someone has to stop it* – the grandmothers rewarded his restraint. He was to call himself a *kahu* – a guardian or priest of the original culture. It was a turning point – and it increased both his responsibilities and his gifts. There were potent dreams and whispered messages – that added mightily to his bank of authentic history, language and culture. It seemed to me that people recognized it in him instantly.

Now I longed for 'Iokepa to be with Ben – and I tried to imagine how I could affect it.

On January 10 – one year to the day from the ancestors' first written message to me on the yellow legal pad – I awakened voiceless.

Let go now, even of your attachment to words. Things happen in their own time, with no help from your hand, or your mouth.

I spent the entire day alone. I lounged in enforced silence in the sunshine on the beach at the Park. Nathan was at school. Ben was in the tent reading. The laryngitis was a reminder of what I'd known instinctively a year ago – I need only receive.

In mid-afternoon Ben emerged from his tent for the first time to swim. He set his beach chair next to mine. We sat next to one another in silence. Then I heard Eleanor's tinkling giggle behind me and I turned. Phil was beside her.

"I'm a messenger," Phil said. "'Iokepa called. He'll be here on Wednesday at 10:45 a.m. He said. 'I'm coming to see Ben.'"

Again, there had not been a word of written or verbal communication between us in the eight days since Maui. I didn't know if he were still at Keone'o'io. He didn't know a single thing that had happened to me since I'd stepped on the plane in Maui, not where I'd been or where I was now, not that Ben had been suspended from school or that the visit had been hard. Logically, he didn't know any of it. Obviously, he did. His gift to my son was this. Ben was worth it.

The next day my voice returned. The day after that 'Iokepa arrived. I met the plane alone. "My grandmothers said I'd see you with entirely different eyes when I got off the plane," he said. "And I do."

He stayed a week with us in the tents at the Park and he was patient, kind, and loving. Before he left he invited Ben to come live with us in Hawai'i. "It's a different life," he said, "but it hasn't done your brother any harm." Ben appeared to soften.

I never loved 'Iokepa more.

TAKING CARE

1999: Late January

When 'Iokepa returned to Maui there was no place – save the rough and tumble Baldwin Park (an enclave of alcohol and drug abuse) and a very cold mountainous state park – for him to legally put his tent.

A ranger from the state Department of Land and Natural Resources had tossed 'Iokepa off the beach at Keone'o'io three times. He threatened him with a $500 fine. 'Iokepa laughed at the absurdity of fining a man who lived in a tent and owned only a sports' duffel of clothing.

He reminded the enforcer, "The Department of Land and Natural Resources was created to protect the land *for* the Hawaiians, not *from* them."

The ranger took the message to heart. "When I go home at night," he confessed, "I'm Hawaiian. But when I put on this uniform in the morning, I'm not Hawaiian anymore."

'Iokepa contemplated Maui – larger by half than Kaua'i – where beach camping for more than a single night was illegal. Twenty years before, the county government had committed itself to attracting tourism away from Honolulu on O'ahu. They made the decision to target only upscale tourism, no cheap motels, condos or camping. Twenty years later, Maui was crammed with rental Jaguars, Porsches, upper-end homes and hotels – and many wealthy Caucasians. On Kaua'i, by contrast, the tourists' rental cars tended toward Ford Escort or Dodge Neon and the locals drove old heaps, rusted in the salt air.

At the exact moment of 'Iokepa's third eviction, a stranger named Fred appeared. It was unforeseen on both their parts. Fred – barreling down a major highway – slammed on his truck brakes the instant he spotted 'Iokepa seated in a park next to the road. The recognition was immediate, he said. He listened to his own guidance – and without a second thought – invited this stranger to stay on his land.

'Iokepa agreed for just one reason. His grandmothers told him to.

He moved onto four acres in Ha'iku – rainforest land owned by this man who'd offered him a place to put his tent. There were no strings attached – and that was the only way he could accept it. Over the years we both became adept at scanning an offer of housing, food, or money – looking at one another in perfect accord – and either refusing or accepting with great equanimity. It was the measure of the *kahiau* – giving from the heart, as the indigenous did, with no expectation of return.

Fred had 175 banana trees – unpicked, un-pruned, un-kempt, and overrun with rats. He owned four acres that he'd ignored for fifteen years. The *'āina* was now a free-form dump for old paint cans, broken ladders, and a half-dozen rusted lawn mowers. Fred's attention was elsewhere – he was a housepainter with a huge heart. He collected stray and crippled dogs (at last count, ten) – and he infinitely preferred their company to human.

A rare friendship was struck between Fred and 'Iokepa – and 'Iokepa set to work on clearing the jungle of God's abundance and man's waste. He would transform, by dint of sweat and a very small machete, four acres of Hawaiian *'āina*. Fred asked nothing of him – but *Ke 'I'oakua* and the grand-mothers did.

He stayed for a few days in Fred's rat infested, flea ridden, dog filled, two room home – while he built himself a platform out of scrap lumber and set a very large, old army tent that Fred donated, on top of it.

Each day that Fred went to work, 'Iokepa stayed home with the dogs. For the next two months he slogged through mud and rain. Inch by defiled inch he chipped away at the undergrowth, the banana trees, and the squalor. For 'Iokepa (for whom cleanliness was perhaps not second to Godliness) the filth of the house where he and Fred ate, showered, and occasionally watched TV was the hard part.

. . .

From the moment Nathan returned from his Dad's in West Virginia he began lobbying for a move to Maui. It intensified after 'Iokepa's visit to Kaua'i.

I was skeptical – *another* move when he was about to finish his first semester? "You'd leave Kaua'i High?"

"I want to see different places. My friends will always be my friends. I'll have friends on all the Islands."

I didn't think it was a very good idea.

When the doors closed to all County Parks on Kaua'i, Phil and Eleanor stepped up with open hands and open hearts. They genuinely saw themselves as conduits. The Creator's gifts passed through them to us. They were to support the prophecy.

Nathan and I moved into their guest wing – for a month. After that there were scheduled guests. The room was spacious, bright, immaculate, and there were distant views of the ocean from our front door. It had a queen-sized bed, a convertible sofa, a small kitchen and a full bath. We were surrounded by Eleanor's gardens.

It should have been an enormous relief – but, peculiarly, it was not. I felt trapped by the walls. I struggled to sleep in the stuffy, airless room – with all three windows open. The refrigerator hummed all night long.

I'd never had trouble falling asleep in the tent – or anywhere else in my life. But now I missed the out of doors: the sunrise, the sunset, the night sky. We no longer had beach, ocean, early morning swims. Nathan, too, felt the constraint.

We took long walks in the evening to escape the four walls. But Phil and Eleanor's home was in the heart of suburbia. As in Portland after that powerful bodywork that led to my vision of the walking dead on the streets of downtown – I could feel the 'āina smothering and grieving under the opulent houses. "It's crying," Nathan said.

"I didn't think I'd miss the Park," he told me. "But I do. I wanted a house, but not now."

I didn't want God to think us ungrateful. I was more than grateful for the hot showers, the kitchen, the food, the soft bed, and the privacy. Nathan loved the TV. Ours was an odd and unexpected ambivalence.

Now, I spoke regularly to 'Iokepa by phone. He'd call me at Phil and Eleanor's. I'd call him at Fred's. I began to feel the synchronicity and symmetry of our lives.

> *Kanaka maoli lived with the land; they built shelter from the gifts of the land. They acknowledged the 'āina, loved it, and with gratitude, used it for food and for nurture.*
>
> *Now others build houses that smother the Earth: Palaces to their egos, mausoleums to their dead spirits. They do not love the land – they conquer it and plant an edifice to their vanity.*
>
> *'Iokepa works the land to find his remembering. With you and Nathan it is offered in the opposite way. You are denied the land (the ocean, the beach, the stars), so you can feel the loss.*
>
> *Together your hearts and minds are fused for a single purpose – the release of the captive land and its people. The soul of this people is within the land – free the people, the 'āina follows.*

Paradoxically, 'Iokepa actively opposed the Nature Conservancy's plans on Maui. He added his ancient name to the document demanding an accounting of the Conservancy's pay off to the old land thieves. What the commendable, land preserving Conservancy saw as protection of native species, 'Iokepa saw as fencing native Hawaiians off their hunting and fishing lands – while padding the pockets of the old missionary, cum-sugar cane families – who no longer found growing sugar cane so profitable.

. . .

School had resumed. Each morning I dropped Nathan off at the school bus stop at 6:30 a.m. To get there, I drove past the 'No Trespassing' sign and the gates of what I now recognized as the back entrance to the National Tropical Botanical Gardens – past a semi-circular pull-off that looked out over miles of splendid gardens directly into the sunrise over the distant ocean.

Now that I lived in Kalaheo – no longer at the Salt Pans – I was too far from the Park where I'd sit in the car every sunrise and write.

So each day after I dropped Nathan at the bus, I asked the grandmothers to tell me the precise place to write that day.

On a Monday in late January, I was led to ignore the 'No Trespassing' sign, drive through the gate, and write from that spectacular lookout. It was an impressive spot – and because I was on a hillside above the gardens, I knew I was doing no harm. I realized, of course, that I was in full view of the administrators, but I believed in my unsullied innocence: I was writing the ancestors' words, and I was simply watching the sun rise.

Again on Tuesday, Wednesday and Thursday the grand-mothers sent me through that gate.

Each day a stream of pickup trucks passed behind me, heading from the main building to the gardens. I never looked up at them: I was busy writing, first in the dark, and then gradually by daylight.

On Thursday morning, I wrote: 'Why is Iokepa at Fred's?'

He is living the largest metaphor of all. He walks through garbage and he removes the remnants of one man's desecration one bucket at a time, one banana tree at a time, one blade of grass at a time. What he has done on these four acres will be done across the Earth.

The Earth will be scoured of man's desecration. What feels like a drop in the bucket (four acres, one man) is not. When the flood begins, the change accelerates. One drop spills over into a flood. One person turns around all human consciousness. You never know which drop, or which soul.

Your job and 'Iokepa's is in the trenches, face to face and hand to hand with the skeptics, the fearful, the hurt, and the angry. In freeing one person's heart, you free every person's.

On Friday, the fifth day that I parked illegally on the National Tropical Botanical Gardens land, I was confronted. One of the passing pick-up trucks pulled off the road and parked next to me. We each lowered our windows and we spoke through them. I prayed for the words.

"This is private property," the man said without a word of introduction.

"*Aloha*," I answered him. "I'm sitting here and writing. Am I harming the land?"

"My grounds crew complained."

"I have trouble imagining someone complaining because I watch the sunrise."

"This is private property."

"This is Hawaiian land – it was family land."

"Well, it's private property now."

He told me that he was the head of the grounds crew; that I was to take this up with the administration, that maybe they'd grant an exception for a writer.

I said that I had nothing to discuss with them.

He left. I stayed. My heart was racing.

You did the right thing. The intention of those who donated this land (including 'Iokepa's Uncle Gideon) was never to keep you or others off it. It was to preserve and protect.

The initial instinct of the County Parks, the state Department of Land and Natural Resources, the Nature Conservancy, and here at the Botanical Gardens was admirable: to protect the land – to keep it from the desecrators.

But that initial instinct has been perverted. Now 'protection' has come to mean fences, boundaries, and separation. It has hardened into 'rules' that imply that no one but who we permit uses it. 'We' becomes the makers of the rules of entry. This was never the plan; it must never be the way.

You will return on Monday; you will stay and write. Nothing more is necessary. We ask you to claim what is

Hawaiian from the enforcers who have forgotten. You pry open the locks for all who follow.

On Monday morning it was raining. I was back in place at the Botanical Gardens, writing to the red streaks of sunlight – my body tensed. I sat and counted. Twelve, fifteen, twenty trucks drove past me – the grounds crew on their appointed rounds. Will this be the one that stops...that one?

I wrote through the darkness, and the rain. I didn't slow down, and I didn't stop.

On Tuesday I returned – and again on Wednesday and on Thursday. It seemed pointless – or else the point had already been made. On Friday morning I felt no inclination to return. But when I asked I was told that I was to finish out the week.

This time it was different, because they'd sent Waihona, who was a *kanaka maoli* – one of the few in the employ of the Botanical Gardens and the only one in a position of authority. He was the curator of native species – and he was nobody's 'boy.' But he was native Hawaiian and because I understood a few things about that, we each got out of our vehicles, hugged *aloha*, and sat together on the retaining wall to speak.

There would be no shouting through car windows this time, no 'This is private property.' He told me his family's connection to that land. I told him 'Iokepa's family's connection. We spoke softly and gently. We did things the way indigenous Hawaiians did them.

He told me that the powers that be had watched me with increasing distress each day I'd parked there. Because I was Caucasian, they imagined I was part of some radical American environmental group. Because I claimed that this had been family land, they imagined a major subversion of their claims.

Every day, they had weighed calling the police. When things grew increasingly tense, Waihona broke through their paranoia and said he'd intervene. They were greatly relieved.

We spoke for an hour before he broached this: "The president of the Botanical Gardens would like to meet you."

When I balked because I refused to accede to bureaucratic authority, he said: "We can go to the office for a cup of coffee or tea...."

Because it was Waihona and I already felt some genuine warmth and understanding between us, I agreed.

It didn't go as well with the President. He began by insisting that I would need to apply for a special exemption as a writer. I told him I didn't see it that way. I told him this was Hawaiian land, and it was not the intention of the Creator, or Uncle Gideon – who'd been one of the founders – to close the doors to the people of the Island.

We were deadlocked.

Then, like many who'd come here before him, he tried to set Hawaiian against Hawaiian. He suggested that Waihona and 'Iokepa must be at odds over whose family had prior claim to that land.

I looked straight at Waihona and I answered. "We know better. We know that neither family owned this *'āina*. We know that our *ohana* were simply stewards of the land." Then I smiled and Waihona solemnly nodded.

I took a deep breath and I asked the ancestors for the right words.

"I'm sorry," I told the President, "that we got off on the wrong foot. I know you are doing a good job here and it is not my intention to undermine it.

"I am simply listening to the ancestors, and writing."

He breathed an audible sigh of relief, and said. "When I looked at you I saw a *haole* from the Mainland."

I heard the answer before I spoke it. "Then you didn't look deeply enough."

THE *KANAKA MAOLI*

Ignored

On one of our conversations, 'Iokepa said. "The *kanaka maoli* are already artifacts. We pride ourselves on how much stuff we can cram in a room at the Bishop Museum."

It seemed that just about everyone who had written about Hawai'i and its native people, had gotten it wrong. The archaeologists – punching random holes for the bones of 'Iokepa's ancestors (with their now discredited, but long-revered radio-carbon dating) – they'd gotten it wrong. These were a people who for thousands of years buried at sea.

The historians – using only early colonialist sources (from mercantile Captain Cook to evangelical Calvinist missionaries – each with something to sell) – they'd gotten it wrong too.

And the native people sat silently by, while what 'Iokepa calls the "Observers" made their observations – observations tainted by the *malihini* (guests') hopes, fears, mythologies, and self-interest.

Who among them came to listen? Listen, not only to the indigenous people, but also to every element of Creation that the indigenous people listened to: the 160 words for the wind, 138 words for the rain. *Kūkulu ka 'ike i ka 'ōpua.* (There is knowledge – there are answers – in the clouds.) Every subtle difference in rain, wind or cloud deserved a name of its own – each one was the answer to a prayer. Ask and you will receive. But you must ask – and you must listen too for the answer.

To be an observer was to be removed from – outside of – that knowing. To be out of touch with what the *kanaka maoli* saw, heard and felt with every breath. But that didn't keep those observers from claiming knowledge superior to that which resided in the heart of the culture – and then, enforcing that claim with technology: the print press and the written word. And because they had the written word, they were able to persuade themselves and others (but never the native people) that theirs was the truth.

"God is here!" the *kanaka maoli* told the first missionaries – and then exhaled. God, of course, was in their breath.

"No!" the missionaries with big black Bible in hand refused them. "God is here!" They rapped their book. Unknowingly, they named themselves.

For then and forever after, white men and women were to Hawaiians *ha'ole*, the people without the breath.

The truth was far different than the written page represented it – Bible or history book. The truth, again and again, eluded the observers who stood behind their insular walls: fenced plantations, gated communities, schools and universities – then and now. Clothed in their Western certainties, they misread the soul of a people they lived among but not *with* – and of a land they built their palaces on but could not speak to.

In 1778 Captain James Cook brought unknown European disease to the healthiest people in the world – and killed three out of four Hawaiians within fifty years. Three out of four mothers, brothers, daughters, fishermen, farmers, priests – those links in the chain of human genealogy and orally transmitted history – dead within a single human lifespan.

They said these are not even a people in their own right – but derivative – settlers of these Islands from other places: Tahiti, Micronesia, New Zealand. *They* said they've occupied these Islands for less than 2000 years. *They* called these people warriors. *They* celebrated their brutal puppet King Kamehameha as the great unifier of the Islands. For 112 years they've told themselves that these Islands belong to the United States. They see all things through the filter of European mythology – which they call *ideology*. (Because only the primitives live by *myth*.) They hear words spoken only in their own tongue. *They* believe, exclusively, only what they can read in books.

. . .

On every one of the Hawaiian Islands, there are *heiau* – sacred sites aligned always with the migration of the stars and moon. At each of these sited *heiau*, stonewalls were constructed (without use of mortar) and many (that have not yet been bulldozed for hotel and timeshare construction) remain these thousands of years later. At these sanctified *heiau* a different hula and chant was offered every night, in accord with the successive phases of the moon. At most heiau, there were two towers (the earliest telescopes wrapped in bark cloth with reflective bowls of sea water at the bottom) to observe the transit of the sun in one – the moon, stars and planets in the other. The *heiau* were the places of high ritual, prayer, ceremony, and observation.

On the Island of Kaua'i alone, there was a consecutive string of thirty-seven *heiau* – a necklace of holy sites that began at the *muliwai* (mouth) of the Wailua River, and climbed with the river to the top of the volcanic mountain, Waialeale. This was the birthing place of the Hawaiian people – and more. All of Polynesia was born here.

At odds with the latter-day accounts of the origins of the Hawaiian people – the *kanaka maoli* know. On every other Island in Polynesia – from one edge of the Pacific to the other, as far away as the Maori in New Zealand – the aboriginal people *know*.

Still throughout the Pacific Ocean, the native peoples repeat the original chant. They chant the celestial navigation (their voyaging map by sea) with only stars for guidance – that tells them exactly how to return to their birthplace at the mouth of the Wailua River. Only on Hawai'i has the chant been abandoned – because this is home.

For thousands of years the original Hawaiians journeyed in their remarkably sophisticated voyaging canoes throughout the Pacific, carrying with them the chant – their map – for the return trip, home.

Hawaiian canoes were built for a single trip – in the direction of the current, deeply V-ed or flat bottomed, depending on destination. Sailing on them they populated the Pacific Islands to faraway Australia and New Zealand.

The chants were the sacred stories, studied, memorized, and passed down to the destined child in every family – the oral tradition was essential and sacrosanct. There was no room for confusion. Sometimes hundreds of years passed before return voyagers followed the map again to the Wailua. But they did, and over thousands of years the family returned and integrated into the existing culture.

. . .

One thousand years ago, all that has transpired in modern Hawai'i was prophesized. Prophesized: the oppression that predated Captain Cook by more than 400 years.

The first foreign colonizers were not European. *Kapu* (taboo) was a political system that arrived in Hawai'i in 1320 – under an autocrat by the name of Pa'ao, from Tahiti. Threatened with death in his homeland, he followed the well-worn chant charting the distance to the birthplace – to the place of compliant people who could imagine no resistance to his ambition.

With a flotilla of armed warriors (selected in part for their seven-foot height), the high Chief Pa'ao and his lieutenant Pili sailed for Lāhui. To an egalitarian people, he brought hierarchy – he established a monarchy, nobility, and a slave class to serve them. He brought gender stratification – the powerful Hawaiian women were separated, humiliated, demeaned. To Eden, he brought war. What Pa'ao brought to the Hawaiian Islands was tyranny and foreign domination. Only the missionaries and their adherents, adding insult to injury, would later call this brutality 'Hawaiian.' It made it easier to convince themselves that these benighted heathens needed saving.

But forty years before the arrival of those missionaries – the people of Lāhui, still suffocating under that enslavement – met their first white man. Captain James Cook, his crew, and the increasingly debauched European sailors who followed him brought unimaginable diseases that wiped out three-quarters of all living *kanaka maoli* in fifty years.

It was then, 500 years after it was imposed, that *Kapu* collapsed under the weight of its own cruelty. The irony was that just a single day after liberation – a divided, frightened, confused, and *dying* Lāhui received their first Christian missionaries. The English and New England Calvinists arrived brandishing an austere, judgmental brand of Christianity – and their corrupted version of Hawaiian history.

And that, perhaps, was the greatest violation of all. Not the laws that incarcerated and murdered the holders of the knowing; that closed down the ritual and prayer; that refused these people even their own names. The greatest violation was the silencing of another people's story. They came, they shut down the native voices, and they wrote their own version of 'Iokepa's family's story. But ignoring the truth does not make it go away.

The Hawaiian Prophecy – held deep in the hearts of these people and their living culture – flicks the speck that was *Kapu*, missionary oppression, and now the greedy raping of their precious *'āina* from their 13,000 year history. Their sacred knowing was passed down all those many years inside the *oli* (chants), the *mo'okū'auhau* (genealogy), and the *mo'olelo* (history) from destined child to destined child.

For 150 years the original people of Lāhui have been silenced. Silenced by the Europeans and Americans who assigned no value and who refused to hear. Silenced finally by shame.

Yet, that which has been endured was purposeful. It had been prophesized that when the *kanaka maoli* remember fully who they are, they will once again be free. They will live once more – as a flame in the shadows for all of mankind – what their ancestors lived before the successive tyrannies. The separation, the shame, the denial, and the deaths were but prologue to the coming together with forgiveness.

"But there can be no forgiveness," 'Iokepa said with conviction. "Until we address what needs to be forgiven. Until we acknowledge the true history, we cannot forgive."

FLOATING

1999: February

In early February, I persistently heard the call: *Maui*. And it was not only from Nathan. I heard it, felt it – and in truth, I feared it.

I very much wanted to live with 'Iokepa again. But I feared a move to Maui on Nathan's behalf. He was doing so well on Kaua'i. Nathan argued, "My confidence is in myself now – not my clothes."

I anguished. School? House? Car? Where? When?

Without saying a word to one another that implied a decision, Nathan and I began preparing. We went to storage and began emptying once again. I gave my fax machine away. He gave his computer to a friend. He packed up three boxes for the Salvation Army; I packed one. I gave away clothing that had never been out of the box since Portland: an umbrella, two baseball gloves, and a bat. *What* had I been thinking? This time, the emptying felt clean and good.

Then the ancestors resolved the uncertainty for me. I was to leave the Camry for Eleanor's use; forward all mail to General Delivery on Maui; keep the rest of our things in storage.

I asked, "For how long?"

I heard: *At least until Nathan finishes the school year.*

'Iokepa intended to make good on last year's promise. "We will never again be apart on Valentine's Day." Although I had a past that was checkered with missed chances and hurt feelings around this silly holiday, I was touched by his sentiment. He planned a five day visit to Kaua'i – then back to Fred's. I hadn't yet shared what I'd heard from the ancestors. He had no idea we'd be returning with him to Maui.

When I finally told him, I could hear his reluctance on the phone. He was anticipating Fred's reaction to our move – and my reaction to Fred's house. Nevertheless, 'Iokepa would never second-guess the grandmothers.

There was really very little preparation required when we travelled with only what we could carry on a thirty minute airplane flight. Only our beach chairs counted as 'excess baggage,' but we weren't charged for them. An inter-island flight at the time cost $25. Phil and Eleanor donated the tickets.

. . .

Fred's house was filthy. There wasn't an upholstered chair I could sit on without a conscious act of will. The wet dog smell and the fleas were oppressive. The kitchen was thick with rat droppings – the stove was encrusted, *all* the dishes were left unwashed. Ten squalid dog dishes were scattered across the floor of the two rooms.

Fred was generous, if taciturn to the extreme. 'Iokepa insisted that Fred had been transformed by my pending arrival: that the entire inside of the house had been painted before we'd arrived, the wooden floors had been scrubbed – 'Iokepa found the new Fred downright chatty. I could only imagine what preceded my arrival.

The man was lavishly talkative only to the dogs. I took to cooking dinner for all of us when he returned from work, trying to clean the kitchen a bit – but Fred refused to eat with us. He'd eat whatever I prepared, later, in front of the TV. He'd come home, roll a fat joint, walk the dogs down the dirt road to the edge of a cliff that faced the ocean, smoke the joint, return and feed them – all before he'd eat himself.

If Fred noticed the miracles that 'Iokepa was performing on his untended piece of land he never mentioned them. He ate dinner without comment. But his heart was big. He was a sucker for strays. Words just weren't his way.

The rain pounded unceasingly in those first weeks in Ha'iku. Our tent leaked badly. But it was the tent – or the two-room, rat infested, flea ridden house. Every morning we awakened to pools of water. There was no sun to dry the wet linens or clothes so we went to bed wet as well. 'Iokepa was like a man possessed, trying to make that flat-roofed decrepit army tent waterproof. Finally, he succeeded.

We rented a car one week at a time and put it on my American Express card – the last remaining credit card to my name.

We showed Nathan the Island. I took him to three of the four high schools while 'Iokepa continued to clear the land. But I enrolled him in none of them because we didn't know where we'd live – and we didn't know how he'd get to school.

Nathan didn't object to an unauthorized couple weeks off between semesters, but he grew tired of our company and of the future's uncertainty. He told us that we could no longer call him *Nathan*. On Maui he had become *Nat*.

"My Natey boy," I reminisced.

"*Our* Natey boy in Hawai'i," 'Iokepa amended.

'Iokepa was trying hard to make a place for Nathan and me in his life on Maui. He built a separate but equal wooden platform for Nathan's tent and chair. He scrubbed down Fred's crude bathroom, and strung a protective tarp where there'd been no door. He brought pineapple juice to the tent for me every morning. I knew we brought changes that weren't entirely welcome.

So when 'Iokepa asked me why I hadn't been writing, and prodded: "Would you mind asking something for me?" I jumped at the chance.

We'd both seen spirits, and auras around certain people at certain times. "Why weren't they accessible to us all the time?" he asked.

Gifts are given only as needed. Not for parlor games to impress others. Only for purpose: to add to human understanding. Seeing and feeling them is secondary to purpose.

The mountains move whether or not we take note. The stone is tossed in the water; there are ripples; the

Earth turns. Know that and trust it even when you can't see the magic.

What you ask for is not cloaked in secrecy. It is there whether or not you are aware of it. Sometimes you see the unfolding. Other times, your attention is elsewhere – as it must be.

'Iokepa grappled, too, with how to tell other *kanaka maoli* that what they'd been taught about their history and culture was wrong – that even the language they spoke had been drastically distorted.

He does not make them wrong. He simply presents a new understanding of what is true, and they will see the light of the new truth. As always, some will accept and some will not. But there is no way in heaven or on Earth that he can speak other than the words we give him to speak.

. . .

At the end of February, 'Iokepa and I took a day for ourselves. Nat had already decided to hitchhike twenty miles to town and go to the Mall. I understood his need for a fix of consumer culture – and time alone.

We drove through the unknown, up-country villages circling the dormant volcano. Then we passed a small country church that literally yanked 'Iokepa in. It was the memorial church to Father Damien.

Father Damien Joseph de Veuster was a Belgian Catholic priest who in 1873 swam ashore to Kalawao, the isolated leper colony on the Island of Moloka'i. There, the sick and suspected sick *kanaka maoli* from every Island were deposited – without family or friend, water or shelter – to die. Once a week, a boat delivered food. It was tossed ashore without human contact.

That story is known. But there is another.

Kalawao was Auschwitz for the native Hawaiians. It was the site of a holocaust committed against healthy *kanaka maoli* who refused to accept the Western customs, laws, and dogma. These were the political lepers.

These intransigents were falsely identified as diseased and given a choice: enforced exodus to Kalawao, or death by gunshot and burial in a pit on O'ahu. Hundreds of indigenous Hawaiians were buried in the pit. Thousands died the slower death at the leper colony.

Father Damien volunteered to go to Kalawao. He devoted his life to turning this deprived – if beautiful – corner of Moloka'i into a thriving community. He was a courageous and outspoken advocate for these people. He died there in 1883 – of leprosy.

Last September on Moloka'i, 'Iokepa looked over the cliffs into the valley that was Kalawao and cried.

Five months later, now on Maui, 'Iokepa swerved our rental car, cutting a sharp and sudden left into the parking lot of this enticing country church. There were three other cars parked there – all identical to ours – white Chevrolet Cavaliers.

We walked tentatively into the Catholic Church. Three tourist-couples – one with a video camera – scattered toward the back. Without exchanging a single word, we walked up the center aisle together and faced the altar.

'Iokepa looked straight ahead – his strong back to the pews – and visibly gulped down emotion. Silently he asked for the words.

He looked over his shoulder then, but I did not – and he saw the seemingly empty pews filled to capacity with ancestral spirits. He knew then that they had been waiting for him. He was in awe of that expectation.

His words rang as loud as a church bell, and as true. At top volume and with rich inflection, he called our Creator by his Hawaiian name.

He chanted three times: *"Mahalo Ke 'I'oakua..."*

The words shook the gothic arches, and reverberated through my feet.

He intoned the genealogical chant – his *mo'okū'auhau* – commencing six generations back, and tracing the maternal and paternal lines to his own birth. It was the ritual of introduction.

"*Ho'omaika'i* (blessings) to Father Damien for his love of our people – and to the ancestors of Maui who fill these pews. I am humbled by your presence.

"We are asked to live *kaupalena 'ole 'ia huikala* (unconditional forgiveness); *kaupalena 'ole 'ia mana'o'io* (unconditional faith); and *kaupalena 'ole 'ia 'ano'i* (unconditional love)."

He spoke interchangeably in English and Hawaiian, for five minutes. I stood stock still at his side until the last of the syllables ricocheted off the ceiling.

The last ones were "grandmothers, grandfathers, *'uhane* (spirits) of this land, *mahalo* for the prophecy.

"*Aloha.*"

Into the continuing vibration I repeated, "*Mahalo...aloha.*"

We turned, and slowly made our way down the center aisle. I felt the solemnity and the glow, like a bride. But I was aware, too, of the tourists transfixed and reverent – and of a video camera on one man's shoulder still running.

. . .

By February the whales had migrated south to Hawai'i. They returned annually to the warm Island waters to breed until spring.

Hawaiians never killed whales. "On the ocean, we were guests of the whales – they were the hosts," 'Iokepa said. "The whales took care of the voyagers – wind or no wind."

The *kanaka maoli* of Lāhui voyaged in highly-developed outrigger canoes with crab-claw shaped *lauhala* sails. They followed the migration of the whales to the top and to the bottom of the Americas.

It was a one-way trip. The very best of the *kahuna* journeyed to plant the seed of their culture's *aloha* among the natives of North America and South America. They stayed and integrated into that existing culture.

In the American Northwest, mountains, rivers and towns still bear their ancient Hawaiian names. Native American tribes, even now, repeat the story of 'the people who came from the sea.'

"At the time of Creation," 'Iokepa said "the whales were charged with taking care of the oceans. The humans were to *mālama ka 'āina* – take care of the land. The whales have done their job – we have forgotten ours."

Since I had arrived on Kaua'i that first Christmas, I'd heard a steady stream of stories about the magic of the *koholā* (humpbacked whales). As much as I yearned, I'd never seen one.

Now on Maui I saw them first at a distance in front of the hotels in Lahaina. I watched an entire beach population converted from apathetic vacationing sunbathers to rigidly alert whale watchers. The creatures transformed humans.

At first, I saw their far off spouts like drinking fountains gone berserk. Then I saw the creatures breaching – their slick, mammoth, black bodies arching above the water, sailing through the air with the grace of a hummingbird. Still, they were at a great distance.

Later, I went into the water, submerged my head, and eavesdropped on their conversations with one another. I could easily recognize the differences between their voices. Floating on the vibration of whale songs, I lost sight of where or who I was. My body and mind slid easily to some other universe. Only when I was beached – my back scraped against the sandy bottom – did I awaken to the dream that was our separate human life. I staggered to my feet. I had to reorient myself to even walk again.

Finally, days later, I saw them up close – for an hour. It was late in the afternoon and we were waiting on the beach at Kihei for the sunset. The whales – more than a dozen – came within forty feet of us and performed their dance for what seemed an eternity. I sprawled on my stomach on the sand, transfixed. I'd experienced nothing like this unity – human and other mammal – in my lifetime.

> *Many humans, being near the whale – seeing the spout, the breach, or hearing the songs – are roused to full memory of who we are, what we have promised, and how far we have strayed.*
>
> *The whales are the irrefutable living example. The whales live what man promised. Man cannot help but feel that in their awesome presence. We think we are moved*

only by the sight of a massive mammal. Instead we are moved by the honesty of the life lived. They live faithful to their promise of unconditional compassion – even for their tormentors.

Whales live what we forgot. They love us regardless of the violence we do them. They vibrate at a level of utter consistency with remembering that promise.

They remind us to root out anger the second we feel it. When we remain vigilant, it will become easy.

It was almost a joke, that first year – but it wasn't. Whenever I'd say to 'Iokepa: 'I've never been happier.' He would answer, 'Uh oh!' Our best times were often followed by our worst.

After two weeks at Fred's – still glowing from the sacraments at Father Damien's church, still alive to our sublime connection with the whales – we stumbled. I hadn't seen it coming.

It seemed to me that 'Iokepa had been stalling at Fred's. There was no end to the demand of the land – even when Nat and I pitched in and hauled branches and cuttings to the massive bonfires. 'Iokepa still waited for direction.

I badgered him. "When would my son be back in school?"

Nat had become increasingly unhappy and rootless without friends. I felt powerless to do a thing about it.

I do not remember the words I spoke to 'Iokepa – but I know they were profane, and I know they found their target. I *do* remember what he said – and it cut me to the quick. "This was a trial couple of weeks. We didn't make it." What I'd seen as forever, he'd seen as provisional? I refused to hear to another word. I would not allow him to explain.

At midnight, I decided I could no longer sleep next to a man who thought that all we'd been through was a *trial* – who wanted me gone – in the morning. Instead, in the pitch blackness – tripping over roots, stumps, and branches – Nat and I rolled up his tent, his sleeping bag, packed my possessions, and filled the trunk of the rental car. We drove to the end of the little road by the cliff, and slept in the car.

I was *very* angry.

I wrote that night. "Thank you for these fourteen months with 'Iokepa. But our words that soothe one another's soul, three days out of four – on the fourth day are poison to each other's ears and hearts. We live the wars of mankind, unable to head them off. We live the opposite of what you teach."

The rental car was due back in the morning. Our possessions filled the trunk of the car. Nat and I had thirty-five cents between us and $20 in the checking account on Kaua'i. Our options were pretty limited. Should we return the car and sit in the airport surrounded by our stuff – awaiting a miracle?

At first light, Nat and I talked. He poured out his heart and I grieved, filled with unspeakable remorse.

"I feel weak when you two fight and I can't defend my mother," he said.

"...You're the one who always apologizes...."

"I don't see you as strong as I once did."

His words were excruciating to hear, but I valued them to my soul. I didn't try to defend myself. I allowed him the freedom to speak his worst – it was all I could do for him at the moment. That, and love him.

We headed for the airport. I asked out loud. "Should I call the rental office and keep the car for another week?" The moment the question was out of my mouth we passed the very rare, rural public phone. I stopped, paid thirty-five cents, called Alamo and asked them to extend the car rental for a third week. I had no idea how I'd pay my American Express bill at the end of the month.

We drove from the rain in Ha'iku towards the sunshine on the south end of the Island. Then we sat all morning in a park fronting the ocean in Kihei, until we got hungry. I went into Foodland and bought sandwich fixings enough for lunch and dinner – maybe breakfast the next morning, a newspaper for the classified housing ads, and some irresistibly self-indulgent strawberries. I wrote a check that emptied the checking account.

Nat and I spent the night sleeping – stiff necks, bent backs – in the car near Keone'o'io. We felt like leaves in the wind. There was a bruise on my left bicep where 'Iokepa had inadvertently grabbed me in the dark tent in his attempted farewell. It stoked my rage.

When I'd told 'Iokepa that I would *never* return, he gloated. "You won't feel that way in a few days." What I heard as his final cockiness hardened my resolve.

I trusted only God and the ancestors. I asked that night – and I was told – Nat and I must stay on Maui. We were not to bail out to Kaua'i.

I agreed, but I required something of them in return. "Your help (as the grandmothers had advised me) *'to root out my anger,'* your help that I *'remain vigilant against it'*."

The next morning, Monday, I'd planned to follow up on house rentals in the paper, but I had no money to make phone calls, let alone pay rent. We showered in the public park in Kihei and sat in the sun waiting for guidance. Each plan I concocted fizzled before I could take the first step.

Finally at noon, I decided to drive to Kahului, the largest town on Maui – halfway between Fred's land to the northeast and Kihei to the south – with what gas remained in the tank. Nat wanted to browse the skateboard shops. I wanted to do something nice for Nat.

Nat quickly tired of my hanging around him in the store – so I took the hint and walked away. With the heavy glass door swinging closed behind me, I looked left at the expanse of shopping center sameness: Eagle Hardware, Office Depot, Sports Authority...and I saw 'Iokepa walking at me, on a collision course not twelve feet away. I froze.

What were the chances – on an Island the size of Maui, in front of a skateboard shop, two days after we'd bitterly parted – that we'd be staring into one another's face again? What was he doing here? What was I?

Short of returning to Fred's – I couldn't have imagined how we'd ever meet again. I was positive I'd never return there. But the grandmothers had their own plan – and it left me breathless.

I stood stock still and watched his familiar face close in on me. Miraculously, that was all it took. We exchanged no smiles, but the plug on my rage dislodged and the hurt simply drained out of me. We hugged effortlessly.

"The grandmothers told me that I had to leave Fred's today," he said. "I had no idea why. They said: *What you are looking for will not come to you here.*

"Fred was driving to town. I got a lift."

Within fifteen minutes of our implausible meeting and our unlikely healing (without budging from that spot) 'Iokepa sold a *puka* shell *lei* for $100. It was only the beginning of a week of wonders.

On Tuesday, after 'Iokepa picked up his belongings from Fred's, we headed west to the town of Lahaina. I felt the push in that direction, and 'Iokepa honored it. But as we arrived in Lahaina, it was he who said, "We're turning here."

We drove two miles up a steep hill. It ended surprisingly for all of us at Lahainaluna, the last of the four public high schools on Maui and by far the smallest. But in this case the last was first. A sign read, 'Founded in 1831.'

The oldest high school west of the Rockies – a boarding *and* day school – set on 500 acres of native species gardens with incredible views of town and ocean. It counted among its alumnae roster the most accomplished *kanaka maoli* from all the Islands.

We knew none of this.

Nat sat in the back of the car, sullen. He was still seething from 'Iokepa and my last fight – and its inexplicable resolution. He resolutely refused to walk inside the fourth school we'd inspected in two and a half weeks. 'Iokepa and I went in alone.

Everything fell into place. There was no question that this was the school.

The registrar was gracious – unlike the other three we'd visited – helpful and astute. She listened avidly to 'Iokepa's words and to mine. She waved her hand and made the paperwork go away, the transfer a piece-of-cake, and the fact that we had no address in the district, inconsequential. She hand-picked Nathan's teachers – and she did a fine job of it.

Nat would begin school on Thursday. I had written on the legal pad only the night before: *First Nat's school, then a place to live.*

Nat was not pleased that the decision had been made while he sat in the car. He let us know that he felt betrayed.

The town of Lahaina was nobody's first choice place to live. The upcountry was more natural, Kahului or Wailuku more convenient. But Lahaina was where Nathan's new school was – not the other three. Lahaina had once been a shipping town – transformed now into a shrine to tourism. The main street boasted a Hard Rock Café, Planet Hollywood, and Bubba Gump's. It couldn't be further from its indigenous Hawaiian roots. 'Iokepa called it the 'first raped.' He said we were there because it was where the work is.

On Maui, you could drive for miles and go for days, weeks, or months without seeing a *kanaka maoli*. On Maui, all things Hawaiian were relegated to the remote town of Hana. It was how the glut of Caucasians viewed things native – 'over in Hana.' Hana was at the end of a winding, narrow, sublimely beautiful, two-hour drive from any other population center. In that way, *Hawaiian* became the name of a theme park.

We slept on Monday and Tuesday in the car. On Wednesday, I prayed hard for a proper room and shower from which Nathan might begin his first day of school. By evening it looked grim. We'd had fish sandwiches at McDonald's; we were standing next to the car. I was propelled (as I'd been pushed through the trees at Keone'o'io last Christmas) to cross the street to two blonde women straddling bicycles and talking.

"Do you know an inexpensive place to spend the night?"

They mentioned a hostel down the street. Then on second thought after they'd already pulled away from the curb, one of them turned around. "The Fountains," she said. "It's up the hill."

We drove higher and higher up the hill and found it. I could not imagine what the blonde bicyclist had been thinking. The Fountains was an opulent Bed and Breakfast with ocean views, swimming pool, and three lavish suites. After dinner at McDonald's, we had $40 left from the *lei* that sold on Monday.

For an hour 'Iokepa told his story to the rapt manager. Nat waited alone in the car listening to his Discman. 'Iokepa offered the manager a *lei* in exchange for the suite for the night. She wouldn't hear of it.

"Just take the room," she insisted, embarrassed that a price had ever been mentioned.

So Nat spent the night before his first day of school in his own bedroom. He had a double bed and a down comforter. I closed his door, turned off the light, and sat on the edge of his bed as I'd done every single night since he was a toddler – exchanging thoughts, fears and dreams, stories and songs. I smoothed his hair, and kissed him goodnight. I'm not sure which of us missed these private moments more.

I drove Nat to school the next morning and returned to a Lazy Susan full of breakfast fixings on a huge round table, across from the other guests. The manager deeply regretted that she couldn't offer us another night gratis – they were booked solid. 'Iokepa insisted that she choose a *lei,* and she finally did. She looked radiant.

Nat, too, was beaming after his first day at school.

The period of grace that sustained us – beginning with our encounter in Kahului – ended with The Fountains. But none of us knew it at the time. We had tents, we would camp. After these days of visible wonders, we were all full of renewed faith.

Over the next three days 'Iokepa acquainted dozens of people with our story. Each one sent us to – what they insisted would be – a wealth of Lahaina church support. The pillars of the local Christian community, we were told, were zealous supporters of the native culture.

The first church woman, acclaimed for her ardent cultural sensitivities, owned a modest hotel. It looked close to empty. Her husband (whom we met first) assured us there were all kinds of long-term rates available. The wife, however, took one look at 'Iokepa's now quite long silver hair and his brown Hawaiian skin and said. "No. No! There is no way I can help you. Try the Hawaiian Church – they give charity."

Before I had moved to Hawai'i, the grandmothers had instructed 'Iokepa to return his thick, shining silver hair to the old ways. He had had his last haircut. The hair would be a recognizable symbol. By now the wavy hair fell well past his shoulder blades – and it was the rare day when some man or woman didn't admire his beautiful hair. He answered always, "It's cultural."

'Iokepa and I smiled at one another after we left the church-woman's hotel. The lesson was invaluable. *Charity* we understood was the snub. There was no word in the Hawaiian language for *charity* because it implied the unthinkable: "I have. You do not."

The second stop was at a Christian church hostel run by a native Hawaiian. We were asked just one question. "Are you married?"

'Iokepa answered: "No, we are more than that."

"Then you can't stay here."

We smiled again at one another. This time we recalled Mary on the night of Jesus' birth.

Our third try was the Episcopal Church camp outside of Lahaina. We'd be welcome there we were told, if we paid a stiff per person per night fee that would wipe out our remaining funds in one night. But at the suggestion of another camper, we set up our tents well beyond the borders of their campground. We were out of sight on a huge tract of former sugar cane land that had been recently sold, and was still two years away from a luxury housing development.

The manager of the Episcopal camp was pretty determined. She tore her nylons and scratched her legs climbing under branches of the thorny *kiawe* trees to get to us. She marched over at sunset and glared at our tents, her hands welded to her hips.

"I'll have to report you to the owners," she said. "Are you squatting on this land?"

Months later, the word 'squatting' still stuck in 'Iokepa's craw. "A *malihini* asking a *kanaka maoli* if he is 'squatting' Hawaiian land," he seethed. "They've forgotten who the guests are."

The fourth church was something called Hawaiian-Christian. The Christian minister was a *kanaka maoli* – an ex convict who ministered to other convicts. He ran a free hostel.

He heard 'Iokepa's story with genuine respect – perhaps awe. The following Sunday, we learned, he delivered a heartfelt sermon on 'Iokepa and the prophecy.

But he offered nothing except his incipient fear that 'Iokepa would settle in Lahaina – which was, after all, his own ministerial turf. There was no room for a Hawaiian *kahu.*

Of the Christianity that had enveloped the Hawaiian Islands, 'Iokepa said: "Jesus was one of the greatest *kahuna* who ever lived. But we had our own. The grandmothers are adamant. The doors will not open until we remember and embrace our own."

Because beach camping was illegal on Maui, we were forced to set up our tents at sundown and roll them up again every morning before we drove Nat to school. It was tedious at the end of a long hot day – and it was frantic every morning before the school bell rang.

We camped either ten miles east of Lahaina in Papalaua Wayside or fifteen miles west at Windmills – both exquisite oceanfront beaches with shade trees. But the wind was so strong at both that the tent stakes would pull out of the soft sand, and as often as not, we'd chase the flapping nylon down the beach.

There was no place closer. We'd awaken to my travel alarm while it was still dark, knock down the tents, head eight miles to the nearest shower and bathroom, stop at Safeway for orange juice, bagels and cream cheese – then drop Nat at school.

On weekends we had the liberty of camping further away on the south end of the Island toward Keone'o'io. But the drill was the same: put up tents, take them down. Sometimes we'd set up only Nat's tent; 'Iokepa and I would sleep in the car. Sometimes we'd put our tent up; Nat would sleep under the stars on his foam mat and sleeping bag. He preferred it to the car – sometimes to his tent as well. It depended on our mood and the weather on any given night.

We spent the weekdays, while Nat was at school, in Lahaina. It was consistently hot, dry and windless. 'Iokepa would spread his *lei* on a stone retaining wall against the ocean, diagonal from the Hard Rock Café. The *lei* were the magnet to his stories.

He began by describing what the *puka* shell represented to his culture. "They're the bones of a living entity. Like ours, they carry the energy after we're gone." He'd segue into true history, genuine culture – always at odds with what the visitors and locals had already read. Sometimes, but certainly not always, he'd speak of prophecy. Occasionally, he'd retell our own story – the prophesized *ten years of grooming.*

Now, of course, 'Iokepa introduced himself as a *kahu.* "A guardian of the *kanaka maoli* history, culture, and religion," he said.

People would ask, "Where's your church?"

He'd answer, "You're standing in it. All of God's creation is my church. Hawaiians didn't need a building for prayer."

Some were mystified, but most were delighted.

Every day, we expected a permanent solution to our camping needs – or a house. Each day we picked up Nat at school with no news and no *lei* sold. I remembered the grandmother's words – *expectation leads to disappointment.*

But my son was sinking under this arrangement. I, too, was worn pretty thin. 'Iokepa increasingly shouldered the responsibility of keeping the faith for all three of us.

Without gas money or food money, the show was grinding to a halt. The ancestors had insisted since we arrived on Maui that we were to dip into Nat's inviolable *bar mitzvah* and birthday fund. This $8000 had been socked away for college – or for whatever Nat chose to blow it on when he graduated high school. It had been gift money from grandparents, uncles, and other relatives since birth – plus the big *bar mitzvah* cash bonanza.

Ben was living on his now.

Repeatedly, I'd heard:

> *Money is to use, not hoard. It will come back to him – in full. He learns in the giving. Your resistance, and 'Iokepa's, are natural – it is about integrity. But you live your integrity every day. It is not an issue.*

But it was not *my* money. Nat, nevertheless, was eager to spend it if it secured him a room where his friends could visit.

The first $20 was the hardest. Up to $300, 'Iokepa and I kept scrupulous records of what we *owed* Nat. But we had to eat; we had to put gas in the car. We'd long since traded the Alamo rental for an Island wreck at a very modest monthly rate. Our 1987 Buick Skylark wasn't pretty – it had no paint and the automatic windows were a sometimes proposition – but it ran well.

For 'Iokepa, spending Nat's money was particularly demoralizing.

For a solid week, we searched for an apartment. But even with the money, we were blocked at every turn. We were living it seemed, exactly as we were supposed to be living – whether we liked it or not.

It didn't get easier. Nat felt abandoned by his faith – though he didn't put it in those words. Essentially our boy felt that God was not delivering. Undoubtedly he held me – and 'Iokepa – culpable too. He was desperately unhappy. I was desperately unhappy on his behalf.

One weekend morning at Keone'o'io, Nat was torn out of sound sleep and sweet dreams by two large, surly men with badges, officers from the state Department of Land and Natural Resources. They stood over the fifteen year old boy, fast asleep on his foam mat in his sleeping bag, and bellowed.

"Get up. You don't belong here!"

Asleep inside our car, 'Iokepa heard and immediately intervened. The officers climbed back into their mile-high truck and shouted at us when they left, "Clean up this mess!"

The place we'd parked was scattered with beer bottles, cigarette buts and condoms – from months, maybe years of misuse. I'd already filled a bag with beer bottles the night before. But to add insult to injury, the paid protectors of the *'āina* couldn't bend down to *mālama* it. It was beneath them.

The shock of being awakened by burly enforcers was like walking into your home and finding it had been rifled by thieves – underwear scattered all over the floor. I'd experienced both in my lifetime and the feeling was exactly the same: violation. I knew Nat was quaking – because I was too.

We all felt, for the first time, genuinely homeless. We were eating far too much greasy fast food – undercooked Kentucky Fried Chicken was the final indignity. We each had expectations that hadn't been met, but our disappointment played out in different ways.

'Iokepa was displacing his – fuming at petty things – a lost sock in the laundry. "Fred turns my clothes brown, and you lose them."

Nat hated himself. He demanded, for the first time in his life, to live with his father. He bought a calling card and phoned his father begging for a reprieve.

For my part, I was swamped by guilt on behalf of my child – and on my own account, I felt lost. I could remember neither who I was nor why I was here.

We were pulling in different directions. It couldn't stay stuck like this. Something had to give.

Standing one morning next to the public restroom while Nathan showered, a lovely, middle-aged Hawaiian woman walked up to me, smiled a beatific *aloha*, and without introduction or prelude she said, "You sometimes wonder what comes next. I'm here to tell you, you're on the right track." That was it. She left, as she had arrived.

Twice in the next week 'Iokepa earnestly apologized to me. "I *am* sorry."

'Iokepa grew more handsome to me – more naturally who he already was. *Kanaka maoli* and locals of every age and gender were greeting him – hailing him in some kind of subliminal recognition. It had been happening around us, without seeming to happen.

> *All of Lahaina is sacred potential. There are places to go and people to meet.*

In the face of Nat's increasing bitterness – "I hate you" an every day epithet – I was desperate. I made a deal.

"I love you Nat," I told him. "We've lived together all your life and I want to live with you until you finish school.

"But I'm willing to make a pact with you. You commit to finish the school year on Maui – without a complaint. At the end of the summer – after your visit to Dad – if you choose to stay, I'll send your school records there.

"But I'm buying you a round trip ticket and I'll expect you home – unless I hear otherwise in August."

He wholeheartedly agreed. Remarkably, from the moment we made our deal and shook on it – his unhappiness dissipated. He had friends; he had a fantastic science teacher who motivated him; and he took up skateboarding with a vengeance.

I took Nat to the State Department of Motor Vehicles to get his driver's permit. We needed a certified copy of Nat's birth certificate (from West Virginia), a certified copy of his social security number (from the federal government), and a Xerox copy of his parents' thirteen-year-old divorce decree proving custody.

There was a third-world quality to the Hawaiians state bureaucracy. It was both absurdly rigid – and infinitely corruptible.

We had ordered and assembled all parts of the required documentation in four months – ever since we'd been turned away on Kaua'i. This time, it had to be a breeze. Nat had studied his driver's manual for the written test. He was itching to drive.

I handed the stack of papers to the woman behind the desk. She disappeared, and then returned. "You need a certified – not a Xeroxed – copy of the divorce decree."

"That's not what they told me on Kaua'i."

"Well, it's what we tell you here."

"Okay," I snatched back the paperwork. "Let's start over. I'm not divorced. Now what?"

Nathan did not get his permit.

We settled finally, though quite illegally, deep in the *kiawe* trees at Papalaua Wayside – invisible from the road and from much else. The ocean was our front window and we were protected from the wind. 'Iokepa cleared the thick accumulation of two-inch *kiawe* thorns off the ground. We set up three tents: Nat's, ours, and 'Iokepa's small one for storage – we strung a hammock. We'd built ourselves a home.

I'm not sure what turned the trick. I think we simply refused to be homeless anymore. From our beachfront home in Papalaua, we still drove Nat to school. But now, after school, he'd visit friends' homes, skateboard with them, or go to a movie – and hitchhike home as he pleased. Occasionally, we'd meet him in town for dinner.

In the beginning, we waited to be caught and expelled from our permanent camp. But after a while, it seemed we were protected.

On April 2, we celebrated 'Iokepa's 49th birthday there. We invited two of his camping friends from Keone'o'io. We cooked and ate in the last of the daylight. We had salmon, *ahi*, and *ono* – 'Iokepa's favorite fish – he grilled them over an open fire. I cooked sweet potatoes and corn together in our one pot. We had dinner rolls and sun-melted butter – store bought chocolate birthday cake and apple pie for desert.

After the birthday cake, all five of us settled on the sand and contemplated the sun dropping behind the distant edge of the ocean. The sky was a brilliant pink. We were riveted, too, by another evening show, a dozen *honu* – huge sea turtles, measuring three feet across – feeding off the seaweed on the corral reef directly in front of our campsite.

Then we stuck candles in the sand and talked into the night. Not everyone agreed on God's plan for the future of Hawai'i.

"There have always been wars and there always will be," our older guest said. "It's in man's nature."

"No," 'Iokepa answered. "*Kanaka maoli* lived a consensus – an agreed upon life. The values were interchangeable with the other side – with the ancestors."

"Tell that to a man with a fist in your face," the man insisted.

'Iokepa described the ancient way. "When two men wanted to fight, they were required to run a footrace against one another instead. Then they'd swim against each other. By the time they'd finished, they'd worked their energy down so they could *listen*, and realize that they sucked the same air."

What 'Iokepa described was one possible outcome of *Ho'oponopono* – the ritual mediation at the heart of the peaceful original culture.

The ritual demanded every man and woman in the community examine his soul for complicity in every other human's misfortune: illness, emotional distress, harm. It had nothing to do with our modern concept of guilt. When we lived the connections, we assumed responsibility for every living thing.

'Iokepa opened his birthday presents. I bought him a new duffel bag to replace the worn-from-wear one he'd bought in Tacoma. I also bought him a book of ancient *'ōlelo* – proverbs. Nathan bought him a gift certificate to Starbucks in Lahaina.

Our younger guest spread his arms and laughed. "You folks sure have a million dollar piece of real estate here." Of course we did. But price-tags belonged to someone else's culture.

It had been a magical night.

It was followed by another.

'Iokepa's daughter Hokulele was a junior in college in Honolulu on O'ahu. During my final year in Portland, father and daughter had exchanged visits several times. But she and I had not yet met.

The day after 'Iokepa's birthday on the beach, Hokulele flew to Maui for a single night. Her twenty-first birthday was April 1; her boyfriend's was a few days later. She wanted to celebrate together: father, daughter and beau.

Finally I met 'Iokepa's daughter and she was everything her proud father said she was – gorgeous, gracious, and smart. It would be yet another year before I'd meet his gentle and handsome son, Malu.

Hokulele was the embodiment of native good looks. She had huge, sparkling dark eyes; thick black hair to the middle of her back; a tender smile.

The young couple stayed overnight with her boyfriend's aunt. This aunt worked in one of the finest restaurants on the

Hawaiian Islands. Mama's Fish House was a class act known for its fresh fish, impeccable service, and secluded beach-front location. She invited 'Iokepa, Nat, and me to join them there for dinner.

Clothing was a huge insoluble problem. All I'd brought from Kaua'i were shorts, jeans, slippers, and walking shoes. There wasn't a single thing I could do about it. I wore my best navy walking shorts, a moderately bright yellow shirt and my new aqua beach slippers. Unsuccessfully, I tried not to feel self-conscious.

Money, ironically, wasn't a problem. In Borders' the day before – at an author's book signing – the writer spotted 'Iokepa and begged to buy the *lei* off his neck. He had $160 for dinner. (We were uncertain if we were to be treated – we were.) We'd brought gifts for all of them – including our hostess. We'd floated birthday balloons next to our table.

In those early April weeks of unprecedented calm, I heard and wrote.

> *The prophecy is a feminine one. 'Iokepa is the la'akoa – the sacred warrior. As a sacred warrior, he brings the female into male form. This time, his 'fight' is for the Creator.*
>
> *It has been a male driven world for a long time. Conquest is male. 'Iokepa will be taught by you about the pain inflicted on the conquered: on women everywhere who have suffered use for male purpose or ego; on an earth that has suffered as well.*
>
> *Through you, he is offered the chance to know – as few men have – the hurt his gender has inflicted on the women they say they love. Only when he sees, hears, and feels that truth, can he truly be a la'akoa: The sacred and the warrior in one. Only then, will he embrace the prophecy fully.*

In mid April, I received a written notice. My fabulous home in Portland – perched high above the trees and city, angled to catch the light, transparent through glass window and skylight – was going to be foreclosed on July 10. The bank was recovering its investment.

Perhaps I'd already relinquished that house the day I began tearing up the bills unopened. Perhaps I'd relinquished it the day I turned the key in the lock last June. But that three-level home – perfectly suited to rearing two teenaged boys and their single mother – and all the life it had held still filled my imagination. I had let it go, and I had not.

It was April, and I knew that the yellow daffodils, blue hyacinths, and white lilies of the valley filled my Portland hillside. It was April, and it would be the first break in the Oregon winter rains. I could recall watching, from my bird's nest desk, the fog filling the Beaverton valley below.

It was April and at Papalaua Wayside, ten miles out of Lahaina, it was hot, dry and indistinguishable from February or March – or, I now suspected, August.

The foreclosure notice had been just another step in the steady progress of handing my life in Portland over to history. It was another step in the recognition that I was living the only life I'd ever really had – the one in this breath. But on the day the envelope arrived, I grieved for the loss of everything that had brought me here.

. . .

We were sound asleep, the three of us, in our home at Papalaua Wayside. It was a Tuesday night.

Before bed, 'Iokepa had played his ancient, tattered Hawaiian *pahu* (drum) given to him by the ancestors a year before – found at the edge of a dump. It was the first time he'd had the courage to play it out-of-doors.

I'd sat on my beach chair next to him and listened with great pleasure to the hurried rhythms he sent into the night. Nat was finishing his homework by flashlight.

By midnight, we'd been asleep for hours.

I remember, first, a very bright light piercing our tent wall. Then a commanding voice, "Get out of the tent." 'Iokepa pulled on his shorts and climbed over me to the door. I pulled on a long T-shirt and followed him.

I stepped into a floodlight pressing against my sleepy eyes. Then it was averted. Two police officers in full regalia were standing directly in front of Nat's tent. One was Caucasian, one was Hawaiian. My heart was beating faster than 'Iokepa's drum.

"Who are in the other tents?" The first officer gestured towards Nat's and the small storage tent.

"*Ohana*," I said, "my son."

Those were the last words I spoke. The first officer faded out of view into the trees. The rest took place between 'Iokepa and the Hawaiian man.

"You can't camp here."

"The beaches are home to the *kanaka maoli*. I am a Hawaiian *kahu*."

"The law...."

"The law," 'Iokepa finished his sentence, "is not Hawaiian law."

Something in 'Iokepa's bare-chested demeanor or in his voice had stopped the officer in mid sentence. He deferred to 'Iokepa's impassioned discourse.

"It is not for *kanaka maoli* to enforce other people's laws. This..." he gestured toward the uniform and the flashlight, "...is not our way."

The officer nodded. "I'm from the Big Island, brother. I understand." He moved in to shake 'Iokepa's hand.

"This is just a warning. But someone else will give you a citation and you'll have to talk to the judge."

Back inside our tent I hugged 'Iokepa gratefully and I said without hesitation. "Then, you'll talk to the judge."

He liked that. "We're going to stay."

Nevertheless, jolted awake and accused by police in the middle of the night in the only home we had left me weaker.

...

The next day, a Wednesday, I was on edge. I could no longer ignore the German shepherd who'd been chained up without food or water since Sunday.

A woman had camped on the beach Saturday night. On Sunday, she'd left her tent, her chairs, and her food – as though she were returning shortly. Her dog, she'd left, chained to a coconut tree without food, shade or water. She never came back.

Either she'd been hit by a car, or she was unbelievably negligent. We'd been picking her windblown stuff out of the ocean and off the beach for days.

By Tuesday, the dog was scared and raging, straining at the end of his chain, looking and sounding as though he'd kill anyone who came within reach. He was baring his teeth – and we cut him a wide circle when we walked to the port-a-john.

Early Wednesday morning, I gathered the necessary nickels, walked a half mile to a pay phone and called the Humane Society. I got an answering machine and left a message.

I was already off-center and I confess that I was not exercising my best judgment when I passed the dog, saw an empty water dish and filled it up for him.

He was tearing at the end of his chain, ferocious.

My thinking went like this: "He wants water. He's watching me fill the water dish. He'll want me to put it where he can reach it." I thought the German shepherd and I were communicating our mutual self-interest when the dog backed off. He stopped barking, walked away from me, and allowed me to enter his circle with the water.

I walked into the circle of the chain, smiled, and laid down the water dish. I turned to walk away.

The dog lunged in a long arc at my right foot which he grabbed top and bottom in the pincers of his jaw. I hadn't seen him coming. He sank his teeth deep into my flesh, veins, and muscle. I screamed, and I passed out.

'Iokepa heard my shrill scream clear across the beach, and he knew precisely what happened. He ran like a panther to me. I lay unconscious on the ground – mercifully just out of reach of the dog – but my foot had been chewed to ribbons.

He picked me up in his arms, carried me to the car, and immediately began screaming at me.

"What a stupid thing to do! What were you thinking?! You couldn't wait for the Humane Society? You could have pushed the water dish to the dog with a stick!"

He drove, and he ranted at me for a solid ten minutes.

I was conscious, of course, and bleeding profusely – weak, but well-aware *why* 'Iokepa was yelling at me. I'd been a mother too long not to understand. I'd done the same.

Three-year-old Ben had been missing from our farm-house – and I'd imagined the worst. When he finally crept out of his hiding place, safe and sound – I yelled, "Don't you ever...!"

It was like that. 'Iokepa loved me dearly and took his job of caring for me (under outrageous conditions) more seriously than anyone had since my father. It killed him to see me hurt.

After he got the fright out of his system, he turned to butter – loving, attentive – and he stayed that way for the next two and half weeks. It was 9:00 in the morning when 'Iokepa scooped me off the ground. It was the beginning of a very long day.

Last June, in what I thought was the final act of letting go of middle class life and conventional comforts, I called my insurance agent and cancelled my health insurance. I'd postponed that call until hours before our plane left – dragging my feet. It felt, more than anything else I'd done, like diving off a high cliff into a rock quarry.

But I was no longer choosing to live with safety nets, and almost $400 a month for health insurance was out of the question. The kids remained on their father's plan.

'Iokepa and I drove to four health care providers from one end of the Island to the other before I got treatment. I was still in the emergency room at 3:30 p.m.

We went first to the public health service in Lahaina. 'Iokepa gathered me into his arms, his back straining against my limp weight, and pushed us through the clinic doors. "No doctor is on duty today," the receptionist said.

We stopped next at the fire department. "A dog bite can be dangerous," the fireman insisted. "You need immediate attention." He sent us to the private clinic in the middle of town.

'Iokepa pulled up to the front of the doctors' office that looked a great deal like one I would have visited in Portland. There were plush furnishings in the waiting room, and a glass partition separated the patients from the busy office staff. It was a thriving, modern practice. Every seat was taken.

'Iokepa set me down, leaning me against a pillar in the middle of the room facing the reception desk. I was pale, woozy, and my foot was still pumping out blood – top and bottom.

"I'll park and be right back."

I stood there for what seemed an eternity without soliciting so much as a passing notice from any of the six women behind the reception desk. I simply didn't have the strength to call for help. I couldn't move.

'Iokepa, meanwhile, faced a packed parking lot. In downtown Lahaina, parking spaces were gold. He was circling.

Another patient – a Hawaiian woman – was the first person in that crowded waiting room to notice me. She walked up and suggested there was an empty chair in front of the reception desk now – and the receptionist appeared to be free.

"I can't walk there," I said.

"Let me help you."

I sat down in the chair at the open window in the otherwise sealed reception wall of glass.

"Have you been here before?" the woman in white asked me.

"No."

"Who is your insurance carrier?"

"I have no insurance."

"Then you'll have to pay for your treatment today."

"I don't have the cash with me."

"Then we can't treat you."

Weakly, I said. "I've been bitten by a dog. I'm about to pass out on your waiting room floor. I'm dripping blood on your carpet – and you are asking me questions? I can't speak anymore until my partner gets here."

As though on cue, 'Iokepa came charging through the front door and across the waiting room floor.

"They won't treat me without insurance or cash in my pocket," I barely whispered.

"This is Hawai'i," his voice announced at a volume that most certainly would have alerted the doctors hidden behind the paper-thin walls. "And this," he waved at the glass wall and the indifferent faces, "is *not* how we treat people in Hawai'i.

"If you choose to live among the *kanaka maoli* – the host culture – then it is your responsibility to understand the culture, and to honor it."

With that, he hoisted me again across his strong arms, and we pushed our way past the contemptuous staff and out onto the street.

Five women in the waiting room jumped to their feet and followed us. They wanted to express their horror at what they'd just witnessed. They wanted to help. One was a paramedic. "A dog bite is a very serious wound," she said. "It's filthy with potential infection. Come back and let me wash it out in the bathroom."

"Thank you," I said, looking down at my sand-encrusted, bloody foot, "but I don't think they want me using their bathroom."

We drove the thirty miles to Kahului. Looking for a hospital, we passed Kaiser. 'Iokepa had learned his lesson – this time he left me waiting in the car. He came back a few minutes later.

"Not here unless you're a member. We're looking for a public hospital."

We waited in the public hospital's emergency room for three hours. Within minutes of my arrival, the receptionist popped out from behind her desk and covered my filthy foot with bandages. It addressed the problem of the growing pool of blood on their linoleum floor. Then they ignored us.

A posted sign above the entrance to the Emergency Room said: 'One visitor per patient – no exceptions.' When the wheelchair arrived to take me through the swinging doors, I said, "I want my partner with me."

"That won't be necessary," the aide said. "You'll only be a moment."

"I insist," I said. "I want 'Iokepa with me." She tried to push me against my will through the doors. I threw myself out of the moving wheelchair onto the floor.

"In that case," she said, "I'll take the next patient." She left me there. When the doors swung open for the next patient, the nurse inside saw me and asked what had happened.

I said, "She took the next patient because I wanted my partner with me." The nurse looked mortified, brought another wheelchair, and invited both of us in.

I was examined, x-rayed, hooked to an antibiotic IV, and a doctor surgically removed any skin, sand, or other foreign particles from each of the five, very deep, puncture wounds – without anesthetic. It hurt like hell and I practiced my fifteen-year-out-of-date Lamaze breaths.

"What a high pain threshold she has," the nurse kept marveling. Then the doctor set out to prove it.

I don't know what I would have done without 'Iokepa. Except during the surgical probing, he kept me laughing.

Perhaps the most endearing part of 'Iokepa's character is his absolutely rare sense of humor. He's completely unafraid to be ridiculous. He's a natural mimic, and depending on the provocation can switch into various European and American dialects that – in juxtaposition with his distinctly Polynesian face – are hilarious. His humor was very physical – he used his body and face in the manner of a Steve Martin. Nathan and I long ago agreed that the laughter was an essential antidote to the Earth-wobbling seriousness of the prophecy.

The doctor offered me a menu of disastrous outcomes from the dog bite that included infection of the bone, rabies, and a litany of other dog-borne diseases. I knew that I was essentially healthy and filled with faith, so I didn't buy into any of it. I just wanted out of there.

I was sent home with a $20 prescription for an antibiotic. I had refused them all my life – for both my sons, and for myself. I tended toward natural remedies. But I was warned I must continue what the IV drip had begun, or suffer the consequences. I agreed. But I was reminded that my father had suffered a severe allergic reaction to Penicillin at my age.

I agreed, too, to buy $20 worth of bandages, Neosporin, Peroxide, and Advil for the pain. I was told to stay away from sand beaches, ocean, and keep the wounds clean.

"But I live on the beach."

I was in very high spirits when we left. The pain had subsided, my foot was wrapped up tight, and 'Iokepa came out of the drugstore with comfort food – a bag of M&Ms and a York Peppermint Patty.

Now, we had all the reason we needed to stay at Papalaua – I couldn't walk. We couldn't move the tents if we wanted to.

The German shepherd remained tethered for two more days, when the young owner returned and responded to 'Iokepa's account with a shrug. "Yeah, my dog is kind of protective." And then, "I thought my friend might take care of him."

After two days of antibiotics, I was considerably weaker, and sicker – and I quit them. My bottom began to hurt and ooze. I treated those symptoms for yeast infection for two days, but they worsened. I switched to aloe plants.

I was burning up with fever now, and it had become unbearable to urinate, or to sit. I was too weak to stand unaided. Lying on my back in the tent was my only option – it was a major exertion to roll on my side.

I used the occasions when I got up to pee to pour the water that we carried in Tropicana orange juice jugs over my lower body in a futile effort to stay clean. Everything I did burned like fire. The hurt now went all the way thorough my pelvis, my stomach, my lower back.

By Monday, 'Iokepa insisted I call the hospital. The phone number that the hospital had given me for a follow-up visit rang at a clinic up on a mountain, an hour and a half from Lahaina. When I asked for the doctor whose name they'd listed, I was told. "He's been gone for two months."

I talked to the nurse. She was empathetic and told me that they had the best Family Practice doctor on the Island. It would cost me $30. I said we'd be there in two hours.

"Wow!!!" the doctor said when he did an internal exam. "You're unbelievably raw. It's not yeast...

"What *was* that antibiotic you took?"

He was genuinely perplexed – and worried that the dog might carry disease.

"Don't go into the ocean. Keep that foot clean! The worst is over – it should clear up in a couple days." He gave me cortisone cream for my bottom.

The cortisone cream did nothing. By Thursday, I couldn't walk, I was incontinent, and I was growing delirious from the raging fever.

My modus operandi throughout the ordeal had been stoicism. First, because the dog bite was my own fault and I felt guilty making others suffer for it. Second, I was the daughter after two strapping sons – macho was the game. Third, 'Iokepa set a formidable example of courage.

When 'Iokepa asked me, which he did often, 'Is it any better?' I'd search hard for the bright side. 'It's a little less raw,' or 'I think the fever broke.' He took me at my word.

Eleven days after the dog bite, I offered to accompany 'Iokepa to town. It took an enormous act of will. He bought me *limu* (seaweed) to eat because I had an indefinable craving for it and nothing else. Then I told him to drop me off at a town park, while he sat with his *lei* across from the Hard Rock Café. I waved him off cheerfully.

Since that first *lei* sold off his neck at Border's, the *puka* shells had been selling steadily – keeping our family in food, gas, and now medicine. 'Iokepa's hands were at all times open. If he had ten dollars in his pocket, he'd hand it off to someone he'd never met without a second thought – always.

Now, he felt the pressure to care for Nathan and me. Sitting with what he called, 'the ancestors' *lei'* took on a breadwinner's immediacy. The ancestors provided.

When 'Iokepa left me at the park, I immediately spread a straw mat on the grass, rolled my sweatshirt under my head and fell fast asleep. When I awakened, I felt like a derelict sleeping off a drunk on a mat in the park. It was dark and I had to urinate in the worst way. I stood and stumbled in the direction of the public restroom – but I didn't make it. Totally humiliated, I peed through my clothes and stood in the puddle of my own urine in the middle of the park. I wanted to cry.

Instead, I changed and tried to drive the car to find 'Iokepa. He was already on his way. He climbed into the passenger seat.

Apparently, my words were slurred and my thoughts disjointed. 'Iokepa hollered, "It's going to your brain. You've got to get to a doctor."

"No," I said. "They can't do anything."

The next morning – after twelve days of gently changing my bandages twice a day, carrying me over difficult obstacles, finding me aloe plants, and loving me without let-up – 'Iokepa took matters into his own hands. He no longer allowed for my judgment.

He registered us in a very nice hotel in town – at half the going rate. "You need a bathtub. You need to soak all day in Epsom salts. You need a bed."

I sank into that bed and that tub like my body had been starved for both – and, of course, it had. But one day didn't come close to doing it, and two days didn't either. Each day, we'd peel off another $75, and each day we'd extend our reservation for one more night. Our spending 'Iokepa's and Nathan's money for the hotel was hard *only* for me. Nathan luxuriated in the HBO movies and the swimming pool.

From early childhood Nathan had felt undermined by my very rare illnesses – it threatened his security mightily. Instead of empathy, he typically showered me with anger at those times. Of course, he knew how sick I was now. This time, however, he left me alone – secure in 'Iokepa's care.

But once I'd sunk into the ease and comfort of my own bathroom, hot water and tub, I couldn't imagine *ever* again sleeping in that tent. The thought of returning to Papalaua, the scene of the attack and subsequent agony, was unbearable.

I began – very slowly – to heal. The pain that shot through my entire lower body began, in tiny gradations, to let up. The sores on my bottom incrementally lessened. I could walk slowly now – from bed to bath and back – on my own. Still I could not sit without unbearable suffering – and still I was sicker than I'd ever imagined in my life.

Long after the story was history, an experienced nurse practitioner diagnosed me with certainty. "You were septicemic – you could have died." The dog's disease had ravaged every organ in my body – and was shutting them down.

Paradoxically, as my body showed its first signs of recovery, my emotions plummeted. Increasingly, I felt hopelessly depressed. It had taken far too long; the signs of healing were much too subtle. I gave up the fight.

I believed, in truth, that God and the ancestors had written me off – that I wasn't worth their effort.

Weeks before, 'Iokepa had been directed by the grandmothers that soon he would leave for Lana'i – the Island within sight of Lahaina. Since then, he'd told me, "I promise I won't leave you while you're still sick."

After three days in the hotel room, 'Iokepa was – to my eyes – visibly restless. Increasingly, it seemed to me, it was harder for him to stay put. My healing was invisible, my melancholy contagious. He adamantly denied – and denies still – that this was ever the case. He still held his healing hands to my sick body and prayed his soothing words. He still held me in his arms and loved me. That was true. But in my state of deep self-loathing, I was sure that more than two weeks of constant care had taken its toll – and I hardly blamed him.

After five nights in the hotel, with no dramatic changes in my body or my spirits, I urged 'Iokepa to leave for Lana'i. But I silently prayed that he would not.

At the very moment of my insincere offer, I got my period. The accompanying PMS gave new meaning to the words *mood swing*. Now my disease-ravaged body revolted with the first migraine of my life. The pain drilled up my spine and into my brain every time I took a step. It showed no signs of subsiding. Emotionally and physically, I was in the toilet.

We were checking out of the hotel Friday morning when it all broke loose. It had something do with my refusal to carry a very light bag. But it had everything to do with 'Iokepa – who had declared me much improved – leaving me, while I was still sick. Even more, it had to do with my horror of returning to that tent with Nathan.

It went from bad to worse. 'Iokepa had disassembled the campsite at Papalaua while we were in the hotel. Now we returned there for him to set up the tent for Nathan and me. But I refused his offer – refused his labor as a salve to his conscience. (That was how I saw it at the time.)

"You're abandoning me," I accused. "You promised."

He answered. "My path is cut and dried. The prophecy...."

Finally he blurted out, as I stood next to him at the ferry crossing to Lana'i. "Puanani *said* you would try to follow me."

"What!?!" I screamed, and the migraine thrashed the inside of my skull. "I'd try to what?"

"Like you followed me to the other Islands."

I breathed in his words and I know I turned white. "Goodbye 'Iokepa," I said *very* softly. "We have nothing left to say."

I drove to the park where I would watch his ferry cross to Lana'i, and I knew exactly how I would kill myself. I'd put Nathan on a plane to his father that afternoon. I'd wait until nightfall. In the dark, I'd swim beyond exhaustion and endurance into the ocean's waves. And I would never come back.

For some men, and some women, there is no alternative. We must scrape the dusty bottom of our reservoir before we can begin the climb into ourselves.

I bottomed out. Then God sent me to the home of strangers to lick my wounds and heal. To rid myself of my unbearable hurt and my remorseless rage. To grow into my own soul again. But first I had to live out that desolation fully.

When 'Iokepa left I was flooded with self-doubt. But I never once doubted the existence of the Creator or the ancestors who reached across the grave to me. I did not, in fact, try to end my life, because I'd already effectively done that in the months before. I'd nullified myself, step by disloyal step.

The night that 'Iokepa left – with Nat asleep in the backseat of the Buick I walked to the edge of the ocean near Keone'o'io, and bellowed an appeal to the wind and waves, to the starless black sky.

"Enough! It's been almost a year – I want to know *why* I'm here. I want to *live* the reason why I'm here."

I felt the heavens listening and I saw the light dawn.

> *Let your human form grow slowly to bear the weight and responsibility of your soul's knowing.*

The migraine was unrelenting. After two nights sleep in the backseat of the Buick, my head and spine hammering out its pain, I began the search for a room to share with Nat in Lahaina. On Sunday, we called three dozen numbers, visited every place that sounded promising, and by day's end had come up empty-handed. The reasons varied. We walked into filth, greed, drugs, noise, and family battle. We slept in the car again that night.

Monday morning after I drove Nat to school I stood at the public phone by the Lahaina harbor, fed change into the box, and called the last two numbers where there'd been no answer the day before. Both were listed under vacation rentals, by definition too expensive for long-term residence. We needed a place for six weeks until the end of the school year.

The first person who answered was delightful. But no matter how he measured his tiny room, there was no room for the two of us, and he regretted it. The second voice I heard – the last number in the paper – was friendly, a woman. She introduced herself: Christina. I stumbled out our story: that there were two of us; that we'd come from Kaua'i; that my son was a freshman at Lahainaluna; that I was a single mother. I'm not exactly certain what else I said to her.

She said: "Come take a look."

Afterwards, she told me: "When I saw you walking up the sidewalk, I knew that God sent you to us. I felt your peace and your honesty."

It's a wonder that she saw peace. I hadn't slept for days. I was still very sick. It was all I could do to put one foot in front of the other. But when I saw the sprawling home set on spacious private lawns and gardens, I felt the hand of the grandmothers at my back.

The home sat on the best street in Lahaina, a block from the beach. It had a private swimming pool, large old shade trees and hedges. It was walking distance from downtown.

Its beauty and refinement reflected the family who lived there. First I met Christina. She showed me around. We were joined by her husband Edward and his mother, who I learned to call Grams. We sat in the living room on down-upholstered antique arm-chairs. They offered me iced tea.

All three of them coaxed me – with warm smiles, tender hugs, and the kindest words – to open up and talk about the faith that was my path. I felt a surge of renewal and I held forth.

"A woman was raped and murdered a few months ago on Kaua'i," I told them. "The next day, the newspapers called her a 'homeless alcoholic'. Her murderer was called the 'Westside Slayer.' As a community, we agreed to distance them – *not us*!

"Well, I don't see it that way," I said. "I *am* Lisa. I am the man who killed her. I am the community that allowed that to happen. *Ho'oponopono.*" I referred to the cultural tapestry that wove the native Hawaiian with every part of creation. *Ho'oponopono* was the ancient ritual mediation founded on that tapestry.

Christina nodded. She answered, "This place is about *ohana* – family." With a glass of tea and an hour of conversation, Nathan and I were part of it.

Edward had been an accomplished artist and a passionate surfer. He'd contracted Parkinson's disease in his early thirties. Ten years later his nervous system had deteriorated severely and yet he was consistently good-natured and optimistic. He didn't complain – ever. He kept up the strenuous physical regime that it took to maintain the house and grounds daily. Only on a surfboard was he free of tremors.

Grams was an eighty-five year old charmer. She'd been a Southern belle who'd married a Dole Pineapple executive in a lavish society wedding. She was widowed young. She reared five children alone in rural Hawai'i – for some years in teepees. We shared that, of course, a life in tents with children.

We shared, too, a love of literature. Her mind was sharp, her poetry accomplished – but her body, after a stroke, was struggling to keep up.

Christina had been diagnosed with cancer the year before. After extensive surgery, she remained irrepressibly lively, funny, and strong.

Christina became my friend: we shared a deep sensitivity for the past and the future of the native Hawaiians. She'd been a poor girl who'd married well. Effortlessly, she recognized my need for privacy and yet offered me the intimacy of a good woman friend. I had sorely missed that.

Christina and Edward waited on Grams hand and foot. Grams worried about Edward and Christina when they were out of earshot. The couple cared for one another with unceasing grace and obvious affection.

This was the family that took us in. They had something to teach us.

For me, there was a guest cottage next to the main house that they rented as a Bed and Breakfast. It was all white lace, with a large bay widow and cushy window seat, a queen sized bed, a private patio, a bathroom that opened to an outside tile shower. It was surrounded by – and filled with – flowers.

"Is it too feminine?" Christina asked me the first day.

I laughed with disbelief, 'You have to be kidding."

The towels were thick and plentiful. It had its own refrigerator, microwave, and telephone. It rented for $100 a night.

A bedroom materialized for Nat at the opposite end of the house – with its own private entrance, next to the hot tub. We were granted full use of their equipped kitchen – and every other part of their home. Cristina offered this bounty at a ludicrous fraction of what the cottage alone rented for. It was ours for six weeks.

Christina had already made up her mind as I'd sipped tea in their living room, she told me later. If God had sent me to them, she would not refuse. Immediately we became at once part of the family – and treasured guests. Nat was delivered from home to school and back again on the school bus. It was nothing short of a miracle. For two weeks, I slept. The physical healing was slow – the emotional healing, slower still. I wrote tirades of fury to the absent 'Iokepa. They all began with, "You!"

"You...didn't love me enough!"

"You...were disloyal."

"You...."

None of it at first had anything to do with me.

I lay in bed staring out at the flowers, trees, and sunshine – and at the end of two weeks I summoned enough energy to write a dozen short letters to old friends in Portland and Virginia. I left a phone message on Lena's answering machine in Portland, and one on Eleanor's on Kaua'i. They both called back instantly. I soaked in their familiar voices – but mostly their empathetic listening. I needed to talk.

"This has been the hardest year of my life," I told Lena. It was no exaggeration; it was important to hear myself say the words. There had been too much denial of what had been required of me.

Lena said simply: "That life is much harder for a woman than for a man."

For the first time, I conceded that truth. I knew that my need to nest was so much greater than 'Iokepa's. I knew, too, that there were things – showering in public, sleeping in the car, using public bathrooms for private moments – that were unbearably humiliating for me, but only mildly unpleasant for him. There was the fine line of respectability that seemed so much more fragile for a woman than a man. There was my son!

There was also a glaring irony. I had chosen this life for my spirit. Yet, I'd been denied the very things that supported my spirit: solitude, privacy, silence – and the deep reaches that silence fostered. I'd been dropped, instead, into the thick of a systemic grief – poverty, racism, addiction – so pervasive that it drained me of serenity.

Ironically: instructed by the echoes of an ancient culture, I faced the pain and horrors of the modern one. In this pain, I learned to my toes the constriction, boredom, un-freedom of my *machutenim* – family by marriage. I came for simplicity, truth, and divine guidance. Instead, I had lived – like the *kanaka maoli* – as a trapped animal among human noise and invention. It is what the natives have suffered for almost 200 years.

Slowly now, I emerged from my isolation. I began, for the first time in an entire year, to read again. Jane Smiley's *The Adventure of Lidie Newton*, Kurt Vonnegut's *The Sirens of Titan*, and Mary Gordon's *Spending*. It was a renewal of my deepest longing.

I began again to walk.

I wrote on the legal pads constantly. With the first genuine distance I could imagine the outline of this book. Finally, there was a hill high enough to see from.

I heard the ancestors' words differently now. The endless stream of words that I'd heard first in my ears, then in my head, had become a reliable part of me. I *understood* the grandmothers' words in a way that would have been unthinkable under those skylights in Portland. So much had been surrendered. In the vacuum, so much had been clarified.

I'd been through the worst.

> *Sickness strips us of the illusion that the body defines the limit of us. In pain, we can choose to define ourselves by the pain ('Poor weak me') or transcend it. ('I am neither this body nor this pain – I am infinitely more.') That is where faith counts. You see it in Edward, Christina and Grams. We are divine spirit only temporarily housed in a cage of bodily pain.*

Beginning in the spring – invisible on Maui but spring nonetheless – my body healed, my heart mended. I reclaimed my own life.

I understood now what Nathan told me after my earliest fight with 'Iokepa that he had witnessed: "Because your *love* and your *destiny* are so linked – the end of the first threatens to destroy everything." I had not been able to imagine one without the other.

Remembering who I was, I felt happier than I had in months – lighter and more alert to my own needs.

For a fleeting moment I imagined a move back to Portland, or to Baltimore. But I was never very serious about it – and not just because my winter clothing had long since disappeared. The guidance was so clearly otherwise.

The ancestors were *still* pouring directions into my ears. After the school year, I would return to Kaua'i. In the fall Nat would be a student at Kaua'i High. It was time to begin the book.

> *You are bone tired from trying to please others. Your greatest challenge has been what others think of you. Forget it. What your mother, your brothers or the people around you think of you is ego attachment of the worst kind. It prevents you from knowing your true self.*
>
> *The last piece is this. What 'Iokepa thinks of you is important only to him – not you. It is exactly what readers*

bring to a writer's book: irrelevant to the writing and the writer.

. . .

By my 53rd birthday on May 12, my carefully cosseted hurt had become irrelevant. My anger at 'Iokepa had dissipated. I honestly knew the journey was about me.

Nat made me breakfast in bed and posted a half dozen signs – 'Happy Birthday Mom!' and 'Happy! Joy! Happy!' – around the room while I was sleeping. He bought a cake and held a party. When I blew out my candles without remembering to make a wish and then suffered seemingly irreparable regret, Nat laughed and convinced me. "It's an old Nordic tradition. *First* you blow out the candles – *then* you make the wish." He gave me an old Motown CD, and one by the Who. "So you'll have music in your life again."

Ben sent me a wonderful and fitting art book, Gauguin's paintings of native Tahiti. He called on my birthday. He'd been washing dishes in a Washington, D.C. restaurant for four months, living in a tiny room he rented in an older woman's Capitol Hill home. He was dying to return to Beloit in August.

Nat took me to dinner at Kimo's, the best seafood restaurant in Lahaina. We had an outside table overlooking the harbor, the ocean, and the Island of Lana'i. Hawaiian musicians played the guitar and ukulele just beneath us. After eight years without, I shocked myself and ordered a huge rare steak. I savored every bite of it. Nat paid the check with cash from his dwindling college savings account.

Christina had given me two dresses the night before. "They don't fit since my surgery." I wore one to my birthday dinner. I'd lost a great deal of weight during my sickness, and the dress (with deep décolletage) was slinky. I draped an orange and black seed *lei* from the Island of Hawai'i around my neck. I'd had my hair cut and colored. I wore eyeliner, mascara, and lipstick.

But the *puka* shell *lei* that I'd worn every day without exception since 'Iokepa sent it to me in Portland for my 52nd birthday stayed stored underneath my socks. I had stopped wearing it when he took the ferry to Lana'i.

I felt like a million bucks. I turned heads. I was remembering.

...

I filed for bankruptcy. Since December, I'd asked the ancestors whether bankruptcy was appropriate. Until now the answer had been, *No.*

Then one Tuesday, for no particular reason, Christina handed me an extra Maui phone book she'd turned up in the garage. I flipped through the Yellow Pages to *Attorneys* that same day. Among the dozens of bankruptcy lawyers Nora's name jumped out at me. I called, and she answered her own phone.

She heard me out: my insecurities, my embarrassment around what had happened in one short year to a thirty-year impeccable credit rating. Four years before, a mortgage banker held up my credit report in her outstretched hand, and said to me in amazement, "You've never even made a late payment!"

"No," I answered her. "I never have."

Nora, it turned out, had been a hot-shot Los Angeles corporate lawyer who opted out of the cut-throat urban legal life five years before – for Maui. She lived, now, in an up-country home, high on Haleakala with ocean views in the distance. She worked out of her home. She was ethnic Chinese, beautiful, smart, and most important to me now – compassionate.

After we'd met and done what needed doing, she had me laughing – hard. On what might rightfully have been one of the toughest days of my life, I stood, then reached down to her with gratitude and embraced her.

"In all my years of corporate law," she said, "I never had a client hug me. That's why I'm here!"

I didn't know how I would pay Nora. Quite understandably, she required money up-front. It felt very wrong to take that from Nat. On the way home from Nora's, I stopped at the General Delivery Post Office box in Kahului. Among the bills, there was a late birthday card from my mother. I had told my family *nothing* about either my illness or our separation.

Inside, she'd tucked a check for an unprecedented odd and large amount of $600. I owed Nora $650.

Clearly it was time.

In the middle of the night, on the legal pad, I was feeling full of myself and rather flippant. Referring sarcastically to the grandmothers' original promise to 'Iokepa, I snickered. "You promised to fill me after I'd been emptied. I imagine that won't be with '*Hawaiian language, history, and culture.*'"

I heard this.

No. That will come through 'Iokepa.

I was stunned. My pen froze in place. Then I asked, "*Still?*"

Still – if you choose him.

"What are the odds of both of us choosing this?"

One hundred percent. It is who you are, why you are.

"I can't imagine an end to the differences that feed hurt and anger."

Then your imagination is too limited. The prepara-tion is nearing an end. It will happen soon – and with ease.

. . .

Nat kept asking me where I'd like to live once he was out of high school. He wanted to pry open my self-limiting horizons. He asked me my favorite places. I answered: "Bali, for the spirit of the people; Machu Picchu, for the spirit in the land; Florence, for the spirit born of man's art." Each had offered me what Hawai'i never had.

The Hawai'i that I'd wandered into Christmas week, 1997 had never fit me.

Living – as I had this year, within the unavoidable crush of Hawaiian tourist culture – saturated with the crassness of

America's most extreme materialism – was at odds with everything I valued.

I was equally alienated from the transplanted American hippie culture – young (and now aging) people drawn to Hawai'i for nothing Hawaiian. They were attracted rather to an escape from America's middle class demands – or from their parents. Living in a drugged haze, they could be anywhere.

Living here this past year had in fact required of me the greatest feat of faith, that I would one day live in a very different Hawai'i – the one which was prophesized. *Ho'omanawanui* – wait in faith. But I understood none of this until now.

It was only the ancient culture – *abandoned but not forgotten* – that touched my soul. I belonged with these people, but only within the culture that the prophecy foretold. When it flowered, I would fit. I'd never claim to be *kanaka maoli.* I'd be proudly Jewish, always. But I could live compassionately, as a guest, within their world. It was, of course, what 'Iokepa's calling was about.

We had lived this past year without home or paycheck – had both given up lives of extreme comfort – to be lightening rods for the wrongs that had been, and continued to be, committed against the indigenous people, their land, and their way of life.

Now the sadness began. For the first time since he'd left, I missed 'Iokepa. Still, I preferred to miss him rather than actually be with him. I feared what I would become in order to be loved by him. I remembered the extreme dependence, amplified finally by my sickness.

> *Never again can you choose a year like this one – being the poor imitation of another soul. Because you genuinely admired him and because he is a formidable personality – you tried to be him.*
>
> *Then you fought him, so you could find your own lost soul – so as not to die of the lie.*
>
> *But, in your differences, there are none that separate. In the future, there will be respect both ways.*

I heard the metaphor loud and clear. I'd been living a tiny paradigm of what an entire people had lived.

Within their *mana'o* (ideology) they were the direct reflection of their Creator. What they lived was a fresh water stream, flowing from Creator to created – and from legions of ancestors who whispered unremitting love into every *kanaka maoli* soul. For almost 13,000 years they had lived this truth – until 700 years ago.

Then in order to accept and be accepted (under prodigious persecution), the people of Lāhui did what I'd done in a small way with 'Iokepa – relinquished who and what they were.

What I had struggled with for a single year, the indigenous people have wrestled for centuries. What I'd done at a soul level, the *kanaka maoli* did at a communal level. They denied themselves to create a false unity.

Hence 'Iokepa's heartfelt words on behalf of his people. "No more compromise!"

Yet there was purpose even here. What we forget, sometimes we remember far better and deeper in the reclaiming. Prophesized: in their remembering, the people of Lāhui would be redeemed – as a lesson to the hungry planet.

. . .

It had been four weeks since I'd last seen 'Iokepa. I had no way of knowing whether he was still on Lana'i – or if there, where? I was in no hurry. I would know his whereabouts when – and if – it was time for me to know.

> *You go Friday morning on the first ferry to Lana'i. Take a small bag with a swimsuit, a toothbrush, and a change of clothes. You are sent to every Island to be God's witness – and 'Iokepa's.*

I balked. I couldn't shake the echo of his words: 'Like you followed me to the other Islands.'

> *Banish fear. You cannot be afraid to live. The healing has ended.*

I walked a mile up Front Street Friday morning, carrying – as directed – one small duffel to the harbor. Nathan was in safe and loving hands for the weekend.

I paid $20 and boarded the 6:45 ferry for Lana'i.

Moloka'i rose above the ocean to my right, Kaho'olawe to my left, and Lana'i was straight ahead as we pulled out of Lahaina harbor. On the forty-five minute crossing, I felt myself floating on top of the submerged land mass that connected them all. Truly, I knew these to be parts of a single Island.

The ferry landed in a small bay surrounded by hillside. I saw a public restroom, a picnic pavilion and nothing else. I wasn't prepared for how small Lana'i was. It had, I'd learned on the ferry, just ten miles of paved roads and 2,500 residents. I was told the town was four miles uphill. There was no other.

I walked up the steep road for about a half mile, stopped, and decided – for the first time since I'd been in college in Italy – to hitchhike. The first car that passed stopped. The driver was a young woman who worked, along with her husband – and almost every other working-age person on the Island – at one of the two posh hotels.

Ninety-eight percent of all land on Lana'i was controlled by a single corporation. It had been for more than a hundred years. The corporation owned most private and public buildings. Like the former Soviet Union, they assigned apartments and houses to the citizens.

Until 1991, the entire Island had been planted in pineapple. Its residents were now overwhelmingly third or fourth generation Filipino, whose ancestors had been imported to work the pineapple fields by the American and European owners.

The minutes of an 1890 Hawaiian Board of Immigration meeting in Honolulu told the story. All ten Board members were missionary offspring, sugar cane or pineapple tycoons, bankers who financed their plantations, and manufacturers who built farm equipment used on their plantations.

Faced with an indigenous population who could not fathom working their ancestral lands for pay, the missionary offspring living in Hawai'i took to importing labor.

At this particular Board meeting, member R.A. Macfie, Jr. said. "European laborers will never be satisfied to remain as mere coolies doing the drudgery of the plantations."

Board member and sugar cane baron Henry P. Baldwin heartily agreed. The minutes quote him directly: "The majority of planters prefer Asiatics. All we want for our ordinary work is muscle without brains."

Member Theo H. Davies qualified his support. "They make very good laborers, but it is undesirable to have too large a proportion of them. It seems to me that they should be imported under contracts, binding them to be sent back at the end of their time."

First the Chinese, then the Japanese, and finally the Filipinos were imported to the Islands and exploited to satisfy the greed of a few businessmen. The plantations succeeded economically beyond the Board's wildest expectations. But they failed in their effort to control the workers they imported. When the contracts ended, the Asian labor force refused (often hiding out in remote mountains) to go home.

For generations, the good folk of Lana'i radiated a deep sense of pride in honest labor on the beautiful, hilly 'āina – and it still showed. Lana'i was a very sweet place. People waved at one another (even to strangers) from their car seats. In truth, there were no strangers here.

In 1991, the land-owning conglomerate abruptly dictated that growing pineapple in Hawai'i was no longer profitable. It could be done cheaper in the Philippines. The real money, they projected, would lie in creating tourism where none existed.

They built two opulent hotels, and booked them solid by convincing a particular brand of moneyed traveler that Lana'i was the elite Island to visit – not available to the ordinary tourist. As a footnote to their greed they shut down the source of four generations of a landed people's pride and livelihood – farming.

If the 2,500 citizens – who knew and cared for one another in the manner of the host culture that had welcomed them – chose to stay in the only home they'd ever known, they'd have to work at the five-star Manele Bay Hotel or at The Lodge at Koele.

They had no choice about the conditions of their labor. They were pitted cousin against cousin for the existing jobs. The beautiful green pineapple fields were left brown and barren. The owners forbade private farming – refused to rent land to their work force. The entire Island's social life and ecosystem had been destroyed. Proud farmers, with a deep attachment to the 'āina, had been turned into busboys and servants.

These were still an engaging, good and generous people. But there was sadness, a trauma that struck the heart of anyone aware enough to see beyond the hotel menu.

Many insist that the best beach on any Hawaiian Island is at Manele Bay. Dolphins romped along unsullied shoreline in the purest ocean water. On one end of the beach were thick terry towels, an over-priced snack bar, beach chairs, and scores of brown men serving hotel guests.

The other half was public – and you had better not step over to the hotel property and touch a towel there – though by state law, the owners could not forbid their servants' families from walking the water's edge.

'Iokepa, it turned out, was camped on the public beach. He was the only Hawaiian there.

I had no idea, of course, when I hitchhiked into town that 'Iokepa was camped just a single rock cliff away from the ferry landing.

When my ride dropped me off at the top of the hill, I asked her, "Is this town?" I wasn't being intentionally rude. I didn't see anything but a sprinkling of houses.

She waved two blocks up the street and said, "The stores will open in a half an hour."

I walked past the tiny post office, the gas station, two very simple restaurants, an aged hardware store, a bank, and two very basic general stores. I had seen town. I set my duffel down in the middle of the town park and left it there. I walked into one of the two restaurants, pulled a newly developed photo of 'Iokepa from my pocket and asked the young waitress. "Have you seen this man?"

She called into the kitchen, and out stepped an older woman.

"He had breakfast here yesterday and the day before. He hasn't been in today."

Bingo!

I walked the town. In front of the post office, I approached a man parked in his pick up truck, and I flashed the photo.

"Yeah," he said. "I've seen him running up the hill. He's probably camped on the beach." He directed me back down the hill.

I picked up my bag, walked two blocks to the corner where I'd been dropped off earlier, and stuck my thumb out. A Caucasian woman in a jeep stopped.

"To Manele Bay."

"The beach or the hotel?"

"The beach."

It turned out she was one of the imported executives at the hotel. I showed her 'Iokepa's snapshot. Without a moment's hesitation, she said, "I know him. He always has a big smile and an *Aloha*. I know exactly where he sits."

We drove and chatted. She circled behind the beach.

"He should be right...there!"

I walked slowly up behind him and at the very last moment I said out loud. "I recognize that beach chair. And that hair too."

He turned and smiled. I leaned over and kissed him.

It was the beginning. There were many important and unimportant words shared. I remember a few.

I said, "No blaming, no complaining. I chose and I choose."

He said, "We don't struggle for power, we struggle for understanding."

And, "Sometimes I think you're like a wild mare. It isn't about conquering her. It's about *appreciating* her freedom."

Finally, he said. "The path to everything is through our own self. I will wait for you to go through whatever you have to go through Inette Gayle. It can't be mine – but I'll be there while you go through it. What brought us together, will keep us together."

I couldn't ask for more.

PART THREE

LIVING FAITH: ONE

June

Alone, I flew back to Kaua'i exactly one year to the day since I had first arrived to make it my home. 'Iokepa stayed behind on Maui. Nathan flew to his Dad's for the summer.

It felt as if someone had lifted a veil. The sunlight on Kaua'i was softer than I remembered and it cast subtle changing shadows over incredibly green mountains. It was a light show constantly shifting. The ocean invited me from every angle and on every road I drove. It was beautiful. Had I missed it before? The Island's embrace was gentle – I felt nurtured by the Mother.

Eleanor and Phil reinvented themselves as my literary patrons and had scrubbed their guest wing top to bottom until it shone. Eleanor welcomed me with a flower *lei*; Phil had set up my computer. The Camry was glowing at the front door.

I bought food and began writing. I barely looked up for the next four months. But when I did, Phil and Eleanor were there for me: inviting me to dinner or offering me fresh baked bread or hushing their friends and neighbors lest they disturb the writer. When Nathan returned in August, they opened a bedroom and bath in their home to him.

Only one week after I returned, 'Iokepa was there and loving. He said he had missed me profoundly.

'Iokepa went about his day – his 'job' – and returned when the grandmothers told him it was time. Sometimes I was ready for a break, sometimes I was not. Day and night, I wrote. He never intruded. For the first time in my life I wrote with another person in the room. I wrote longer and I wrote better.

At the end of each day I read him the day's prose. He often cried over the ancestors' words.

Sometimes after dinner we danced to Aretha. I followed his lead and I felt the submission of resistance – but no longer of self.

The relationship had been reborn, perhaps as it had been in the first breath, perhaps deeper.

I doubt that anyone observing us during any part of those first years together missed the sexual charge. He'd tease me with truck driver double entendre and idiom I'd never heard. He'd play with words that he knew would shock me, exhilarate me, make me recoil, and then laugh like a school girl. But he kept his promise. He never swore. He was more than politely bawdy – but never profane.

In some ways he appeared stereotypically male – but in fact he was something else entirely.

"The reason some Hawaiian men are like *this* now," he parodied the strut of muscle-bound machismo, "is because they are like *this* with women." Here, he shot both arms straight out and pressed his hands away from his chest. I laughed at the pantomime.

"Only in inclusion," my grandmothers say, "will the prophecy happen."

He paused a few seconds and listened for the next words. "In cultures where women are removed or neglected – where they are secondary – there is war. War is what happens when men are searching for what they've lost – their female half. There is no balance – *kaulike'ole*.

"We don't have to *do* anything to make women equal – or to make men sensitive and inclusive. We are already half our mothers. We have only to recognize what God created. See it and live it."

I listened and I remembered the grandmothers' words. *The prophecy is a feminine one. Through you, he knows the hurt men have inflicted on the women they say they love.* Through my pain 'Iokepa had become more deeply compassionate.

The unspoken communication between us was forceful. Regardless of distance 'Iokepa called me to him – using neither phone nor written message. He called me by practicing his remembered mantra: *Manifest your magic with mana and faith.* Whether he was across the room or across the Island, I'd hear the summons at whatever remove and effortlessly find him.

He'd think it; I'd hear it. Sometimes I'd ask, "Did you say something? Were you speaking to me?" It was *that* loud. A dozen times a day in a dozen important and trivial ways we spoke – explicitly and without words.

Since I'd returned I was repeatedly told, 'You look ten years younger.' A rabbi's wife I met, in her mid-thirties, did a neck-snapping, double-take when I told her my age. "Well," she said, "this life sure agrees with you." I didn't know whether to laugh or cry.

I thought long and hard before I answered her. "I suppose you're right – but it's not because I haven't fought it."

'Iokepa asked me, "Would you do it again?" Would I have chosen this life, knowing what I know now? The answer is spiritually meaningless. Thank God, I had only to make that particular choice once. There are other choices for other times. The choice I make now – knowing what I know – comes from a different place.

> *An unchallenged faith is no faith at all. An unchallenged life is surface and shallow.*

In Phil and Eleanor's guest house we were joined by an idiosyncratic spirit. Every night we'd close the gate to our garden, setting the heavy latch in place. In the morning – every morning – it had swung open.

> *Before the houses were built on these hills this was his playground. He misses what was. The open fields are strangled now with fences and gates. In your vision of the future he sees his past. He leaves the gate open as a reminder.*

"*Hele laulā,*" 'Iokepa reiterated. "We act with freedom.

"No one can throw us out of our house, fire us from our jobs, or empty our bank account. After we've given everything away, what can they take from us? We are servants only to God."

August

In August, when 'Iokepa was gone again (this time to Honolulu) I did some quick math. In our fifteen months together on Hawai'i we'd spent five apart.

That had not been the plan back in Portland when 'Iokepa spoke of our home. It would be a simple Hawaiian cottage: wooden floors covered with woven mats; no walls, just wide-open screens. The house would look out on papaya, banana, avocado and mango trees – on irrigated fields for growing *kalo*. We never expected to own it. Unfailingly, it would be open to others.

Now I imagined, we'd have to wait a little longer for that. There was, first of all, these *ten years of grooming* – that preparation of the messenger to carry the message.

But apart, for one month in three, had definitely not been the plan as I understood it. 'Iokepa had spoken of Linda and Paul McCartney, who in their thirty-year marriage never spent a night apart. "Like that I'll come with you on book tour. Like that you'll travel with me around the Islands."

Yet that was not what God and ancestors had in mind. It had taken me a year to reconcile our expectations with theirs. I'd fought the separations every step of the way. I'd literally fought my way into each of them. But I was reconciled to them now. Time apart was uninterrupted time to work. Time apart was precious, inimitable time with Nathan.

Still I missed 'Iokepa, and I suspected it would always be harder for me to choose time apart if I were able to choose time together.

Public reaction to 'Iokepa permitted very little middle ground. He was respected and he was reviled – with equal force. In his absence I'd been accused by a man who detested 'Iokepa, who felt threatened by the prophecy, by the force of 'Iokepa's convictions. He targeted me. "You are blinded by love."

I opened my heart to the grandmothers. "Am I?"

> *'Blinded by love' is actually its opposite. It is opening the eyes and seeing God in the soul of another. It is really a matter of 'blinded by no love' – by a closed heart.*
>
> *On the other hand, worshipping, woman to man, is not what we want. It idealizes, it distances. You have not done that with 'Iokepa. You contain him fully human and imperfect in your heart – and you 'worship' who he really is.*
>
> *When you met Christmas morning, you each worshipped the soul within the other. It was recognition, not blinding.*

When Nat had left in June to spend the summer with his Dad, our deal was still on the table: he could choose to live with him. But by the time he flew to West Virginia, there was really no question that he would return to Kaua'i in August.

Two weeks into his eight with his father, he called to reaffirm. "You and 'Iokepa are the only adults I know who aren't stuck, who aren't afraid to take risks. I admire you." I was propelled for weeks on the power of his fifteen year old words.

He returned shortly after 'Iokepa had left for O'ahu. He was thrilled to be back on Kaua'i and reunited with his surfboard and his best friend Erik. He was less than eager to start school again in two weeks.

. . .

'Iokepa flew to Honolulu as usual, with just a ticket from Phil and $20. No one save the grandmothers expected him.

He traveled as the ancestors had decreed. It was at the core of his culture. *Carry only what you can hold in your hand.*

Before he'd left we heard this cautionary tale. A Hawaiian fishing canoe sailed from Ni'ihau and encountered very rough seas. It rocked deeply and took on water.

The *kupuna* – elder – demanded of his crew. "Who has extra?"

A young man emptied the seashells from his pockets and threw them overboard. The sea calmed; the boat stayed its course unharmed.

'Iokepa headed now for the same no-name hostel he'd been dropped at by a shuttle bus driver on his first day in Hawai'i, two and a half years before. Unpredictably on that first visit, he'd discovered the hostel was owned by a third or fourth cousin whom he'd never met.

This time the desk clerk said he could not stay. The hostel had been converted to an international one – open only to those with foreign passports. "But I'll call your cousin."

His cousin by chance – *there is no such thing as coincidence* – had access to a vacant apartment two blocks off the beach in Waikiki. He gave it to 'Iokepa, stocked the refrigerator, and connected the phone.

The cinderblock apartment building was notorious – the site of hardcore heroin traffic, prostitution, and mayhem. Neighbors complained bitterly to police about fistfights, bloodshed, and all night pandemonium. The building's ownership was hung up in a court dispute. It was in legal limbo until the court decided its fate.

Shortly after 'Iokepa arrived a number of the tenants were evicted, the locks were changed, and security guards were posted around the perimeter. They called it a raid and it made the TV news on Kaua'i.

But we both knew the real reason that the apartment was available to him. The grandmothers wanted 'Iokepa right smack in the middle of the drama.

"Alcohol and drugs were something else that was brought here," he told me by phone. "My people can't handle them."

In the beginning he had no bed. The two rooms plus bath were filthy. He slept then on a futon on top of the solitary piece of furniture, a desk. With copious amounts of Clorox he scoured the walls, floors and ceiling. His cousin found him a narrow cot, linens, lamp and chair – from the hostel.

In the empty kitchen cabinets 'Iokepa found a single item. It was a ceramic mug engraved on its ornate sides, *"Grandmother."* He kept it. He has it still.

'Iokepa was elated to be exactly where he was. He ministered by example. It had never been about lecturing; it had always been about radiating a visible alternative – and he did. He was perhaps more visible in Honolulu with his flowing silver hair, his wide Hawaiian brown face, his huge *puka* shell *lei,* and his bare stout calves than he'd been anywhere else.

Honolulu had pretensions to be a modern, urban American city – populated overwhelmingly by ethnic Japanese. Men and women dressed, wore jewelry, and owned automobiles that solidified their upscale status. In contrast, 'Iokepa looked in dress and manner as out-of-the-ordinary as someone released from a Polynesian Disney movie into the middle of Wall Street.

He was told:

> The flag – American or Hawaiian – is a symbol. Yet you can buy it, cut it into pieces, or hang it upside down. But you are a symbol too – and you cannot be changed unless you agree to be.

'Iokepa would not let urban diffidence or indifference prevent him from lavishing his beautiful smile or his warm *'Aloha'* on strangers on the crowded city sidewalk. He savored their reactions.

Once, when a drunk asked 'Iokepa for twenty-five cents he answered. "I have only seventy-five cents and I'm giving it all to you."

The man was taken aback. "But I only asked for twenty-five cents."

"Listen to me. I won't say this again. I am giving you every cent I have. Take it or leave it."

He took it.

Immediately after, 'Iokepa – who had been without food for several days – walked with empty pockets and an empty belly for a mile. He passed a five-star hotel. Two Hawaiian women stepped out in front of him – they'd just taken part in a craft fair. They couldn't miss 'Iokepa's striking *lei.* The women admired it – and bought two. He had money to eat.

When your hand is emptied, it will always be filled.

'Iokepa didn't believe in *teaching* or being *taught* – he'd stop me every time I used the word. "Everything we need is already within us – given at Creation."

The Head of Collections at the prestigious Bishop Museum insisted against his objection that he, like she, was a *teacher.*

He responded. "I'm just the opposite of you. I assume everyone knows. You assume no one does."

Later when he called me at Phil and Eleanor's he told me. "The Bishop Museum's staff is assumed to be expert; you're not supposed to challenge their authority. I asked them where their knowledge came from. It's all out of a book.

"What they're protecting isn't Hawaiian culture at all. It's the Western *idea* of Hawaiian culture."

Paradoxically, in these past years while 'Iokepa depended solely on his ancestors' wisdom – and found his answers in every element of nature – he'd become a voracious and eclectic reader.

"We are in this world now," he explained, "challenged by other cultures. We need to know about those cultures."

He read extensively from early American history.

"Thomas Jefferson, Oliver Wendell Holmes, Benjamin Franklin. We must remind the United States how it was represented at the beginning – and hold it to its best."

'Iokepa explained the counterpoint to his reading. "*Now* we have to read Freud for psychology, Jung for dreams, Goethe for philosophy, and Cicero for human responsibility!" (He had, by then, read each of them – and deeply.)

"But you and I have lived what we've lived because the ancestors lived in the elements – and in the elements *are* psychology and philosophy, theology and human responsibility!"

In attempting to live the ancestors' example, 'Iokepa was sometimes caught short.

There were two different men whom 'Iokepa routinely passed on a Honolulu sidewalk near his apartment. Every morning without fail, he greeted each one with '*Aloha.*' Both ignored him. The first man sat stock still in front of a store and looked through 'Iokepa, as though he were invisible. The second man, fixated in another direction, behaved as though he hadn't heard a word.

Each day, 'Iokepa grew increasingly indignant. Every day, he persisted. Finally, he decided to call the men on their refusal.

The first man, he discovered to his chagrin, was recovering from eye surgery. He couldn't see 'Iokepa at all – had no idea that 'Iokepa was addressing him. That man turned out to be 'one of the warmest human beings.'

The second man was hearing impaired. It took a near-by shop owner to let 'Iokepa know.

'Iokepa told me (and later, others) this story on himself. "How quick I was to judge. What a jerk I was." He'd laugh and shake his head.

After three weeks, 'Iokepa was smothering inside his cinderblock prison. He was kept up all night by screamed obscenities, tripping over broken beer bottles on the stairwell, and feeling smashed up against airless views of other cement walls. He yearned for the '*āina.*

He is in Honolulu to feel the land, even when it is bur-
ied under office buildings, stores, automobiles, and con-
crete; to feel the heart of his people even when they are
buried under foul language, greed, and drugs. Both his
land and his people are there – only hidden.

Nothing and nowhere, on the Island – or on Earth – is
to be written off as lost. No one is lost to God.

'Iokepa sat on his tiny balcony – facing across a narrow river of concrete to another decrepit building (eight floors of pink wall and rotting windows) – and beat the ancient rhythms, day and night, on his tattered *pahu.* He sat, too, on the tiny scrap of grass that constituted a park in the middle of a busy boulevard – and hammered out the heartbeat of his people and his land.

"Drums reverberate," he said on one of our nightly phone calls. "Even after you stop playing them, you can still feel their vibrations in the air."

"So does every word we speak," I answered.

Perhaps the highlight of 'Iokepa's month alone in Honolulu was his visit with family. His father's only living sibling was ninety-one year old Uncle Gideon – a highly educated Hawaiian who'd been an articulate spokesman for the *kanaka maoli.* He was equally fluid in both English and Hawaiian – and this was rare. He'd straddled two worlds.

He had served in almost every school on Kaua'i and Ni'ihau as teacher, then principal. He'd also been a celebrated *lapa'au* – a practitioner of traditional medicine, using the healing herbs and plants.

He lived now with 'Iokepa's cousin in Honolulu.

Uncle Gideon's name had paved a wide path for 'Iokepa. The man was revered. Despite generous success in a Western world, he'd never forsaken what was Hawaiian.

'Iokepa's visit to his patriarchal uncle two and half years before – when he'd first arrived in Honolulu – had gone badly. His uncle insisted that his own mother ('Iokepa's grandmother) would never instruct a man to quit his job, relinquish his worldly goods, and come to Hawai'i empty handed. It seemed at the time that Uncle Gideon feared his own esteemed position might be compromised by a penniless nephew who spoke to spirits.

This time the visit was a whole different story. Gideon deferred to 'Iokepa on all matters sacred and seemed genuinely honored by his nephew's presence. He worried only about one thing. "Among all the false voices, how will they know you?"

"The one who lives the example," 'Iokepa answered, "the one whose words match his deeds. We always hear the truth. But fear is a mighty obstacle."

His uncle, past ninety but sharp as a tack and handsome to boot in his pressed Oxford shirt and khaki slacks, nodded his agreement. "It is."

Taking our truths back to source – in this case human source, family – is always pivotal. It is measuring our growth against those who remember us in a different way. No false notes would have gone undetected. With family he had to ring truer than a piece of crystal.

After three weeks apart, 'Iokepa invited me to spend some time with him in Honolulu. I spent a week. Except for changing planes at the airport, I'd never been before.

I had not been to *any* city for fifteen months and I wasn't sure that I was up to it – the noise, the crime, the pollution. But I was quite wrong. I loved every minute of it: the neon lights, the street performers; people-watching tucked under 'Iokepa's arm on a bench in Waikiki. I loved the restaurants and the glitz.

We slept on our sides together on the narrow cot in 'Iokepa's apartment. Every twist or turn in bed was a twist or turn for both. But after three weeks without him, I refused to let him sleep on the floor as he'd offered.

'Iokepa took me to meet his Uncle Gideon. We spoke for an hour and a half. It was a forceful exchange, and I was touched by his interest.

"The Hawaiians *know*." I said.

"But so many do not speak, so many are silent," he answered.

"Because they've been shamed," I said. "Shamed into silence."

I thought of how the cream of Hawaiian youth (the best and the brightest including Uncle Gideon) had been skimmed off the native population for more than a hundred years, and fed into a select, tuition-free, boarding school in Honolulu.

The Kamehameha School was the missionary's ideal of civilized Christian education, and that coveted, respected institution drained the lifeblood from the Hawaiian people.

A friend on Kaua'i – now sixty-five and a retired engineer – told us his story. He'd been proud and privileged to be selected from a remote Westside village at age twelve. "You had to be Hawaiian," he said. "But when I got there, there were no Hawaiian history, language, or culture classes. I was shocked!

"You couldn't eat unless you spoke in English.

"After five years, I graduated. I could no longer speak our language. I was ashamed of being Hawaiian. I could sing *Oklahoma* – and I just wanted to be American."

At Uncle Gideon's, I remembered the words on the simple black button with white letters that I'd bought ten years before at the Holocaust Museum, in Washington. 'Never Again!'

Despite the tyranny, the defilement of their homeland, and the corruption of all that they traditionally valued – they remember still. Tell me how I – a *Jewish* woman – could not understand that about the Hawaiian people?

Most evenings, 'Iokepa drummed for me on his balcony. It felt enchanted. The *pahu* spoke tangible words. Our conversations too seemed inspired. We tripped off one another's ideas.

I remember a few thoughts that we shared.

"The asking *is* the destiny," he said. "We already know before we ask for it."

And: "You can't live miracles unless you're human. They are only miracles to human eyes."

I recalled, on that balcony, the infuriating encounter we'd had with an Englishman, the day before. The traveler bragged that when the natives saw the English three-mast, sailing schooners three-hundred years ago, they must have enthused, 'Beautiful!'

'Iokepa, brimming with barely suppressed emotion, replied.

"Maybe the *first* one – Captain Cook's ship – but not after that. Not when those schooners brought epidemic and death. They wiped out most of my ancestors. You're speaking about my family!"

The Englishman took 'Iokepa's measure and without a shift in expression said. "That's the way the cookie crumbles."

I was livid. I leapt out of my café chair before 'Iokepa could stop me. Toe to toe with the imperious lout, I said. "You and I, sir, are guests here! I don't know how *your* parents reared you, but *mine* insisted that I honor the people and the home I am a guest in."

On that balcony, we spoke of anger – and its twin, forgiveness.

"Anger is reactive. It's intrinsically weak," 'Iokepa said. "It is playing their game on their field."

We agreed. The *kanaka maoli* will not be free as long as violence is an acceptable response. The same was true for 'Iokepa and me. We fought one another that first year to learn the weakness of the fight. We fought and learned, also, the hypocrisy of the fight – healing a people without healing ourselves.

I remembered a time we visited a Hawaiian man we knew well. To 'Iokepa he said. "I admire your defense of gentleness in the face of all that's been done." The words were particularly poignant because our visit took place in a high-security prison. This loving father and gentle husband, under the tragic influence of misdiagnosed drugs, had killed his landlord.

They took away the religion, language, personal identity – and replaced it with their own. It is reasonable to feel righteous anger – but it is not acceptable to conduct yourselves with anger. It is not within the culture.

"With *kanaka maoli*," 'Iokepa told me, "I can be loud and passionate about our language and culture – and they get it. But with *malihini* I am immediately labeled the *'angry Hawaiian.'* It was true, and I had to be watchful of myself on his behalf. Any number of times I'd been passionate – and loud – about the plight of the indigenous people. 'Iokepa sat silently. But later we'd hear a very different version of the event: "I'm told 'Iokepa was rough on..." *My* impassioned words were without exception attributed to him.

On the last morning of my visit, we sat again on that little concrete balcony. He leaned into the listening. He heard that he was to return to the Island of Hawai'i.

I flew back to Kaua'i, to Nathan, and to my writing.

. . .

For the next three nights and three days 'Iokepa did not sleep at all – his raucous neighbors were in high gear. For those last three days he spent in Honolulu, he had neither money nor food. I asked him by phone, "Do you feel virtuous when you look at a time of deprivation and say, 'I did it.'?"

"No," he said quietly, "just responsive to the responsibility of faith."

Without food, sleep, or money he used the single return ticket Phil had given him when he'd left Kaua'i, and flew to Kona. In the absence of other guidance, he stayed put that day and then that night in the Kona airport. The security guard asked him to make himself inconspicuous.

Without food or sleep he told me that he felt the opposite of weak. He told me he felt 'armed for bear.'

The next morning he walked three miles from the airport toward town, before he got a lift into Kailua. He set up his beach chair on a tiny scrap of Town Park, and slept. Over the next few days, hostile drug dealers and mean drunks challenged his right to live on their turf. One particular young punk led the verbal assault. Police, seeing just another brown-skinned, trouble-maker intermittently told him to move on. He washed himself in the sink of a filthy public restroom – astounding the thugs by leaving every scrap of his possession outside for the snatching. No one touched them. He sold his *lei* when he needed to eat.

"The *kanaka maoli* are the tough guys – for all the wrong reasons," he said. "They smoke *paka lōlō* (marijuana) and they drink. It emboldens them. But our ancestors were the real tough guys – they didn't do either."

There were breakthroughs.

"People passed me in cars stuck in their half-soul syndrome," he described the vacuous stares. "But they'd melt down and actually smile at the sound of the drum."

Out of the blue, his former antagonist, the leader of the pack blurted out. "You're the chosen one aren't you?"

"That's not important." 'Iokepa answered.

By tradition, every child's name carried his or her future. 'Iokepa Hanalei 'Īmaikalani means in the grandmothers' words: *The best from heaven – who is God – has chosen you to work to bring the people together* . 'Iokepa claimed nothing more. But he claimed nothing less either.

I asked the grandmothers: "Why, 'Iokepa?"

> *What 'Iokepa sees as privilege, others see as hardship duty. To the one who fits the glass slipper, it is a perfect fit. To others the fit is painful. There wasn't a crowd clamoring for the job. Others are occupied elsewhere, with other tasks.*

September

I was thrilled that once again God returned 'Iokepa to us for the Jewish High Holy days. It was a complete surprise. He was home for *Rosh Hashanah*.

Nathan hadn't seen 'Iokepa for almost four months. Their reunion took place on a public street. Nathan was hitchhiking and 'Iokepa happened to be driving past.

'Iokepa pulled over, stopped the car, and waited for Nathan to notice him. Then he climbed out and let Nathan make the first move. That move was the rare, unhesitant public bear hug from a fifteen year old boy. Some things were definitely worth the wait.

In synagogue the next morning, the Rabbi held forth (as every Rabbi on Earth held forth that day) about the story of Abraham – the *Torah* portion for *Rosh Hashanah*. Every year, I struggled with what God asked of Abraham, the sacrifice of his son, Isaac. What kind of God would ask this of his faithful? I wasn't the only member of the Jewish community to struggle with it.

The Rabbi turned the discussion of God's intentions over to the congregation, and nothing new or inspiring had yet been offered. We were all groping.

'Iokepa leaned respectfully over me, and whispered, "Do you mind if I...?"

I smiled, "Of course not."

And he – alone among the seated congregants – stood up in his place. The rabbi acknowledged the sole Hawaiian in the synagogue.

"In the Hawaiian culture...we do not own...our children." He paused between words and delivered them as they were delivered to him. "We know that our children...belong only...to the Creator."

Nathan and I grinned at one another across 'Iokepa's back.

Afterwards, he explained the pauses. "The grandmothers wouldn't let my mouth get in front of my heart."

. . .

In late September, Phil and Eleanor closed down their home and moved to the Island of Hawai'i to be near their son, daughter-in-law, and granddaughters. I boxed up my computer and packed it away in storage. Nathan, 'Iokepa and I were back in tents at Kaheka – the Salt Pans.

I confess it felt like a physical withdrawal for me – the removal of my writing instruments and my daily labor, once again. Tenting still carried more than a few unpleasant memories.

But the weather was beautiful, the sunset, moon rise and falling stars were compensatory. We – all three of us – adjusted well, and waited for whatever came next.

October

It was a particularly beautiful October evening. I was in desperate need of a walk. 'Iokepa had run ten miles that afternoon, and was exhausted, so I was on my own. It was perhaps an hour before dark.

I parked the car in the cul-de-sac of a solidly Caucasian subdivision that had been farm land the year before, and I told him I'd be back before dark. 'Iokepa had an enormous world mythology book on his lap; he settled into the driver's seat to read. I wandered off down the road, in a direction open to impulse.

The evening was breathtaking. A rainbow greeted me at the first corner. The sky was streaked with shades of rose after sunset. I walked on, thinking and then speaking out loud. I misjudged the time of the return trip. So by the time I turned around to head back to 'Iokepa, it was pitch-black, and had been for a half an hour.

I started jogging. This is what I saw when I reached the car.

'Iokepa was standing outside the car, bent in half, with his hands on the rim of our open trunk. Two police cars were parked behind, their headlights blasting him. Several burly officers leaned in around him, shouting questions.

This is what happened.

A transplant from California who lived three houses away near the end of the cul-de-sac saw a middle-aged native Hawaiian sitting in a car near her home, reading – and thought he posed a threat to her safety. She called the police.

When I jogged up – white and American – and smiled, the police backed off immediately, even apologized to 'Iokepa. It was a curt, "I'm sorry sir." Clearly they wanted the incident to go away.

But before I'd arrived, they had insisted 'Iokepa was lying. That there was no wife walking – that he'd fought with me, maybe even beaten me, and he was refusing to admit it.

"*Where* is she?"

"Walking."

"But *where?*"

"I don't know where. She'll meet me here."

"Why don't you go look for her?"

"Because then I wouldn't be here when she gets back."

But *now* the police were backing away from 'Iokepa, taking the first steps toward their cars – obviously wanting this to end quickly.

To me: "Well, *you* would do the same thing – a strange man parked in front of your home..."

I'd gotten as far as, "I would *not*..."

'Iokepa interrupted with the last words on the matter. "I'd have asked him to come in and eat with us."

And, of course, he would have.

The four officers slammed their car doors, left us sitting in the Camry, and drove away. This was a small Island, we would see them again.

. . .

We were savoring one of our rare solitary mornings – sitting at Kalapaki Beach where 'Iokepa had played as a child across from his grandmother's house. I was reading a book aloud to 'Iokepa.

To get to that beach, we'd made our way through the public beach access to the public parking lot that the Marriott Hotel was mandated by law to provide. We carried our own beach chairs and sat at the far end of the Marriott's grass, at considerable distance from the hotel – an area that the Marriott provided to keep the local population out of sight of their guests.

We'd arrived before eight, taken a swim, and settled our beach chairs in the shade of a large bush. The breeze was perfect, the story I was reading aloud was stirring – we hadn't been to this beach in more than a year.

Abruptly, a huge wall of a security officer appeared from behind the bush.

"We're setting up for a *Lū'au* tonight. There's a sign – you can't be here."

"Oh," I said, "we got here before the sign went up, we didn't see it. We'll move as soon as I finish reading this paragraph."

He pulled out a cell phone. "I'm going to report you!"

So I stood up, conciliatory. I saw what looked like a Hawaiian name on his shirt. I said: "Is that your name?"

"No!" he shouted in my face. "I'm *not* Hawaiian, and I'm glad of it!"

I finished the page and we moved to the water's edge on the sand of the adjoining public beach. The guard's summoned supervisor appeared. I explained what had happened: reasonable people, reasonable story. He listened, and then pulled out a citation – already prepared.

We were forbidden from retrieving our car in the parking lot. The police were called and arrived to lead us to our car. There, we were told we'd been barred from stepping foot on the Marriott's graciously landscaped grounds for one year. My appeal to the hotel's General Manager by phone left us empty-handed. "I support my staff."

('Iokepa had not uttered a single word, and yet this was all about him. So much about him that when the same security officer – until then a total stranger – spotted 'Iokepa at a shopping mall a month later, he screamed obscenities at him and threatened to beat him up.)

Meanwhile, several dozen, very recognizable residents of Kaua'i (in no way pretending to be hotel guests) were sprawled on the Marriott's restricted-to-guests-only beach chairs next to the swimming pool. They were white.

I knew that many Americans looked at the racial mix in Hawai'i, and smiled benevolently at the *melting pot* – the diversity that had become one. They liked to imagine Hawai'i as a munificent example for the rest. It was an innocent enough daydream. I, too, once believed it.

What outsiders imagined as an enlightened example of integration, *kanaka maoli* knew was not. The native Hawaiians were the invisible minority: ignored politically, economically and socially; paraded as tokens only – for tourist entertainment.

Stereotypically (and at obvious disservice to each culture) – Japanese were called the smart ones. (The state's civil service, school system, and political arena were overwhelmingly Japanese.) Caucasians were the rich and powerful ones. (The multi-million dollar beachfront homes were dominantly theirs. The original sugar cane families still held sway.) Filipinos, the last ethnic group imported for labor, were labeled hardworking, in the way of recent immigrants – and fecund. (They filled almost all hotel service jobs.) Hawaiians weren't part of anyone's equation.

'Iokepa elaborated. "People come here saying, 'We're all One' – and they feel virtuous for saying it. But the ones who say it are the same ones doing the taking."

The grandmothers made the distinction.

Not: 'We are all One.' But rather: We are a multitude of ones, created by the One.

"Culture comes from survival in a particular place," 'Iokepa said. "Ritual is the gratitude for that survival."

If we accepted the story that we are all the same, then there was truly no reason to preserve or celebrate aboriginal culture. The goal becomes, instead, the obliteration of differences – the eradication of our unique gifts.

. . .

From the grief comes the birth of the Hawaiian nation.

Since 1972 when the oppressive laws were dropped, men and women of good heart and good intention have championed the Hawaiian sovereignty movement. In identifying the need for an independent Hawaiian nation, and in courageously dedicating their lives towards that elusive goal, the sovereignty leaders – and they have been many, and varied – offered *kanaka maoli* a focal point for pride, a reminder of self-esteem.

To these men and women is owed the awakened memory of the Hawaiian nation. To them is owed reawakened interest in the language, cultural immersion classes, rebirth of *hula hālau*, and the Hawaiian voyaging canoes (in the manner of the ancient voyagers). To them is owed gratitude for every struggle to reclaim every parcel of land that had been usurped and desecrated.

They have been blamed for their diversity. 'Iokepa and I had often heard, 'The Hawaiians can't even agree among themselves.' It was both, an accusation – and an excuse to do nothing.

'Iokepa's unswerving enthusiasm confounded the critics. 'Isn't it wonderful? All that energy – different paths to the same goal! That's how you build a nation! It'll be exciting, when it all comes together.' That it *would* come together, he entertained no doubt.

But his walk has been solitary – *kū ka'awale*. He joined no group (not even a canoe club), because it had been proscribed by the grandmothers – though their members and leaders were among his friends, family, and allies. Of each, he said. "They are passionate about our culture." He would not bad-mouth his *ohana*.

Jonathan Kamakawiwo'ole Osorio, among the newly emergent *kanaka maoli* historians wrote: "Having identified themselves with America, most residents of Hawai'i do not understand that our self-definition as Hawaiians has little to do with trying to gain political and economic advantage over them. It has everything to do with kinship."

Throughout aboriginal history, land ownership in Lāhui was an oxymoron. Until 1848, all land was held in stewardship for the Creator – cared for by unending generations of *kanaka maoli*. But in 1848, foreigners with insatiable sugar cane ambitions (children and grandchildren of the first Calvinist missionaries) manipulated and bullied a series of hospitable monarchs – and changed that overnight.

By 1891 a few dozen Europeans and Americans owned sixty-six percent of Hawai'i. Along with ownership, the land barons created taxation. The *kanaka maoli* didn't know what taxes were and, of course, they had no money to pay them – unless they agreed to work for the sugar cane lords.

The land transfer of 1848 hypothetically offered the native people of Lāhui an opportunity to make ownership claims on the land of their ancestors. In fact, the claims were required to be made in person, in Honolulu. It involved filling out pages of incomprehensible paperwork. Even this murky offer evaporated after just a few months. This: to a people who had no word in their language for 'ownership.'

For hundreds of years, the native Hawaiians have been the back-drop for other peoples' aspirations – the tool for others peoples' dreams. First the despot Pa'ao, then the whalers, the missionaries, the sugar cane barons, the land developers, the New Age healers – they came and they come still to save the *kanaka maoli* (from their barbarism); to sell *to* them (Christianity and a Western legal system); and to sell *them* body and soul (to tourists).

There have been sovereignty groups who lobbied Congress; others who petitioned the World Court or the United Nations. Regularly, there have been protest marches in front of the last Queen's palace in Honolulu – and in front of the Capital building in Washington, D.C.

Since the early 1990s, approximately two thousand native Hawaiians have renounced their U.S. citizenship as part of the sovereignty movement. Some have done it individually; some as part of political organizations. All have struggled with institutional pressure in claiming a nation that is as yet unrecognized internationally.

Yet the existing sovereignty movement never had the numbers. In some ways it remains an elite gathering of idealists who never actually believed they would live to see the nation they championed. It failed to touch hearts in the numbers essential for the change they advocate.

On an evening in late October, we revisited *Poli'ahu heiau*. It was the long delayed and sentimental return to the place where we'd met. We offered our gratitude.

We left the *heiau* and we were directed to turn *left* instead of right. We headed with no idea *why*, due north. Not a single traffic light slowed our progress. On this typically congested Friday night we drove on an empty highway. We knew we were on track because absolutely nothing stood in our way.

After twenty minutes we found ourselves at the public park in Anahola. Three large tents had been set up, where sovereignty leaders from Oʻahu were laying out provisions for the new Hawaiian nation. It was dry, legalistic, and boring. We turned and recognized an activist we'd met picketing on the streets of Honolulu. He remembered ʻIokepa as the *prophet.* ʻIokepa remembered him as the man who'd studied American law on Wednesday nights and International law on Thursday – so as to best the Americans at their own game.

ʻIokepa honored the man and his goal, but not his methods. Because ʻIokepa was an old pugilist, he knew. "You can't win when you fight your opponent's fight. I do not know politics – Hawaiians were never politicians. But I know Hawaiian history, language, and culture. That's our strength."

And we both knew first-hand that when a person is stirred, when his or her soul is touched by the Creator, when he is ready to reclaim his birthright – no American government and no United Nations can facilitate that claim – or prevent it.

"You can't impose unity – you can only awaken it!" ʻIokepa said.

December

Nathan turned sixteen with a vengeance. It brought extravagant changes. He was inordinately tired of waiting for his life to begin. He was exceedingly tired of living someone else's idea of how he should spend five days a week (trapped inside a high school), someone else's notion of what constituted an education (mindless paperwork and sterile instruction), and someone else's idea of who he'd surround himself with for companionship (other angry, confused adolescents). He wanted out of school entirely.

But that had never been part of the plan. The plan he'd set for himself since grade school was Harvard – with an already published novel under his belt, several musical compositions, and some grand technological design that drew on both his art skills and his mathematical ones. They weren't idle plans. He thrived on unstructured time – he was completely self-motivated. He set goals and he used his free time well to fulfill them.

But Nathan now insisted that school (which only last year he'd relished) was draining his motivation, sucking him dry. He was certain that spending eight hours, five days a week heading toward, returning from, or zoning out of the bedlam and boredom that was school was depriving him of an education. I wasn't sure he was wrong. But I thought school was the obstacle course all of us were required to negotiate. I was unable to define a different course.

I was the child of a solidly middle class Jewish family who took education very seriously. Schoolwork was the bedrock. Everything else was a frill. With me, Nathan was beating a dead horse.

But Nathan wasn't without resources to reshape his destiny. At the end of the first quarter, he brought home his usual exemplary grades. By the middle of the second quarter, he was failing every class. I was shocked. He wasn't at all surprised. Each teacher had summoned him and said, "I can't pass you if you don't come to class."

So, it wasn't about tests, homework, or grades, and it wasn't about drugs, alcohol or sex. It was about: climbing on the school bus every morning and spending his days elsewhere – not the first teenager to do it. But this was Nathan! We argued.

> *Love the boy – ignore the behavior. Forgive him, so he may forgive himself. You owe him no less than you offer the rest.*
>
> *You are the perfect adults for Nathan now. You live your truth. It is all that parents can do.*

Into the thick of the fray, a family of transplanted Californians arrived: Mom, Dad and four children. They camped near us at the Salt Pans. The oldest sons were sixteen and eighteen.

They were, as they explained to us 'no schoolers – not home schoolers.' Their bible was *The Teenage Liberation Handbook*.

They were beautiful, creative, wholesome, smart, well-behaved, enthusiastic young people. They agreed that Nathan didn't belong in school either.

Nathan now had a social world at the park. In addition to the 'no schoolers,' there were two girls, a year younger than Nathan, who'd found him reason enough to spend every non-school hour at the park. We'd send them home after dark.

Now Nathan put it on the line. He refused, he said, to live a lie. He wanted to take charge of his own education. He wanted, once again, the adventure to begin.

As I lay next to 'Iokepa in our tent that night, I stared wide-eyed at the blank nylon wall. My stomach was churning; I was filled with anxiety. I had only questions – no answers – for Nathan or for me. But the ancestors did.

> *You can put Nathan on the school bus, but you can't make him go to school. You always said you trusted Nathan: Praised his maturity, intelligence, perseverance, and kindness. Now is the time to live what you speak.*

At 'Iokepa's suggestion, we committed our thoughts to paper. We wrote what we agreed was a two-page contract between us – signed and notarized it for no other reason than to vest his decision with the seriousness it deserved. Clearly we were not looking for legal recourse, just upping the pressure on Nathan. He didn't flinch.

In our contract, we first spelled out our resistance, doubts and concerns. Then finally, "We have agreed to Nathan's decision because Nathan's judgment is sound and he is capable of making the best decision on his own behalf."

On his last day of school Nathan told each teacher his plan. Some offered him private instruction. By state law, attendance was mandatory until eighteen. I signed him out at the registrar's office – and checked the box that said we were moving out of the district.

Nathan asked permission to spend his first week without school alone at the most remote beach on the Island – Polihale. He packed his tent, guitar, books (Sartre's *Nausea*, Kafka' *Metamorphosis*, Kurt Cobain's biography) and a stack of paper to write and draw on. We filled bags with food for him and drove him through the cane fields to the pristine beach.

'Iokepa had to peel me off of Nathan. I was hovering with gratuitous advice on where to pitch his tent.

"Not *there*, Nathan. It's too windy."

It was hard to let go.

But that was *nothing* compared to what came next. Fast on the heels of his week alone at Polihale, two days before leaving for Christmas vacation with his father – he let me know he was not coming home on January 3.

He'd done his research: his air ticket would be good for another two months; the train from his Dad's to Wisconsin would cost him $60 of his recent $400 birthday and *Chanukah* stash. He planned to stay in the apartment with Ben and Ben's girlfriend – they'd agreed. He was not asking my permission.

I freaked. Then, I got it. Free of school, he wanted more than Kaua'i. Ben's was a safe first bet.

At the Park, his new friends – both girls – cried when they heard. The older boys cheered him on. At the airport, his best friend Erik was grim. "You're coming back aren't you?"

"Sure, I am." But the 'When?' was left open.

In the end, I didn't laugh or cry. But I felt as though someone had pulled the heart out of my body. This was two years too soon.

For weeks after he left, I grieved. There is no other word for it. I felt emptied. But when the phone calls began, I heard what every mother wants to hear.

"I'm really happy. You have no idea how much school took out of me," he said.

"I love you Mom, but I don't miss you. When I screw up now, it's mine – when I do something good, it's mine. There's no parent between me and my decisions."

It turned out, he was good for Ben. He reminded his big brother of a responsibility beyond himself, at a time in Ben's life when the reminder was crucial. Ben, it turned out, was good for Nathan too. He loved his little brother and created a home for him.

Nathan got a night job bagging groceries at a supermarket. I thought of his lifelong organizational challenges and imagined the fresh eggs under the tomato juice. I laughed, but I was proud of him.

He was writing like crazy, reading books off Ben's college bookshelf, and making himself helpful. My grief evaporated, replaced by genuine satisfaction. My boys were no longer with me – but they were with one another, and certainly with God.

January, 2000

Only in experiencing loss, can you begin to understand the Hawaiian people. You write from loss – but you also write from strength. They are not exclusive – for you or for the kanaka maoli.

I thought I had moved to Hawai'i to make a life with 'Iokepa – and in one sense, of course, that was true. But the real reason took me almost two years to understand. I moved to Hawai'i to listen.

I wasn't raised to listen. I don't think modern American culture reared me in that subtle necessity. It is a noisy culture – and not just for the diversions: television, cinema, telephones, and traffic. It is a culture that values sound, and labels silence negatively. A lull in the conversation means a *failure* to speak; a quiet person is *timid*; a lack of activity is *passive.*

The *kanaka maoli* knew otherwise. In silence, came the answers. The Earth spoke in a myriad of voices: the bird songs, the ocean tides, the fog, and sometimes too, in the words we humans exchanged.

The people of Lāhui were isolated on this tiny piece of land in the middle of the Pacific Ocean. Their sole corridor to knowledge lay in their breath. They sucked it in with every inhalation, released it effortlessly in every exhalation – and were reminded by it, of their connection to the Creator.

God gave us all, it seemed, this uncomplicated path to remembering who we are and what we promised. It happens without thought or exertion. And yet we forget.

> *The purpose of human life is to be who we were born to be at all times, with all people. To be 'lightened' of human mask or charade. There is a unique signature to each soul. It is how we recognize one another – the light by which we see past human form.*
>
> *Imagine, for a moment, a world where every soul in human form is so lightened. That is hāʻupu – remembering who we are, as a prelude to reclaiming life itself.*
>
> *But making 'enlightenment' a human goal is wrong. We do not beat a bud for not yet being a flower. Instead we celebrate the sporadically 'lightened' human in embryo.*

Neither ʻIokepa nor I look back on our first year together in Hawaiʻi with pride in our erratic words or actions. Each of us would have preferred to purge parts of that year from our hearts, minds, and the written page. But not only could that not happen – for the purposes of the Hawaiian prophecy, it must not. This is the story of the human possibilities of spirit. But it is equally the story of the human path, burdened with fears and doubts. I lived it, and I have exposed my weakest. But it is (for all of us on Earth) just the short pause in our steady return to remembering.

Finally, I had found home. It turned out not to be a place on any map. The confusion of identity, the fear of being an appendage to the man I loved, were long gone. So was the resentment. Neither ʻIokepa nor the ancestors had ever asked me to give away pieces of myself. On the contrary, they'd never stopped telling me to claim my own. Home, finally, was me. It was a powerful challenge. I live to fulfill it.

Today, I am no less the journalist, the witness to history, than I was for twenty years. It was and is one of the important reasons I am here.

I am no less the writer – though I do not get to choose the time, place, or frequency that I once did. There was a tradeoff. I now own the story of a lifetime. That, too, was why I have chosen (and been chosen for) this particular pathway: to tell the tale.

I am no less Jewish and no less a woman than I was before – quite the contrary. Because I am a Jewish woman, I understand oppression. And as far as I understand, the only gift of oppression is an unwillingness to tolerate it in any shape or form – to any people.

"The function of freedom," Nobel winning author Toni Morrison said, "is to free someone else."

Naturally, I am no less a mother. I bring to my mothering a depth of faith. I know that Ben and Nathan are protected by more powerful forces than my own. I have faith, too, in my sons, in their good judgment, good hearts, and integrity. I regret deeply the times we are apart – but they are young men now on their own voyages. I straddle that line all parents do: being present for them with my opinions, ideas, ways of doing – and allowing them their own.

I mother many now who are not biologically my own – nor by strict definition, even children. It is the responsibility of a *kupuna*, or elder. That too, is part of the job.

I was a *malihini* embarking on a rite of passage that asked me to walk naked in someone else's homeland – on foreign terra firma. I didn't always behave with wisdom or with dignity. That acquisition continues to come in fits and starts.

I was mute during that first year, but I am no longer shy about telling my story. I know that I have been prepared by the work of my lifetime for the job I am asked to accomplish now.

. . .

"It did not feel good," Maxine Hong Kingston wrote in *Hawai'i One Summer*, "to be a writer in a place that is not a writing culture, where written language is only a few hundred years old."

I understood what she was saying. I am a writer. I massage, pleasure in, and lavish affection on the written word – but I do not idealize or idolize it. It is not my god. I do not believe that which is bound in leather (or cardboard) is therefore true or authentic. I know better.

The rich oral traditions are lost to our Western world. We've made false idols of the written word. We assumed that what was written carried a weight that what was spoken did not.

I know, too, what has been lost from the rich subtle shadings of the spoken word. It is as if we have broken a leg – we limp to one side. When we hear 'oral tradition,' we assume it is unreliable.

But the indigenous Hawaiians knew another way. The oral transmission was anything but haphazard. It was exact.

In every family, and to every generation, there was a child born to be the carrier of the chants – the history. They were those ordained to remember – and repeat – the genealogy. It took that child half a lifetime to acquire the transmission; the remainder of that life, to pass it on. He or she embraced the skills of memory and the gifts of living oratory.

'Iokepa said. "When the written word came, the aboriginal culture ended. The aboriginals saw it for what it was: in 'black and white' – hard and fast – it no longer changed in a breath. It was no longer alive and true in this moment.

"It marked the devaluation of living experience. We no longer depended on community for transmission. (We could be alone with our book.) We no longer needed our grandmothers."

In deifying the written word, we give ourselves away to others – to their greater knowing. We celebrate scientists, at the cost of our own knowing. We venerate words on the page, at the cost of words written on our soul. We make gods of human invention, so as to take God away from our own human heart.

The book *Grandmothers Whisper* is written, and it is bound. It wasn't researched in a library. It wasn't spoken by living *kupuna*. It was received from the ancestors, snatched from the *mana* in the airwaves, and played on the living instrument that is breath.

If it rings true, it is simply because in our effortless breath we have remembered – the intention, reason, and grandeur of *Aloha.*

KA WA MAHOPE (WHAT CAME AFTER)

Two Years Later

In total – now four years after we met at the *heiau* – we've gone through nine tents and eight air mattresses. The tents were destroyed in turn by wind, rain, *kiawe* thorns, and unrelenting ultra-violet sunlight. From the day Nathan left, 'Iokepa and I have not slept apart.

In the Millennial year 2000, we slept merely under towels on Hapuna Beach on the Island of Hawai'i. We hitchhiked in with no money and no food. For three days we ate nothing and drank only water. Then, like a violent tornado on a quiet beach: $460 worth of *lei* sold to a half dozen people, in an hour.

In August that year, an improbable royalty check arrived from Germany, for a book I'd written fourteen years before. It was $1,868. To-the-dollar, it was the amount needed for airfare to visit my mother and my sons. The ancestors were precise.

My mother, who was wary to the extreme of meeting 'Iokepa, was ultimately won over by his not-inconsiderable charm. For his part, he found her 'adorable in every way.'

She was disarmed by his humor.

"Nobody knows what happens after we die!" my mother insisted.

"*You* know, Hannah," 'Iokepa grinned across her breakfast table. "And *I* know that *you* know."

They both laughed.

When we left, my eighty-eight year old mother gave him a huge hug, and gushed. "I didn't think I was going to like you. But you're really a swell fella'."

This year, 2001, we slept only fourteen days inside of walls. We slept forty-six consecutive nights in the Hotel Camry – a memorable record for discomfort and displacement.

The grandmothers instructed 'Iokepa: *Make no more lei. Go deeper in faith. Something else will come.* He made no more.

Between us, we lost forty-two pounds. There was very little food.

One month, I had no money to buy tampax. I made do for five days of very heavy bleeding with the thin, ragged toilet paper from the public bathroom at a Westside beach.

The ancients lived a spiritual and cultural consensus. They fit comfortably into the heart of their community. We do not. It's a thornier time to be living what 'Iokepa and I are asked to live.

Our lifestyle was not universally embraced. To many, it seemed – and seems – extreme, fanatic, *suspect* even. Many who respect 'Iokepa still struggle to connect our seeming deprivation with a prophecy fulfilled.

As 'Iokepa picked up confidence, words, and steam – so did the institutional oppression.

Handcuffed, shackled, and fingerprinted – 'Iokepa was held in jail for twenty-three hours on a bogus charge by an "Anonymous" witness. He was released, without indictment, for "Insufficient Evidence." No witness ever materialized.

The arrest was arbitrary. That charge was murder. The imagined victim was me! My reappearance from a solitary walk in the sugar cane fields simply altered the charge to abuse. They were determined to arrest him.

"I walk ten miles every day," 'Iokepa said afterwards. "I have long silver hair and a brown face. The police know I'm a sovereign Hawaiian, and they couldn't figure out why they didn't have me in their system. Now they have me."

When one of the dozen officers (and half dozen police cars) that surrounded him, told him he was suspected of *murder* (and snapped the handcuffs on his wrists), he whispered to 'Iokepa, "I'm sorry…"

'Iokepa looked him in the eye and said: "Do me a favor. Don't say you are sorry – it's the wrong use of the word."

He remained rock-solid, calm throughout the ordeal. "God gives us wisdom and instincts. I knew I was there for a reason." He used his time well: counseled both inmates and guards in those hours of confinement.

He pondered the unimaginable.

"I don't know what it would feel like to not have a culture. The image I get is that your feet aren't on the ground, you're tugged in all directions, there's no stability. You have no history to draw on – good, or bad."

INETTE GAYLE MILLER
AND
ʻIOKEPA HANALEI ʻĪMAIKALANI

Lovingly invite you to join us,
In a family and community affirmation
Of our enduring marriage.

The ceremony, within the spirit of the Hawaiian Kingdom,
Will be held at Poliʻahu Heiau
Wailua, Kauaʻi

Wednesday, the twelfth of December,
Two thousand and one,
At eleven oʻclock in the morning.

I realize that on some unspoken level, I assumed that ʻIokepa and I would marry soon after Nathan and I moved to the Island. But for the next four years, I may have learned a level of commitment that transcended marriage. I learned to live with trust in a challenging relationship.

Early September last year, 2000, when we were walking for five miles under the searing sun on a stretch of beach at the far western end of Kauaʻi – Mana. – I asked ʻIokepa. "Do you think about marriage?"

He said, "I do. But I don't know what a marriage in the authentic spirit of the ancient culture *looked* like. I haven't been shown yet."

On the afternoon of Wednesday, September 5, 2001 – *exactly* one year after our earlier walk and in the exact same spot – ʻIokepa and I were playing in the waves under that searing September sun. Abruptly, ʻIokepa grabbed me up, wrapped his arms around me, and kept us both afloat while he paddled his legs.

He said: "The ancestors just gave me a precise vision of what a marriage – *in the spirit of the Hawaiian Kingdom* – looks like."

Every single word, he explained, and every single image needed to make that happen had just been handed to ʻIokepa in a breath.

He was jubilant. He described a chanter, two hula dancers, his own *ki* leaf skirt – the place, the time, my *dress*. He said: "We will marry at 12/12 at noon."

A few minutes later he let me go and I swam back to shore speculating on what that vision meant for us. I sat in the shade of a pavilion watching him swim a while longer and then return to join me. He walked slowly across the sand dripping salt water. He stopped suddenly, obviously listening. His grandmothers, he told me moments later, were prodding: *You haven't asked her yet!*

So, in his black and white surfer trunks still dripping wet, 'Iokepa got down on bended knee and asked.

"I didn't know I could love someone so much," he said. There's a sanctuary I feel in your arms, Inette. I know it's what the ancestors have provided.

"I don't just love you. I honor you. I honor how you see things. I honor what you've been through.

"You've grown into more of who you already were. From a thoroughly Jewish woman – you've embraced and under-stood a life within Hawaiian culture. It's beyond what humans expect of one another. But it's exactly what God expects."

He took a breath and paused.

"No one can point a finger at you and say, you've done this for yourself. You've given up your books, your home, and your comfort. You've been forced to live apart from your children and your family. These are not your people.

"Sure, we can get along separately. But together we're stronger, we are whole. It is what the prophecy is about."

He paused again, held my hand tighter and asked. "Inette, will you marry me?"

I was choked from chest to throat with an inexpressible joy. My eyes were brimming. I answered only, "Yes."

But when we would exchange vows, four months later, I had my chance. The ancestors gave me the words.

'Iokepa had literally seen and heard our wedding cere-mony that morning in the ocean at Mana. That vision – and my own longing for the day almost immediately began to unfold.

I'm a woman. Of *course* I thought first of my wedding dress – and immediately found it frustrating and impossible to find anything acceptable on our little Island. But, 'Iokepa had already been shown it. So when he spotted an effervescent white dress in a tiny store window while we walked on a sidewalk in Kapa'a – he recognized it at once and took me inside to look. It was lovely. He knew: I would wear a *po'o lei* –

a circle of white flowers and green *maile* leaves around my head. I would be barefoot.

For himself, he knew he'd be dressed only in a *kī* leaf skirt, tied at the waist with braided *hau* bark – barefooted, bare-chested, bedecked with seven flower and seed *lei* (each one signifying a populated Hawaiian Island). He knew he would weave the skirt himself from the leaf and bark inside another *heiau*. He began gathering and preparing the bark within days of his revelation at Mana.

For me, having all four children present was imperative. And they were: wholeheartedly, lovingly.

'Iokepa knew that on December 12 ("*12/12 at noon*") in the middle of the typically wet Kaua'i winter on a volcano that claimed to be the rainiest spot on Earth – it would be a perfectly sunny day. He refused to consider a tent. He was right.

The wedding unfolded just as 'Iokepa had seen it. He heard the incredible native chanter invoking the ancient parables to the echoing mountains. He saw the magnificent *hula* dancers – a single male and a single female – enunciating the ageless *kahiko* with their hands and their hearts. He heard the trident conch shell sound a cry across the *heiau*, assembling the scattered guests to witness this history.

He saw us walking together across the green grass field toward the *heiau* where we'd met – towards our assembled friends and family. He heard, too, the sounds of Hebrew chants – a Cantor in *tallit* and *kipah*. He knew he would break the wineglass under his bare foot: A traditional reminder at the conclusion of a joyous Jewish wedding, of the pain and oppression of our peoples. A shard left just a fine thread of blood to remember the moment.

I spoke the words that I had been given by the grand-mothers four months before:

"On the first day I set eyes on you 'Iokepa, in this very spot, the spirits of your grandmothers, my father, and this *'āina* surrounded us – and I knew then that you were the soul with whom I would spend my life.

"What I did not know was how much that would ask of me.

"Now – four years later – I know. And with an unrestrained heart, I accept the challenges and the adventures of the path of a prophecy that will return your people to their knowing and their freedom – a life by your side.

"I feel as though every moment of my life so far has prepared me for what is now asked.

"So 'Iokepa, I willingly and eagerly bring all the gifts of my own culture, and my unique soul, to bear on the fulfillment of the Hawaiian prophecy. With all my heart, I join my life with yours."

Just as we had hoped, each of the children wove their love into the ceremony.

Beautiful, soft-spoken, self-reliant Hokulele was there. Now a college graduate, she worked in Honolulu. We'd seen her just three months before the wedding. At the ceremony she spoke extemporaneously. Her words were soft; her emotions amplified them.

With tears rolling from her dark Hawaiian eyes, she said. "I've seen the changes in my father, and I admire him more than I can find words to express. I have always loved him, before and after.

"I didn't know what to expect in Inette. I couldn't have expected her wonderful energy. She is unlike any woman my father has ever been with. They are perfect together."

'Iokepa's oldest, his son Malu, was there. Malu was a college volleyball coach in Idaho. I'd met him for the first time at Hokulele's graduation. He was tall, fair, slender and handsome – the physical and emotional complement of his Dad. They cherished one another.

I'd been dazzled by Malu's solidness and generosity, when he and a girlfriend camped with us for a couple weeks the year before.

Malu was the backbone of our wedding: utterly dependable, easy-going, smart, funny and respectful. He greeted the guests at the ceremony, made sure the chairs were in place, even remembered to pick up the broken glass shards from the smashed wine glass.

Ben was there. I hadn't seen Ben since our visit to Wisconsin the year before. But we spoke by phone every few weeks – for hours. My mother kept us in telephone calling cards just for that purpose. Ben had returned to Beloit the fall after his suspension. Now on a *voluntary* leave from school, he lived in Madison, worked a series of jobs – most recently as technical support for Palm Pilot. Not a bad fit for a computer-obsessed kid. He was in a committed relationship with a wonderful woman he'd met at school. All of it looked good on Ben. He was happy, communicative, loving. He'd grown up.

Last spring, in a rare letter for my birthday, Ben had written me. "Any doubts about how much 'Iokepa loves you are nicely erased and I can now honestly wish the very best for *both* of you. Be happy together."

At the wedding, Ben volunteered to handle the Hebrew prayers. In *tallit* (ritual prayer shawl) and *kipah* (ritual skullcap) he chanted the *Kiddush*, the blessing over wine – offering us grape juice out of the ornate silver *Kiddush* cup that had been given by his grandparents at his *bar mitzvah* eight years before.

"My mother, my brother, and I," he told our fifty assembled guests, "come from another proud and ancient culture. We observe the rituals and traditions of our people. We too, honor our ancestors."

Nathan had grown taller, and cut his hair short. In the *tallit* and *kipah* from his *bar mitzvah* five years before, he chanted the seven Jewish wedding blessings, in Hebrew and in English.

Neither of our mothers – both eighty-nine – could travel to witness the wedding. But both convincingly yearned to be there.

My mother's generous wedding gifts were $4000 and her heartfelt blessing.

'Iokepa had known, too, that without a rehearsal of any kind, we would conclude our vows precisely at noon. *Kau ka lā i ka lolo, ho'i ke aka i ke kino.* When the shadow retreats into our body – then morning (which is male), and evening (which is female) – are one. It was a time of great *mana*.

He was right, of course – about all of it. How could he not have been?

. . .

My mother's generous wedding gift paid the airfare for our four children, and for Ben's girlfriend, Elizabeth. The remainder paid for our reception brunch and a lavish condominium we'd rented for two weeks for our children, and for 'Iokepa and me. With other wedding presents, we stocked the pantry full of food. It was a precious time with our children.

For Nathan, the wedding was also a return *home*. It had been exactly two years since he'd left and a year since we'd been able to visit him. Three weeks before, he had turned eighteen. He stayed with us for more than a month.

He visited old friends. On his second day home, he slept over his friend Erik's and together the young men plunged into the rough North Shore winter ocean. Nathan was carried out to sea by a fierce riptide.

Erik's girlfriend frantically called the rescue squad by cell phone when she saw Nathan disappear.

But Nathan made his way to shore without them, and laughed about it at dinner. "I almost died today," he grinned over pasta.

He was alive enough to tell the tale. We might say this about much of what Nathan has lived – and because he is a writer, he will someday tell his tale.

Nathan now lived in Madison, Wisconsin – a mile from Ben's apartment. He despised the frigid winters, but he loved the public library, the city bus system, the rock concerts, and the freedom. He had unearthed a remarkably progressive public high school named Shabazz for 'academically motivated students'. Shabazz called itself a 'mini-university'. All classes were seminars for eight to ten students; there were no grades; the teachers wrote student evaluations; the students wrote teacher evaluations.

Nathan was a merciless evaluator. "I will hold them to what they claim to be," he said. He supported himself after school and on weekends by making sandwiches at Schlotsky's Deli. He asked no one for a dime.

Even after Nathan got his own apartment, he continued to stop by Ben's place daily after work carrying excess deli meat. Through bouts of illness, unemployment, and occasional heartbreak, the boys have supported one another.

Nathan expected that Madison was the first stop of many, on his journey to independence.

In the extravagant condo our newly-blended family cooked together: sharing breakfasts, dinners, and late night talks under the stars next to the hot tub. Our time with the children passed like lightening. 'Iokepa and I cried copious tears at the airport, first, when Hokulele left, then Malu, then Elizabeth and Ben.

Finally it was just Nathan.

Together we saw the movie Lord of the Rings. I'd read that entire trilogy to the boys at bedtime, as children. Nathan pronounced the film: "Different than I pictured it, but amazing nonetheless."

We took long walks together – alone and with 'Iokepa. We three talked literature, Karl Jung, friendship, intimacy and sex. We read parts of James Joyce's *Ulysses* aloud to one another and some Thomas Pynchon too – Nathan's suggested reading.

Nathan's last two weeks were appropriately and nostalgically at the Salt Pans inside our tent. We slept nearby, in the Camry.

I write now exactly thirteen years after my life was irrevocably altered on a distant *heiau* on the Island of Kaua'i.

We are in a different Camry now. It is flawlessly black with a grey leather interior, gold aluminum wheels, a sunroof (that works), and it gets 34 miles to the gallon. In its first year, we put 26,000 miles on that odometer, not one of them on our Islands. Never once have we had to sleep on its comfortable, forgiving seats.

We are now living – my husband and I – the calling for which he spent ten years in the "grooming" required by the grandmothers, and in which I spent a number of those years struggling to understand.

In Sarasota, Santa Fe, and Manhattan, in our former hometowns (Roanoke, Portland, Seattle), in college towns and industrial cities, we tell the grandmothers' story and invite others to share the journey.

This calling, these gatherings, were named *Huliau* – **The Return Voyage** – by the grandmothers. Return Voyage is the metaphor for the necessity to reclaim that which all of us were born knowing. It was also the literal truth of the Hawaiian voyagers for 13,000 years: They did not need to know *where* they were headed – but it was essential to know *how* to get home.

It is that home within each of us that Return Voyage honors and insists upon.

We began the Return Voyage in September, 2007 after a dazzling and head-spinning few months when the grandmothers told us, *"The time is now."*

The time of living in the Camry, of hunger, of uncertainty was complete. The new direction was imminent. How it would unfold – we could not imagine.

Almost immediately the grandmothers acted.

On Day One of the grandmothers' decree, our old friend Phil, now living on the Island of Hawai'i insisted, 'You will need a website. I will build it."

I remember that 'Iokepa and I both roared, "A website!?!" We hadn't had a phone, a television, an internet connection, or a house in ten years. What on earth would we do with a *website*?!"

On Day Two: Visiting friends from Canada persisted. "You'll need a laptop. We'll have one built and delivered in three weeks."

On Day Three: Friends on Kaua'i put us on their Verizon family plan. We had a cell phone.

Two supporters cashed in their frequent flier miles to get us to Seattle.

In the next two months, the website was built, the computer arrived, and the airplane seats were reserved.

We left the Islands on September 5, 2007. Our last act was to give away our then sixteen-year-old "Hotel Camry," to Jacob, the big-hearted mechanic who'd kept it running long past its life expectancy. We assume that he disassembled it for parts.

In Seattle, we told a Toyota dealer – a perfect stranger – the grandmothers' message and our story. He gifted us with the use of a brand new Camry for as long as we were in the Pacific Northwest.

Two months later, in rural Washington state, an elderly couple met us and then read the new Return Voyage website. They conferred with one another and agreed: The sleek black Camry they had kept hidden in their garage for the past eight years (that we soon named, "Dark Horse") was to be ours. The maintenance records were immaculate. "We have been taking care of this car all these years for you," they told us.

· · ·

The grandmothers reminded us that our *walk of faith* was life-long. Their guidelines were absolute.

We were to gather during that first year, in intimate numbers only – in strangers' homes. In later years, the venues would get broader and the numbers greater. We would neither push nor promote Return Voyage gatherings. We would wait to be invited.

We were to charge *nothing* for our work – and stay for a couple nights in the home of each of our hosts. A discreetly placed donation bowl would pay for our gas, our food and our occasional need for a motel.

'Iokepa would not stand on an elevated platform and hold forth. He and I would be one of the assembled: eye level, a circle.

For each Return Voyage gathering, 'Iokepa and I now sit side by side in a circle of strangers.

I introduce myself first. It feels right for us to begin this way, because we think it important that 'Iokepa focus directly on culture. I speak:

"For most of my adult life I've been a writer, a writing teacher, a single mother. Thirteen years ago, I was living in Portland when I met *this* man..." (I smile and gesture to my right) "...on my rare vacation without children.

"I had no idea how that would change my life." I often laugh.

Then I introduce 'Iokepa and share his story:

"'Iokepa was forty-six years old and a successful businessman when his grandmothers visited him and asked that he relinquish all that he had worked for his entire life to fulfill his destiny. Two weeks later, he'd returned to the Islands carrying only what fit inside a Nike sports duffel: T-shirts, bathing suits, flip flops – and $100 in his pocket.

"From that moment until this one, he has lived only on faith. He has worked only for his Creator."

I then ask each person in the circle to introduce themselves and tell us why they think they are there.

Their reasons for being in that circle run the gamut.

"My wife made me come."

"I lived in Hawai'i – they were the most incredible years
of my life."

"I had no intention of coming. I found myself at the door."

"I've *always* been interested in indigenous cultures."

These gatherings are highly interactive. Conversations
typically linger well after the three-hour Return Voyage ends.

Every Return Voyage circle is entirely fresh, utterly de-
pendent on the hearts and minds of those gathered that
evening. The grandmothers told us that they would be, *As
different as the waves in the ocean.*

Many of these strangers have become dear friends. There
have been, in these Return Voyage circles: mayors, city
managers, Native American elders, research physicists, heads
of university chemistry departments – and plenty of people
who are best defined in ways that are neither their occupation
nor their ethnicity.

When the circle of introductions is complete – we stand,
grasp hands, and 'Iokepa belts out a chilling and heart-felt
Hawaiian chant. Then we begin.

We speak about a Hawaiian people who lived without
war for 12,000 years. We share the ways they accomplished
that. We speak of the tapestry of human and tree and rock and
earth and sky and ocean. We speak of the possibility of
miracles; we speak of the debt of gratitude.

Afterwards, when 'Iokepa and I are dissecting that particular evening's gathering with one another, we're amazed at
what *wasn't* even mentioned. Return Voyage changes with
every breath.

We, and everyone else in that circle, continue to learn
how important it is to fearlessly accept change – and welcome
it.

We never intended to tell our personal story. We expected to speak only of culture, spirit and the indigenous
wisdom. But we were kidding ourselves. Almost from the first,
it has been what 'Iokepa and I have lived these past ten years –

our journey – that has awakened confidence in our listeners in what was possible. It seems that our walk of faith validates our message, our words.

'Iokepa and I have come to know that, really, all we have to offer is the authenticity of our own experience. Perhaps it is all that any of us have to offer. We offer it with a prayer that it empowers each person, inside that circle and out, to claim his or her own.

Increasingly, we speak with Native Americans. From nation to nation, we hear them reverently whisper to one another: 'He's on a *journey*.' It is a term we embrace literally and figuratively.

This journey, this "Walk of faith" took a deeper turn on the American continent.

When we must travel the 2,441 miles from the Florida Keys to Sedona, Arizona, it takes gas. When we get stuck in a blizzard in Wisconsin, it takes a motel room. We have always and only had just enough.

We depend on the miracles – and the good graces of our friends and strangers. The mechanic in Flagstaff who said he'd forgotten his checkbook at the gathering, and wanted to make a donation, wound up replacing the Camry's $700 timing belt – gratis. The gifted healer, who insisted on treating and fixing my immobile right arm, a month after a hard fall on the ice in Minnesota – and refused to speak of payment. The wonderful family in Baton Rouge who made certain that we were on a flight to 'Iokepa's mother's funeral.

We ask for none of it. When we describe our stripped-to-the-bone life to friends and strangers – and tell them of receiving just enough, they sometimes marvel.

"My culture is not for sale," 'Iokepa still says. We do not charge for Return Voyage gatherings. Money will never be a deterrent to hearing our stories. Always, the intent of the stories is *inclusion*.

The website alone – and word of mouth – inspires invitations. We accept the invitations as the grandmothers guide us. From breath to breath, we truly do not know where the grandmothers will lead us, or where Dark Horse will carry us. The ancestral Hawaiian wisdom speaks to incredibly diverse hearts and minds in places we would never have imagined visiting.

"We *all* come from indigenous people," 'Iokepa says. Return Voyage is about building confidence in that which all of us are born knowing.

We continue to work to awaken awareness of the ancestral wisdom within the Hawaiian culture – and respect for the *kanaka* maoli, the aboriginal holders of that wisdom.

We hope to build a consensus around those ancient values: our connections and our responsibilities for those connections, human and natural.

We could not have foreseen the collapsing world economy.

But we know this: security is our birthright. We do not lose our compassion, our responsibility for one another, our ability to give and receive – our very lives – unless we agree to it.

No circumstance and no person can take away what we were born with – our deep connection to every part of creation and to one another – unless we agree to surrender it.

. . .

www.ReturnVoyage.com

WITH GRATITUDE

I am stymied. The life we live *daily* owes in a hundred ways – and to a dozen different people – the deepest gratitude. These are people who have cooked us a meal, given us a night in bed or a hot shower, offered us a place to launder our clothing, filled the Camry's gas tank, bought us stamps or a calling card, and pressed a $20 bill or a $100 bill in our hands. I have lived now fully thirteen years on the strength of these daily acts of *kahiau* – giving from the heart with no expectation of return. May their *mitzvoth* – meritorious acts that express God's will – be returned a hundredfold. They deserve to be listed here by name, but they do not expect it, and their number prohibits it.

On the other hand, I will list by name those men and women who were specifically patrons of the book. *Grandmothers Whisper* was written, over thirteen years, in their homes. In every case I seized the moment – a week, a month, four months at the longest – and I wrote.

Thank you. Chronologically: Mary Ellen Lee-Crooks; Anita and Eugen Basic; Gordana and Tom Leonard; Layna Larot; Lonnie Johnson; Johana Lee; Phil and Julie Williams; Jean Bradley and Rick Philips; Diane Ray; Tim Dineen and Natalia Ippolito; Chris Evatt and David Williams; Nicole Lawrence; Betty Ann Clifford; Marlene and Ron Czajkowski; Miles and Melissa Greenberg; Christy and Bill Clinton; Janice Mahannah and Robert Casey; Diane and Bill Elliot; Samuel Miller Conte and Elizabeth Hazel; Renu and Michael O'Connell; Veronica Rose and Walter Cannon; Bonnie Nelson.

Computers: In the early years, Carmel Hawn took time from her frantic business to make house-calls to the finicky computer I brought from Portland. Later, Lou Pignolet shipped a phased-out, laptop from the University of Minnesota's

Chemistry Department when my computer bit the dust. Still later, Bruce and Wendie Schiebelbein sent a state of the art laptop from Canada. When it died, David Williams stepped up and bought another. Bonnie and Gerd Winkler supplied essential printer cartridges and added us to their family – so we'd share their cell phone service. We still do. Jayne Grace and Morgan Magras donated emergency printer paper and much more. Lorri Lamb, Michael Kader, Victoria House, and Scott Goold each contributed to keeping this train on track. Tom Leonard built the Return Voyage website and keeps it up to date. Hamilton Gregory kept me apprised of the ever-changing realities of publishing technology – no small feat. He's also responsible for scanning all photos in this book and on its cover. Zach Giezen remains our devoted computer guru – he takes care of us *remotely* – as we travel. Amazing watching that cursor move across the screen from Denver!

Writer Emily Horowitz was my earliest reader. Writer Daniel Miller Conte read this in its middle stages. Attorney Phil Williams read with his razor-sharp eye for logical discrepancies. Editor-writer Hiyaguha Cohen read the first sixty pages for clarity and flow. Maya Muir did a line edit that axed sloppy commas, inappropriate colons and more. Chalanta O'Connell nailed the elusive subtitle during a week-long brain-storming session. Literary agent David Dunton spent a full year of unflinching *belief* in the project. His heart resides in Hawai'i.

Merrell Gregory was my editor. This book is infinitely stronger for her wisdom, her graciousness, and her honesty.

Not a single one of these fine folks took a dime for their labor.

To Michelle Shane at Infinity, to the friends and family who inspired and lived these pages but bear no responsibility for the idiosyncrasy of my experience or the quality of my narrative: Thank you.

HAWAIIAN GLOSSARY

'Ahi poke (āh hee poh kāy): Raw tuna, cut into cubes and
seasoned.

'Ailona (eye lōh nah): Sign or omen.

'Āina (ēye nah): Land or Earth.

Aloha (ah low hā): In the presence of God in every breath. (In
greeting: recognition of the soul.)

Hā (hah): To breathe, or the breath.

Ha'ole (hah-ōh lay): Without breath. (From missionary
avowal: God was in Bible – not in the breath.)

Haole (hōw lee): White person, foreigner. (Derogatory
variation of ha'ole.)

Hau (how): Lowland tree that forms impenetrable thickets.

Hā'upu (hā-oo poo): To remember.

Heiau (hāy owl): Sacred sanctuaries of ancient worship.

"He kahakū wau no kēia 'āina, ia'u o uka ia'u o kai:" I may
go where I please on this Land; inland is mine,
seaward is mine."

Hele laulā (hēll ay) (l ōwl a): Act with freedom.

Honu (hōh noo): Sea turtle.

Ho'ohanohano (hōh-oh hāh noh hāh noh): Honor, glory.

Ho'omaika'i (hōh-oh my kā-ee): Blessings.

Ho'omanawanui (hōh-oh ma nā wah nōo ee): Wait in faith.

Ho'oponopono (hōh-oh pōh noh pōh noh): Traditional
mediation ritual.

Hula hālau (hōo lah) (hāh l'ōwl): Gathering place for dance
instruction.

Huliau (hōo lee ōwl): Turning point. Time of change.

Hūnā (hōo nāh): The original (pre Christian, pre Kapu)
religion and culture of Lāhui.

'Ike Hānau (ēekay) (hahn ōwl): Instinct. Birth knowledge.

'Ike Pāpālua (ēe kay) (pāh pah lōo ah): Commune with the
spirits.

HAWAIIAN GLOSSARY

'Ili 'ōuli *(ēe lee) (ōo lee): Goosebumps in reaction to the presence of spirits. Sign or omen.*

Kaheka *(kah hāy kah): Salt Pan.*

Kahiau *(kāh hee ōwl): To give lavishly from the heart, with no expectation of return.*

Kahiko *(kah hēe koh): The authentic, ancient language, hula, and culture.*

Kahu *(kā hoo): Priest or guardian of Hūnā.*

Kahuna *(ka hōo na): Accomplished practitioner of Hūnā (Uses the universal energy – or mana.)*

Kalo *(kāh low): A staple of the native diet. Both root and leaf are eaten from hundreds of varieties.*

Kama'āina *(kāh mah-ēye na): Born in Hawai'i, but not native Hawaiian. (Now means: Any resident.)*

Kanaka maoli *(kah nāh kah) (mōwl lee): Indigenous, aboriginal people.*

Kapu *(ka pōo): Taboo. A political system imposed by force on the kanaka maoli, in 1320.*

"Kau ka lā i ka lolo, ho'i ke aka i ke kino:" *The sun rests on the brain; the shadow retreats into the body.*
High noon: the time of great mana.

Kaupalena 'ole 'ia huikala: *Unconditional forgiveness.*

Kaupalena 'ole 'ia mana'o'io: *Unconditional faith.*

Kaupalena 'ole 'ia 'ano'i: *Unconditional love.*

Ka wa mahope *(kāh) (wāh) (mah ho pāy): Past. (The time in front of or before.)*

Ka wa mamua *(kāh) (wāh) (mah mōo ah)): Future. (The time behind, or after.)*

Ke 'I'oakua *(kāy) (ēe-oh ahkōo ah): God Almighty.*

Kī *(kee): A woody plant. The leaves were put to many uses: food, clothing, shelter.*

Kiawe *(kee āh way): Mesquite from South America.*

HAWAIIAN GLOSSARY

Koholā *(koh hoh lāh): Humpbacked whale.*
Koko *(koh koh): Blood.*
Ku ka'awale *(kōo) (kah-ah wāhlay): To stand apart, independent; an iconoclast.*
"Kūkulu ka 'ike i ka 'ōpua": *There are answers – knowledge – in the clouds.*
Kupua *(koo pōo ah): Hero.*
Kupuna *(koo pōo nah): Elder, ancestor.*
La'akoa *(lah-ah koh ah): Sacred warrior.*
Lāhui *(lāh hoo ee): Nation, race, tribe. What the kanaka maoli call their homeland (not 'Hawai'i').*
Lānai *(lah n eye): Porch or patio.*
Lapa'au *(lāh pah-ōwl): Traditional medical practice using natural herbs and plants.*
Lauhala *(l'ōwl hāh lah): Pandanus (screw pine) tree. The leaves were woven into canoe sails.*
Laulau *(l owl l owl): Meat or fish wrapped in kalo leaf and ki leaf and then steamed.*
Lei *(lay): Garland of seeds, shells, nuts, or flowers*
Limu *(lēe moo): Seaweed.*
Lo'i *(loh-ēe): Irrigated terrace for growing kalo.*
Lū'au *(lōo owl): Hawaiian feast.*
Mahalo *(mah hāh low): Gratitude. Thank you.*
Mahina poepoe *(mah hēe nah) (poiy poiy): Full moon.*
Maika'i no *(my kāh-ee) (nō): Fine.*
Maka'āinana *(māh kah-ēye nāh nah): People of the land.*
Makani *(mah kāh nee): Wind.*
Mālama *(mah lāh mah): To take care of.*
Mālama ka 'āina *(mah lāh mah) (kāh) (ēye na): To take care of the land.*
Mālama pono *(mah lāh mah) (pōh no): Make right.*
Malihini *(māh lee hēe nee): Guest, unfamiliar with customs.*

HAWAIIAN GLOSSARY

Mana *(māh nah): Divine power, energy of the universe.*

Manahune *(māh nah hōo nay): Original people, who effortlessly used the universal energies.*

Mana'o *(mah nah-ōh): Thoughts, ideas, opinions.*

Mo'okū'auhau *(moh-oh kōo-ōwl hōw): Genealogical succession.*

Mo'olelo *(mōh-ōh lāy low): History.*

Mo'opuna *(mōh-ōh pōo nah): Grandchild.*

Muliwai *(mōo lee w'eye): Mouth of the river.*

Na'au *(nah-ōwl): Guts, intestines.*

Nalu *(nāh loo): Wave, surf.*

Ohana *(oh hāh nah): The human responsibility for every element of creation. (Now used as family.)*

Ola *(ōh lah): Life.*

'Ōlelo *(ōh lay low): Speech, oration.*

Oli *(ōh lee): Chant.*

Ono *(ōh no): Large mackerel type fish.*

Pahu *(pāh hōo): Drum.*

Paka lōlō *(pāh kah) (loh loh): Marijuana.*

Pehea 'oe *(pay hāy a) (ōiye): How are you?*

Poi *(p oiy): The Hawaiian staff of life, made from cooked kalo root.*

Pōhaku *(poh hah koo): Stone, rock*

Pono *(pōh noh): Goodness, uprightness.*

Po'o lei *(pōh-ōh) (lay): Garland of flowers worn around the head.*

Pueo *(poo ay oh): Hawaiian owl.*

Puka *(pōo kah): Hole, opening. (A puka shell, left by a mussel, has an opening in it.)*

Pule *(pōo lay): Prayer.*

Pu'uwai *(pōo-ōo why): Heart.*

'Uhane *(oo hāh nay): Soul, spirit.*

Wai *(why): Water, body fluids, sap.*

Wānana *(wah nāh nah): Prophecy.*

HEBREW AND YIDDISH GLOSSARY

Aliyah: *The honor of being called up before the Torah.*
Bar Mitzvah: *A young man's rite of passage into cultural responsibility at age thirteen.*
Barucha: *Blessing*
"Baruch atah adonai elohenu melech ho'olum, asher kidushanu b'mitvotov vitzivanu, l'hadlich n'er shel Shabbat."
    Blessed art thou O Lord our God, King of the Universe, who commanded us to light the Sabbath candles.
Bashert: *God's choice of mate.*
Bima: *Altar or pulpit at synagogue.*
Bris: *The ritual male circumcision, at eight days old.*
Challah: *Ritual egg-twist bread.*
Chanukah: *The eight-day holiday commemorating the ancient Temple miracle of light.*
Chayah: *Life.*
Kiddush: *The prayer and ceremony that sanctifies Jewish holy days. (Said over wine.)*
Kipah: *Ceremonial skullcap worn in conservative and orthodox synagogues.*
Machutenim: *Family by marriage.*
Mazel Tov: *Congratulations. Thank God!*
Menorah: *The eight branched candelabra lit daily on Chanukah.*
Mezuzah: *An oblong container with a sacred Torah blessing affixed to the doorpost of a Jewish home.*
Mitzvoth: *Meritorious acts, that express God's will.*
Neshamah: *Soul.*
Pesach: *Passover – the holiday commemorating Jewish freedom from Egyptian slavery.*
Rosh Hashanah: *The Jewish New Year.*
Ruach: *Spirit of the wind.*

HEBREW AND YIDDISH GLOSSARY

Seder: *The Passover ritual meal, where the story of Jewish slavery and freedom is retold.*

Shabbat: *The Sabbath – from Friday evening at sunset to Saturday at sunset.*

Shalom: *Peace. A greeting.*

Shamash: *Leader. The top candle on the Chanukah Menorah – it lights the other eight.*

Shofar, *Shofarot (plural): The Ram's Horn that is blown at the close of Yom Kippur synagogue service.*

Tallit: *Prayer shawl worn in Orthodox and Conservative synagogues.*

Tanakh: *Hebrew acronym for the holy scriptures of Judaism.*

Torah: *A parchment scroll containing the Five Books of Moses.*

Yom Kippur: *The Day of Atonement. The most solemn day of the Jewish calendar.*

Yom Tov: *Good day. As a greeting: Happy holiday.*

HAWAIIAN NAMES (Phonetic Pronunciation)

Haleakala Kunao Lota 'Īmaikalani *('Iokepa's grandmother):*
(Hah lāyah ka lāh) (Kōo nah oh) (Lōh ta) (Ēe mai ka lāh nee)
Hokulele ('Iokepa's daughter): (Hōh koo lay lay)
'Iokepa Hanalei 'Īmaikalani (Ēeoh kepa) (Hāhna lāy) (Ēe mai
ka lāh nee)
Israel Kamakawiwo'ole (Songwriter, Bruddah Iz): (Kah māh
kah wee woh-ōh lay)
Jonathan Kamakawiwo'ole Osorio (Native Hawaiian
historian): (same as above)
King Kamehameha (Kah māy hah māy hah)
Puanani ('Iokepa's oldest sister): (Pōo ah nāh nee)
Leilani (On Island of Moloka'i): (Lay lāh nee)
Lo'ika ('Iokepa's great grandmother): (Lōh-ēe kah)
Malu: ('Iokepa's son): (Māh loo)
Moki (Councilman on Island of Kaua'i): (Mōh kee)
Momi (In fishing village, Island of Hawai'i): (Mōh mee)
Nani: (From Island of Ni'ihau): (Nāh nee)
Pa'ao: (Conqueror, 1320, from Tahiti): (Pah-ōwl)
Pili): (Lieutenant to conqueror, Pa'ao): (Pee lee)
Waihona (Native species curator at Botanical gardens):
(Why hōh nah)

HAWAIIAN PLACES (Phonetic Pronunciation)

Ahukini Landing: *(Ahoo kee nee)*
Anahola: *(Ahna hōh la)*
Ha'iku: *(Hah-ēe koo)*
Haleakala: *(Ha lāy ah kah lāh)*
Hanapepe: *(Hahna pāy pay)*
Hapuna Beach: *(Hah pōo nah)*
Hawai'i: *(Ha why-ee)*
Honolulu: *(Hoh noh lōo loo)*
Kaheka: *(Ka hāy ka)*
Kahului: *(Kā hoo lōo ee)*
Kalaheo: *(Kāhlah hāy oh)*
Kalapaki Beach: *(Kah lah pāh kee)*
Kalawao: *(Kāh lah wowl)*
Kamehameha School: *(Ka māy hah māy hah)*
Kapa'a: *(Ka pāh-ah)*
Kaua'i: *(Cow ah-ee)*
Keone'o'io: *(Kāy oh nay-ōh-ēe oh)*
Kihei: *(Kēe hay)*
Kipu: *(Kee poo)*
Kona: *(Kōh na)*
Lahaina: *(La hīgh na)*
Lahainaluna High School: *(La hīgh na loo nah)*
Lāhui: *(Lāh hoo ee)*
Lana'i: *(Lanāh-ee)*
Lihu'e: *(Lee hōo-ay)*
Makena: *(Māh kehna)*
Mana: *(Mah nāh)*
Manele Bay: *(Mah nēh lay)*
Maui: *(Mōwl ee)*
Miloli'i: *(Mee loh lee-ee)*
Moloka'i: *(Moh loh kāh-ee)*

HAWAIIAN PLACES (Phonetic Pronunciation)

Na Pali Coast: *(Nah) (Pāh lee)*
Nawiliwili: *(Nah wee lee wee lee)*
Niʻihau: *(Nēe-eehowl)*
Niumalu Park: *(Nēe oo māh loo)*
Oʻahu: *(Oh-āh hu)*
Opaekaʻa Falls: *(Oh pie kāh-ah)*
Papalaua Wayside: *(Pah pa l ōwl ah)*
Pauhana Inn: *(Pow hāh na)*
Poliʻahu Heiau: *(Poh lee-ah hoo) (Hay owl))*
Polihale: *(Pōh lee hāh lay)*
Waialeale: *(Why ah lay ah lay)*
Waikiki: *(Why kee kēe)*
Wailea: *(Why lēy ah)*
Wailua River: *(Why lōo ah)*
Wailuku: *(Why lōo koo)*
Waipiʻo Valley: *(Why pēe-oh)*